Progress

ENGLISH LANGUAGE
GCSE for AQA
Student Book

Clare Constant, Imelda Pilgrim and Bernard Ward

Series Editor: Imelda Pilgrim

CAMBRIDGE
UNIVERSITY PRESS

University Printing House, Cambridge CB2 8BS, United Kingdom

Cambridge University Press is part of the University of Cambridge.

It furthers the University's mission by disseminating knowledge in the pursuit of education, learning and research at the highest international levels of excellence.

www.cambridge.org
Information on this title: www.cambridge.org/ukschools/9781107453135 (Paperback)
www.cambridge.org/ukschools/9781107453142 (Cambridge Elevate-enhanced Edition)
www.cambridge.org/ukschools/9781107453173 (Paperback + Cambridge Elevate-enhanced Edition)

First published 2015

Printed in the United Kingdom by Latimer Trend

A catalogue record for this publication is available from the British Library

ISBN 978-1-107-45313-5 Paperback
ISBN 978-1-107-45317-3 Cambridge Elevate-enhanced Edition
ISBN 978-1-107-45303-6 Paperback + Cambridge Elevate-enhanced Edition

Additional resources for this publication at www.cambridge.org/ukschools

Cambridge University Press has no responsibility for the persistence or accuracy
of URLs for external or third-party internet websites referred to in this publication,
and does not guarantee that any content on such websites is, or will remain,
accurate or appropriate. Information regarding prices, travel timetables, and other
factual information given in this work is correct at the time of first printing but
Cambridge University Press does not guarantee the accuracy of such information
thereafter.

....

Message from AQA

This textbook has been approved by AQA for use with our qualification. This means that we have checked that it broadly covers the specification and we are satisfied with the overall quality. Full details of our approval process can be found on our website.

We approve textbooks because we know how important it is for teachers and students to have the right resources to support their teaching and learning. Please note, however, that the publisher is ultimately responsible for the editorial control and quality of this book.

Please note that when teaching the GCSE English Language (8700) course, you must refer to AQA's specification as your definitive source of information. While this book has been written to match the specification, it cannot provide complete coverage of every aspect of the course.

A wide range of other useful resources can be found on the relevant subject pages of our website: www.aqa.org.uk

Contents

Introduction

You are about to start your GCSE course in English Language. It is likely that you have already studied English for many years, steadily developing your skills in reading, writing and spoken English. This text book will help you:

- build on the skills you already have
- equip you with the English Language skills you need for further study across a range of subjects
- prepare yourself for your GCSE exams.

Your GCSE exams are based on assessment objectives (AOs). This student book develops the skills outlined in these assessment objectives. Each unit provides instruction and tasks, enabling you to build your expertise, and ends with an 'Assess your progress' section which allows you to check how well you have done. In addition to this, there are tests designed to reinforce your learning across a number of units, a 'Spoken language' unit to help you give a formal presentation, and an exam section that provides sample papers, expert advice, annotated sample answers and suggestions for purposeful revision.

The source materials in this text book have been carefully selected to interest, engage and challenge you. They include a range of genres and text types drawn from the 19th, 20th and 21st centuries. You will also find two 'Wider reading' units, which are designed to extend your interest and independence in reading, as well as further the development of specific reading skills.

The tasks set for reading, writing and spoken language are varied. You will be asked to work on your own, or in pairs or small groups. You will examine detail, meaning and writers' techniques and styles, and will learn how to answer questions about these. You will also develop your own writing skills to target your purpose and audience, and organise and express your ideas clearly and effectively.

We hope you find it an interesting, enjoyable and rewarding experience and we wish you all the best with your studies.

The author team

How to use this book

Each unit targets a clearly defined area. This is indicated at the beginning of the unit you are studying with the symbol (AO1).

There are 32 units and an additional exam preparation section in this student book. As you work through the units, you will explore different aspects of reading, writing and spoken language. Most units end with an 'Assess your progress' section, which allows you to test your understanding and check how well you have progressed throughout that unit. You will also find 'Test your progress' units that give you the opportunity to test yourself on what you have learnt over the previous units under timed conditions.

The exam preparation section provides sample papers, advice, annotated sample answers and suggestions for revision to help you get ready for your exams.

Working on Cambridge Elevate

As you work through the book you will find links to Cambridge Elevate, the Cambridge University Press digital platform. At these points, you are invited to complete a task, listen to an extract or watch a video to help you reinforce your learning.

 When you come across this icon, watch a video.

 If you see this icon, listen to an audio extract.

 Complete an activity when you see this icon.

  These icons indicate sections dealing with grammar and links to spelling activities later in the book.

Unit 1
Identify and select information

Make progress

AO1

- identify information in different types of texts
- select relevant information and ideas to answer questions
- use detail to work out what a writer is suggesting
- answer questions in clear sentences.

USE YOUR SKILLS

Every day you identify information and ideas in texts – when you use a TV guide, for example, or glance at the cover of a book before you look inside.

Watch a video about reading skills on Cambridge Elevate.

ACTIVITY 1

1 Look at the picture below. What information would someone new to this area need in order to find two places to eat? Identify and list three key details that would help them.

2 Show your three details to a partner.

    a Could they find the places using only the information you gave them?
    b Which detail was the most helpful?

FIND KEY DETAILS IN A TEXT

To show your understanding of a written text, you need to:

- identify key details
- select the correct key details to answer questions.

Read Source A, an extract from a guide book. It describes how to walk from one tourist attraction to another.

1 Answer the following questions:

a   Which way should you turn when you leave the Quay?
b   Which road should you take after the first roundabout?
c   What will you find at the end of Marine Terrace?
d   How far must you travel along Pendennis Rise before you pass a leisure centre?
e   Is the sign for Pendennis Castle before or after Pendennis Point?

2 Which **five** details from the text would you **not** need to find the castle?

3 Compare your answers to Questions 1 and 2 with a partner. If they are different, work out the correct answers together.

Source A

CUSTOMS HOUSE QUAY to PENDENNIS CASTLE

Leaving the Quay, turn left onto Arwenack Street. Walk for 400 yards until you reach a roundabout. To your right is Avenue Road; straight across is Marine Terrace. Carry on along Marine Terrace. This will take you past the barracks. Sea-scouts meet here on Thursday. At the end of Marine Terrace is a second roundabout. The left-hand turning leads to flats. College students live here during term time. The right-hand turning leads up Pendennis Rise. Take this road. In 200 yards you will pass a leisure centre on your right. This houses a pool and gymnasium. The road curves to the right, passing Pendennis Point where refreshments are available from ice-cream vans during the summer. Continue for 600 yards. On the right you will see a turning signposted for Pendennis Castle. The castle was built by Henry VIII to defend the coast from Spanish invaders. Take this turning. In 100 yards you will reach the entrance to the castle.

MATCH DETAILS TO THE WRITER'S PURPOSE

The main **purpose** of Source A is to give directions. Recipes often have two main purposes. The writer wants to:

* tell the reader how to make something
* encourage the reader to have a go at making it.

Activity 3 will help you work out which details suit which purpose.

ACTIVITY 3

Read Source B, a recipe for porridge with sticky banana topping. Then answer the questions that follow.

Source B

Porridge with sticky banana topping

SERVES 1

Porridge can certainly be a healthy and nutritious breakfast, and will probably keep you full at least until lunch! About half a cup of porridge oats to a cup of milk per person is just about right. Blast it in the microwave for about 5 minutes, then cover it and leave it to stand for another 5 minutes or so. After that, stir it, and you have a perfectly creamy porridge. Then pour on the delicious sticky banana topping and you'll have a wonderful morning treat to please all the family.

* **a knob of unsalted butter**
* **1 tbsp brown sugar**
* **1 small banana**

In a frying pan, melt the butter and brown sugar over a medium heat. Meanwhile, slice the banana and add to the buttery, sugary mixture and cook for about 3 minutes until caramelised and sticky.

Transfer the porridge into a bowl and add the cooked banana on top.

1 List the important details for making porridge with sticky banana topping. Be careful – some of the details you need might be in the introduction.

2 Which details has the writer included to encourage the reader to have a go at making this recipe?

3 Look at the following phrases. Explain why each of the underlined words might encourage the reader to have a go:

- a <u>nutritious</u> breakfast
- <u>perfectly</u> creamy porridge
- a <u>delicious</u> morning treat.

IDENTIFY DETAILS IN DESCRIPTIONS

You have seen that writers include different details for different purposes. So far, you have looked at texts where the main purpose is to give instructions. Now you are going to consider how details can be used for a different purpose – to describe someone.

ACTIVITY 4

1 Think of a celebrity. Don't tell anybody who you are thinking of. Now make a fact file about your celebrity:

- Think of five to ten key facts about them.
- Write your facts down in a table in **note form** – a single word or phrase to help you remember each one, like this example about Andy Murray.

Celebrity fact file: Andy Murray

Category	Facts
gender	male
occupation	tennis player
age	in his 20s
appearance	
achievements	

2 Use the categories from your fact file to come up with **five** questions. Each question should be designed to help you work out the identity of an unknown celebrity – for example 'Is the celebrity male or female?'

3 In pairs, take it in turn to ask questions to identify each other's chosen celebrity. Listen carefully to the answers and make notes on them.

4 If you still cannot identify the mystery celebrity when you have asked your five questions, think of some more. Continue asking questions until you are successful.

5 Tell each other which facts were most useful in helping you identify the mystery celebrity.

Source C

On his shaven head the old man wore a **puggree**. His eyes were quick and like a bird's. On his upper lip were a few thin wisps of long grey hair which he thought of proudly as his moustache. The yellow brown face was scored. Straight across his forehead the deep lines ran, and in a twisting confusion across his cheeks. In between the skin was marked with a mesh of delicate wrinkles. When he smiled the lines seemed to leap, and move and grow deeper. The boy liked to watch them, and sometimes as he did he wondered whether his face would ever be like that.

5

From *Old Mali and the Boy* by D. R. Sherman

UNDERSTAND HOW WRITERS USE DETAILS IN A DESCRIPTION

Writers often give details about characters directly to their readers. However, sometimes they suggest or imply things about characters. This means that the writer does not state the information directly. The reader must work out what is being suggested.

> **Vocabulary**
>
> **puggree:** the commonly used word for a turban in India.

ACTIVITY 5

Read Source C, an extract from a children's novel. The writer describes a gardener called Mali, who is being watched by a boy.

1 Answer the following questions to help you identify details and work out what they suggest:

    a   What did the man wear on his head?
    b   What was his 'moustache' like?
    c   What was his skin colour?
    d   What details does the writer use to suggest that the gardener is old?
    e   What detail is used to suggest that the boy admires the man?

2 Compare your answers with a partner. Have you both:

    a   identified detail correctly in a, b and c
    b   worked out what the detail suggests in d and e?

WRITE CLEAR ANSWERS

You should always make sure your answers are clear and written in full sentences. For example:

Q: What did the man wear on his head?

A: *The man wore a puggree on his head.*

If you need to use words from the text, you should put quotation marks around them.
For example:

Q: What details does the writer use to suggest that the gardener is old?
A: *The writer suggests that the man is old by writing about the 'long grey hair' in his moustache. He also says he has 'deep lines' in his forehead and that his skin was marked 'with a mesh of delicate wrinnkles'.*

The only time you do not need to write in sentences is if the question asks you to make a list.

ACTIVITY 6

1 Look back at your answers to Activity 5. Check that you have:

    a   answered clearly and in full sentences
    b   placed words taken from the text in quotation marks.

    Now read Source D, the next part of the passage, in which the writer describes the thoughts and impressions of the boy.

2 Answer the following questions about the passage. Use the sentence starters to help you answer in clear sentences. Remember to use quotation marks if you quote directly from the text.

    a   What did the boy think might have caused the old man's lines?
       The boy thought the lines might have been caused by …
    b   How did the man's hands show his age?
       The man's hands showed his age because …
    c   What is unusual about Mali's right hand?
       Mali's right hand is unusual because …
    d   Why was Mali's finger missing?
       Mali's finger was missing because …

Source D

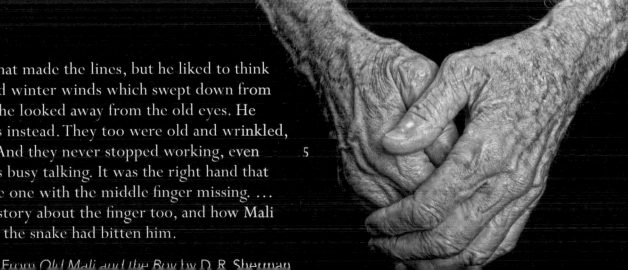

He never knew what made the lines, but he liked to think
that it was the cold winter winds which swept down from
the Himalayas … he looked away from the old eyes. He
watched the hands instead. They too were old and wrinkled,
just like the face. And they never stopped working, even   5
when the man was busy talking. It was the right hand that
fascinated him, the one with the middle finger missing. …
And he knew the story about the finger too, and how Mali
had cut it off after the snake had bitten him.

From *Old Mali and the Boy* by D. R. Sherman

Source E

The first watery beams of sunshine were slanting into the forest gloom when they set off once again. They walked as before, the old man in the lead, the boy following. But with one difference now. The old man carried the pack and the boy carried the strung bow at the ready in his left hand.

'Move silently,' the old man called across his shoulder. 'And from here we do not talk.' 5

'Yes Mali,' the boy whispered.

He tightened his grip on the bow, and he could feel the excitement shivering in his legs as he picked his way carefully over the ground.

'One thing Mali,' he whispered fiercely.

'Yes?' 10

'If they are too far for me you must shoot, but if they are close I will kill them myself.'

The old man bobbed his head in agreement and the boy heaved a sigh of relief. He had practised continuously with the bow, and he did not doubt that he could place an arrow where he wanted, but it was still a big bow.

From *Old Mali and the Boy* by D. R. Sherman

 Assess your progress

In this unit, you have:

- identified and selected information and ideas
- used detail to work out meaning
- answered questions in clear sentences.

Source E is also from *Old Mali and the Boy*. In this extract, the old man, Mali, and the boy have gone to the forest to hunt deer, using a bow and arrows that Mali has given to the boy. Read the source carefully and answer the following questions. Use details from the text to support your answers.

1 What time of day is it when Mali and the boy set off? How do you know this?

2 How does the boy feel about hunting?

3 What **two** pieces of advice does Mali give the boy about the way they should move and behave in the forest?

4 What does the boy ask Mali to do if the deer are too far away? Why do you think he asks this?

5 What can you work out about the relationship between Mali and the boy from this passage?

How did you do?

Swap your answers with a partner. Check that your partner has:

✔ selected and used relevant information
✔ worked out what is being suggested
✔ answered in clear sentences.

 Complete this assignment on Cambridge Elevate.

FURTHER PROGRESS

Find out what happens when Mali and the boy go hunting by reading the full extract. If you enjoy it, read the complete story *Old Mali and the Boy* by D. R. Sherman.

READING
Unit 2
Select, interpret and collate information

USE YOUR SKILLS

When you read, you identify details in a text. You then interpret the details and use them to work out other things.

For example you can look at a TV guide for the times of programmes. You can then work out whether you will be able to watch all the programmes you want to, or whether the schedules clash.

Look at the bus timetables in Source A and the facts about Tom and the journey he needs to take. Then answer the questions that follow.

Facts
- Tom lives by Malvern Railway Station.
- He has a 20-minute appointment at the health centre at 9.15 a.m.
- Then he is going to a cricket match at the Worcester Ground, which is five minutes' walk from the bus station. The match starts at 10.30 a.m. and finishes at 6.30 p.m.
- He must be home by 7.30 p.m.

Source A

Service No.	44	44C	44	44	44	44	44C	44	44	44C
Malvern, Railway Station	0749	0759	0807	0817	0822	0845	0901	----	0921	0931
Prospect View, Health Centre	0759	0809	0817	0833	0833	0854	0910	0920	0930	0940
Powick, Hospital Lane	0818	0828	0836	0851	0851	0911	0927	0937	0947	0957
WORCESTER, Bus Station arr	0836	0846	0853	0908	0906	0927	0943	0953	1003	1013

Service No.	44C	44	44	44	44	44C
WORCESTER, Bus Station dep	1812	1842	1945	2045	2145	2315
Malvern Link, Co-op Store	1837	1904	2004	2104	2204	2332
Prospect View, Health Centre	1841	1907	2007	2107	2207	2335
Malvern, Railway Station	1850	1915	2015	2115	2215	2343

Adapted from
www.firstgroup.com

1 Write a clear set of directions for Tom, telling him the numbers and times of the buses he must catch to complete his journey.

2 Check your directions with those of another student. Do you agree on the details of Tom's journey?

IDENTIFY IDEAS

An idea can be suggested by a single piece of information. For example you might see the phrase 'polar ice-caps' and think of 'coldness'. An idea can also be suggested by linking several pieces of information in a text. For example:

Information in the text	Specific idea	General idea
polar ice caps	coldness	
the ice caps melting	climate change	global warming
sea levels rising	floods	

ACTIVITY 2

Read Source B, a magazine article about holiday destinations.

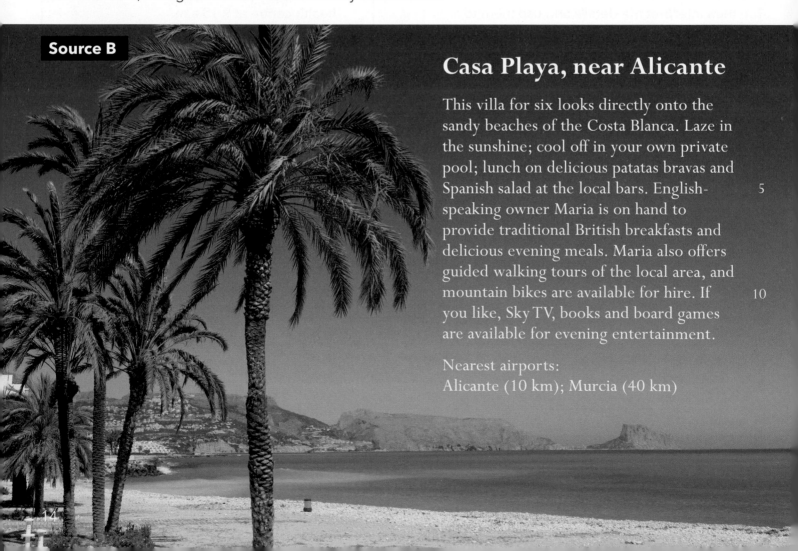

Source B

Casa Playa, near Alicante

This villa for six looks directly onto the sandy beaches of the Costa Blanca. Laze in the sunshine; cool off in your own private pool; lunch on delicious patatas bravas and Spanish salad at the local bars. English- 5
speaking owner Maria is on hand to provide traditional British breakfasts and delicious evening meals. Maria also offers guided walking tours of the local area, and mountain bikes are available for hire. If 10
you like, Sky TV, books and board games are available for evening entertainment.

Nearest airports:
Alicante (10 km); Murcia (40 km)

1 Find and write down details linked with each of the following ideas:

   a geographical location   **b** food   **c** things to do.

2 Check your details with a partner. Have you missed anything?

COLLATE INFORMATION FROM A TEXT

When you 'collate', you identify and bring together several pieces of information. Read Source C, a description of a bus journey written by a student who lives in India. Then complete Activity 3.

Source C

The Cuttack-Balikuda Bus

The Cuttack-Balikuda Bus was due to start at 6am, so I reached the bus-stand at 5 in the morning.

I booked a lower class ticket and got into the bus. The bus was big and it had a capacity of 30 passengers. The bus was served by three employees, titled as Conductor, Driver and Cleaner.

I saw a lot of men at the bus-stand. Their relatives came to see them off. Many hawkers and pedlars were busy selling their goods. There were some tea-stalls where the passengers took tea   5 and tiffin. Some people were busy purchasing tickets. Some were busy getting their goods loaded on the bus. So, I found a noisy scene at the bus-stand.

By 6am the bus was full to capacity. The driver took his seat near the engine. The conductor and the cleaner came inside. The cleaner closed the doors. The conductor pulled the string of the bell twice. The driver sounded his horn. At first, the bus moved slowly. Then it speeded up.   10

While the bus was running I looked outside the bus window. Our bus passed many travellers on bicycles, rickshaws and bullock carts, who were coming from and going to Cuttack. The bus passed through Hazipur, Biridi and Balia. At 9am it reached Basantpur. Here I got down. The green bus drove out of sight on its way to Balikuda.

This journey by bus was very joyful for me. It was not festival time, so there was no heavy rush in   15 the bus. Also the road was good and there was no discomfort at all.

Adapted from www.publishyourarticles.net

💬 **Vocabulary**

hawkers: street-sellers

tiffin: a light snack

rickshaw: a three-wheeled passenger cart

ACTIVITY 3

1 Collate details from the source to answer these questions. Use full sentences.

    a What details do you need to work out how long it takes the writer to travel from Cuttack to Basantpur?

    b What makes the scene at the bus-stand noisy and busy?

    c What other ways of travelling are mentioned?

    d Which five places does the bus stop at after leaving Cuttack?

2 Check your answers with a partner. Have you included all the detail you need to answer the question?

USE EVIDENCE TO SUPPORT YOUR ANSWERS

In Activity 3, you collated details in order to answer questions. For example:

Q: What other ways of travelling are mentioned?

A: The other ways of travelling are by bicycle, by rickshaw and by bullock-cart.

Questions are not always worded in the same way. Sometimes you need to use detail to support the answer you give. For example:

Q: Is bus the only way of travelling between Cuttack and Balikuda?

The simple answer is 'no'. However, you are expected to **explain** the simple answer by using evidence from the text. For example:

A: The bus is not the only way of travelling between Cuttack and Balikuda. The writer describes how people also travel by bicycle, by rickshaw and by bullock-cart.

Another way of answering this question is to quote directly from the text. For example:

A: The bus is not the only way of travelling between Cuttack and Balikuda. The writer tells us about other forms of transport by mentioning 'many travellers on bicycles, rickshaws and bullock-carts'.

Remember: you should write in clear sentences when you answer questions and you should always use quotation marks (' ') when you quote directly from the text.

The following table contains a range of phrases that will help you write answers in clear sentences. Copy the table in your notebooks for future reference.

The writer tells us …	by referring to …
The writer suggests …	by mentioning …
The writer shows …	by using the phrase(s) …
We learn that …	this is suggested by the phrase(s) …
	this is shown by reference to …

ACTIVITY 4

Look at this question:

What is the scene like at the bus stand?

The simple answer is: 'The scene at the bus stand was noisy and busy.'

1. Rewrite the simple answer in a clear sentence, using evidence from the text to support it. Remember to use quotation marks.

2. Is Basantpur the only stopping point for the bus? The simple answer is 'No'. Rewrite this answer as a clear sentence, using evidence from the text to support it.

3. Did the student enjoy the journey? The simple answer is 'Yes'. Rewrite this answer as a clear sentence, using evidence from the text to support it.

4. Read your answers to Questions 1–3 again and check that you have:

   a   used relevant evidence from the text
   b   written your answers in clear sentences
   c   used quotation marks correctly.

   Add evidence or rewrite your sentences if you need to.

COLLATE INFORMATION FROM DIFFERENT SOURCES

You are now going to select and use information from **different** sources to answer questions. Read these four extracts from different websites. Then complete Activity 5.

ARNDALE CENTRE

For the best city centre shopping experience, you can't beat the Arndale Centre, with over 200 retailers. And it's right at the heart of the city. Shops are open 9 a.m. to 8 p.m. on Mondays to Friday (until 7 p.m. on Saturday). Sunday opening hours are 11.30 a.m. to 5.30 p.m.

mosi | Manchester's Museum of Science and Industry

OUR NEWEST GALLERY – Revolution Manchester – is waiting to impress you with its interactive exhibits.

WATCH A SHOW in our 4D theatre – as long as you like moving seats, water spray and air blasts!

OPEN DAILY 10 a.m. to 5 p.m. Adults £4, concessions £3. Closed 24–26 December.

Manchester City

Fixtures 2014

Tuesday 25 November	19.45	Home	Bayern Munich	Uefa Champions League
Sunday 30 November	13.30	Away	Southampton	Barclays Premier League
Wednesday 3 December	20.00	Away	Sunderland	Barclays Premier League

MANCHESTER
Christmas Markets

Arrive any time after 7 November and be dazzled by a Manchester Christmas.

Once you've gazed in awe at the Christmas lights, make time to visit over 300 Christmas stalls in seven different locations throughout the city. European and local produce – buy your friends something different this Christmas!

Opening times: November 10 a.m.–7.30 p.m., December 10 a.m.–8 p.m.

ACTIVITY 5

1 When could you watch Manchester City play at home and visit the museum?

2 What are the differences in the opening times of the Arndale Centre and the Christmas Markets?

3 Which places are definitely closed on Christmas Day?

4 Why might you need to walk further if you shopped at the Christmas Markets than if you shopped at the Arndale Centre?

 Assess your progress

In this unit you have:

- identified and interpreted information
- used detail from different sources to answer questions
- collated detail from different sources to answer questions.

Read the following paragraph about the Peterson family:

The Peterson family are planning a trip to Manchester on the weekend of 29–30 November. They want to see the Christmas lights and they hope to see a match at the City ground. The oldest children, Mike and Kate, want to do some clothes shopping, while Mrs Peterson is hoping to buy some unusual Christmas presents. Kane, who is seven, has been promised a visit to the 4D theatre.

1 Answer these questions:

   a Will the Petersons be able to see the Christmas lights? Give evidence for your answer.

   b Will they be able to watch a Manchester City match? Give evidence for your answer.

   c Where could Mike and Kate go to do some clothes shopping?

   d Where should Mrs Peterson go to get some unusual Christmas presents?

   e When is the 4D theatre open?

2 Collate detail from the four texts to answer this question fully: **Will the Peterson family be able to achieve everything they want to on their weekend visit to Manchester?**

How did you do?

Ask your teacher or another student for feedback on how well you have:

✔ identified and interpreted information correctly
✔ used detail from the different sources to answer questions correctly
✔ collated detail from the different sources to answer Question 2 fully.

 Complete this assignment on Cambridge Elevate.

FURTHER PROGRESS

Imagine you work in the Manchester tourism office. The Peterson family have asked you how they could all get what they want from their weekend stay. Write a short guide for them explaining what they could do and when they could do it. Make sure your details are accurate and that your explanation is written in clear sentences.

Unit 3
Interpret and comment on meaning

Make progress **AO1**

- interpret information and ideas
- comment to show understanding of explicit and implicit detail
- support your answers by using evidence from the text.

Source A

USE YOUR SKILLS

If something is **implied**, it means it is suggested rather than directly stated. If you come into your science class and see a pair of safety goggles at each seat, the **implication** is that you are going to do an experiment that could be dangerous. If there is a pair of safety gloves with each pair of goggles, the **evidence** for that interpretation is even stronger.

You interpret information and ideas all the time. For example you interpret how someone feels from their body language – their facial expression and their gestures.

ACTIVITY 1

1 Work with another student. Look at the images in Source A.

   a How do you think each character in the images is feeling?

   b What is it about their body language that makes you think this?

2 Now look at this photograph of a scene from a film:

Can you work out what is going on from the body language of the characters in this scene?

3 Use your skills to interpret detail in short messages.

a Your friend is having a birthday party on Saturday. You receive a text message from her on Friday saying: 'CU tomorrow?' Does this imply that:

- she is planning to come to your house tomorrow?
- she is checking that you are going to her party?

b You get home from school and find a note on the fridge door: 'Tea in the microwave. See you later. Dad.' Does this imply that:

- your Dad will not be home in time to make tea for you?
- your Dad will be home by tea time, but cannot be bothered to cook?

c You pass a builder's van parked on double yellow lines. There is a note on the windscreen that says: 'Working at no. 64'. Does this imply that:

- the builder is working in a nearby house and does not realise he has parked on double yellow lines?
- the builder is working in a nearby house and this is the only place he can park?

IDENTIFY IMPLICIT MEANING

Writers often rely on readers to work some things out for themselves. They may imply things but not say them directly. To work out implicit meaning, you need to use evidence in the text and knowledge gained from your own experience.

ACTIVITY 2

Source B is taken from a 19th-century text. The writer advises young ladies on how to behave when travelling and staying in hotels. Read the passage, then look at the extracts that follow. For each one, decide what is being implied.

Source B

The hours for meals at a hotel are numerous, so it is best to mention the time when you wish to eat. I know from experience how unpleasant it is to go hungry. It is essential to be ladylike when dining. For instance, a lady shouldn't drink wine at dinner, even if her head is strong enough to bear it. After eating, wait in the parlour whilst the chambermaid tidies your room. Before leaving   5
the room, be careful not to leave money or trinkets lying about. I have lost several valuables that way. When out walking don't drag your dress through that mud-puddle! But take care! You mustn't raise your dress too high. It is said that only a raw country girl will show her ankles!

Adapted from *The Ladies Book of Etiquette* by Florence Hartley

1. 'It is best to mention the time when you wish to eat'. Does this imply that:

   a   meals are available at all times?
   b   you could miss your meal?

2. 'A lady shouldn't drink wine at dinner, even if her head is strong enough to bear it'. Does this imply that:

   a   it is unladylike to drink?
   b   you should not drink wine because you may get drunk?

3. 'Be careful not to leave money or trinkets about'. Does this imply that:

   a   chambermaids should not be trusted?
   b   you could forget where you have put your valuables?

4. 'It is said that only a raw country girl will show her ankles.' Does this imply that:

   a   country girls need to raise their dresses to avoid the mud?
   b   country girls are not ladylike?

5. You can also work out things about the writer. What evidence can you find to support the following deductions about the writer of Source B?

   a   The writer has made mistakes when travelling in the past.
   b   The writer seems to look down on chambermaids and country girls.

ASK QUESTIONS TO WORK OUT MEANING

When you read a text, you need to think hard and ask questions to help you work out and interpret the meaning.

Read Source C, the opening of a book about the slums in Mumbai, India.
The questions in Activity 3 will help you identify explicit and implicit meaning.

ACTIVITY 3

1 Work with another student. Discuss the following questions to identify explicit meaning. Make notes on your answers – you do not need to write in sentences at this stage.

    a   Who is coming for Abdul and his father?
    b   Where do Abdul and his family live?
    c   What is Abdul's role in the family?
    d   What does Abdul call himself?
    e   What does Abdul do with most of his waking hours?
    f   Where does Abdul decide to hide?

Source C

Midnight was closing in, the one-legged woman was grievously burned, and the Mumbai police were coming for Abdul and his father. In a slum hut by the international airport, Abdul's parents came to a decision with an unusual economy of words. The father, a sick man, would wait   5 inside the trash-strewn, tin-roofed shack where the family of eleven resided. He'd go quietly when arrested. Abdul, the household earner, was the one who had to flee.

Abdul's opinion of this plan had not been asked, typically. Already he was mule-brained with panic. He was sixteen   10 years old, or maybe nineteen — his parents were hopeless with dates. Allah, in his wisdom, had cut him small and jumpy. A coward: Abdul said it of himself. He knew nothing about eluding policemen. What he knew about, mainly, was trash. For nearly all the waking hours of nearly   15 all the years he could remember, he'd been buying and selling to recyclers the things that richer people threw away.

Now Abdul grasped the need to disappear, but beyond that his imagination flagged. He took off running, then came back home. The only place he could think to hide was in   20 his garbage shed.

Adapted from *Behind the Beautiful Forevers* by Katherine Boo

2 Now answer the following questions to work out **implicit meaning** (what the writer suggests about Abdul):

   a Which details in the text suggest that Abdul's family is very poor?

   b Re-read this sentence: 'Abdul's opinion of this plan had not been asked, typically.' What is suggested by the use of the word 'typically'?

   c Abdul is described as being 'mule-brained with panic'. What does this image suggest?

   d Abdul could be sixteen or 'maybe nineteen'. What does this detail suggest?

   e Abdul calls himself a coward. What does this suggest about the way he feels about himself?

   f Abdul has been buying and selling trash 'for nearly all the waking hours of nearly all the years he could remember'. What does this suggest about the life he has led?

   g 'The only place he could think to hide was in his garbage shed.' What does this suggest about Abdul?

3 Compare your answers with those of another pair of students. Talk about any differences and add to your notes if you need to.

USE YOUR INTERPRETATIONS TO WRITE COMMENTS

You have identified explicit detail about Abdul. You have also worked out some of the things the writer suggests about him. Now think about this question:

What do you learn about Abdul from the opening paragraphs of *Behind the Beautiful Forevers*?

To answer this question well, you need to show that you can interpret the detail. Here is the opening of one student's answer to this question. The yellow highlights show the detail. The green highlights show the student's interpretation of the detail. The student's use of quotations are in bold.

The first thing I learn is that Abdul and his father are being chased by the Mumbai police which suggests they have done something wrong. It is obvious that Abdul's family is poor as they live in a **'tin-roofed shack'** and there are eleven of them living in it. Abdul is the **'household earner'** which makes him sound important in the family. However, he's not asked about the plan and the word **'typically'** makes it sound as though he's never asked about important things.

ACTIVITY 4

1 Copy out the student response. Use your notes from Activity 3 to help you continue the answer. Remember to:

- comment on and interpret the details about Abdul
- use quotation marks to quote directly from the text.

2 Swap your answer with a partner. Highlight or underline the comments your partner has made that show interpretation of the details.

Assess your progress

In this unit, you have:

- identified implicit meaning
- interpreted information and ideas
- developed comments to show understanding of explicit and implicit detail
- supported your answers by using evidence from the text.

Complete this assignment on Cambridge Elevate.

Read the next two paragraphs from the opening of *Behind the Beautiful Forevers* in Source D. Then answer the questions that follow.

Source D

He cracked the door of the family hut and looked out. His home sat midway down a row of hand-built dwellings; the lopsided shed where he stowed his trash was just next door. To reach this shed unseen would deprive his neighbours of the pleasure of turning him in to the police.

He didn't like the moon, though: full and stupid bright, illuminating a 5 dusty open lot in front of his home. Across the lot were the shacks of two dozen other families, and Abdul feared he wasn't the only person peering out from behind the cover of a plywood door. Some people in this slum wished his family ill because of the old Hindu-Muslim resentments. Others resented his family for the modern reason of economic envy. 10 By doing waste work, Abdul had lifted his large family above poverty.

Adapted from *Behind the Beautiful Forevers* by Katherine Boo

1 Answer these questions:

    a Why does Abdul want to reach his shed unseen?

    b Why is the full moon a problem for Abdul?

    c What is suggested by the sentence: 'Abdul feared he wasn't the only person peering out from behind the cover of a plywood door'?

    d What effect has Abdul's work had on his family and his neighbours?

2 Use your answers to help you write a detailed response to this question:

What dangers does Abdul face as he tries to leave the family hut?

Remember to:

✔ use detail from the text
✔ comment on the detail to show your skills in interpretation
✔ use quotation marks when you quote directly from the text.

How did you do?

Highlight your use of detail in one colour. Use a different colour to highlight comments that show your skills in interpretation. Underline any quotations you have used and make sure you have used quotation marks.

FURTHER PROGRESS

1 Look again at Source C and Source D. The story is set in the slums of Mumbai. Read the following question:

What do you learn about what it is like to live in the Mumbai slums from reading the opening paragraphs of this story?

In answer to this question, you could write about:

    a what you learn about the possible dangers
    b what you learn about the way people live
    c what you learn about the different people who live there.

Now write a detailed response to the question.

READING
Unit 4
Examine how writers use language to influence readers

USE YOUR SKILLS

The **purpose** of a text is what the writer wants to achieve. The writer of an advertisement, for example, may want to inform the reader and persuade them to buy a product. The writer of a ghost story may want to frighten and entertain the reader.

ACTIVITY 1

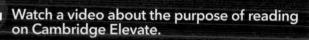

Watch a video about the purpose of reading on Cambridge Elevate.

 1 In pairs, look at this diagram. Match the opening sentences (A) to the type of text it is (B) and then the purpose of the text (C). One has been done as an example.

A1 Enjoy the ultimate driving experience with our powerful new saloon.	**B1** News report	**C1** Persuade
A2 Protestors occupied the council buildings in Truro yesterday. Officers from Devon and Cornwall constabulary tried to keep them at bay.	**B2** Advertisement	**C2** Advise
A3 Take care when opening the box. Carefully remove the contents. Dispose of all wrapping safely. Keep away from young children.	**B3** Story	**C3** Inform
A4 Dawn broke, brisk and cold, and with it memories of the previous night flooded back. It was a bright cold day in April, and the clocks were striking thirteen.	**B4** Instructions	**C4** Entertain

2 Discuss which features of each opening helped you identify the type and purpose of each text. These may relate to content and language use. Here is an explanation of A1:

> *'Enjoy the ultimate driving experience with our powerful new saloon' – this is about a car. The two phrases, 'ultimate driving experience' and 'powerful new saloon', both create a picture of a car that readers would want to own.*

3 Write an explanation of A2 and A3.

IDENTIFY AUDIENCE

The writer's **audience** is the intended reader or readers of the text. A newspaper article, for example, is usually intended for adults who want to know what is going on in the world. A review in a teenage fashion magazine is aimed at young people who are interested in current trends in clothing. A report on a football match is likely to target fans – young and old – of the teams involved.

ACTIVITY 2

Work with another student. Read Sources A and B, then answer the questions that follow.

Source A

WIN OUR FAVE NEW BOOK!

The Forest of Lost Souls is in shops this Thursday – for more info check out www.oksapollock.co.uk!

WIN! WIN! WIN!

We're giving away six copies of this amazing book – we know you'll just love it!

To enter, all you have to do is finish this sentence: 'If I could wear anything to school, I would wear …' and email your answer along with your full name, age and address. Good luck!

The closing date for entries is 2.59 p.m. on Friday, 14 March!

Adapted from www.shoutmag.co.uk

Source B

Many first-time parents experience difficulties. It's understandable. For nine months you've waited and planned … and then reality strikes. You, and you alone, are responsible for this tiny, precious life. Don't despair. This book will give you all the help and guidance you need to make sure that you and baby survive and thrive together. Grab a few free moments, put your feet up and read on.

1 Identify the purpose of each text:

   a What do you think the writer of Source A is hoping to achieve?
Why do you think this?

   b What do you think the writer of Source B is hoping to achieve?
Why do you think this?

2 Identify the intended audience:

   a Who is Source A written for? Why do you think this?

   b Who is Source B written for? Why do you think this?

UNDERSTAND THE IMPORTANCE OF PURPOSE AND AUDIENCE

A writer's purpose and audience directly influence what the writer says and how
they say it.

ACTIVITY 3

1 Read the following commentary on Source B. Parts of it have been
highlighted in different colours. Which colours show where the student:

   a identifies purpose

   b identifies audience

   c gives evidence to support points

   d identifies features of language?

> The writer of Source B is targeting first-time parents who may be struggling with
> their new baby. The writer wants to sound understanding so he says things like 'It's
> understandable'. He speaks to them directly when he says 'You, and you alone' and
> 'Don't despair'. His main purpose though is to encourage them to read his book. That's
> why he tells them it contains 'all the help and guidance they will need'. He uses the
> catchy phrase 'survive and thrive' to sound positive and give his readers hope.

2 Now write a commentary like this for Source A. The information in the
following table will help you to develop your ideas.

Purpose and audience	Evidence	Comment
Purpose 1: to publicise the book	'our fave new book!'	The use of 'our' includes the reader.
Purpose 2: to encourage readers to enter a competition	'Win! Win! Win!'	Repetition and exclamation marks emphasise that this is something readers can and should do.
Audience: young people at school	Subject of sentence: 'If I could wear anything to school …'	Informal language is used, such as 'fave' and 'info'.

EXAMINE HOW WRITERS TRY TO INFLUENCE READERS

Writers often select detail and use language to influence their readers' view of something. Writers may also choose to leave out details that would alter a reader's view.

ACTIVITY 4

1 Read the following extract from a report on an incident. With a partner, find and list the facts included in the report.

In protest at recent pay cuts, 500 protesters attempted to occupy the council buildings in Truro yesterday. Forty-two officers from the Devon and Cornwall Constabulary used batons and pepper spray to stop them. In the exchange that followed, 12 civilians and eight policemen were injured.

2 In your pairs, read two more reports on the same incident. For each one, identify:

a the facts that have been included
b the facts that have been left out
c words the writer has used to influence the reader
d what the writer wants the reader to think.

A Nearly 500 protesters stormed the council buildings in Truro yesterday. Forty-two officers from the Devon and Cornwall Constabulary battled bravely to keep them at bay. Eight officers of the law were injured in the skirmish and required hospital treatment.

B Almost 500 protesters valiantly occupied the council buildings in Truro yesterday in an attempt to make clear their frustration with recent savage pay cuts. Forty-two police officers, armed with batons and pepper spray, were deployed to stop them. Twelve civilians required hospital treatment.

UNDERSTAND WRITERS' LANGUAGE CHOICES

Good writers think carefully about every word they choose and how it will influence their reader. When you are reading, think about the words the writer has chosen and the effect the writer is aiming to achieve.

ACTIVITY 5

The following diagram shows how one of the words ('stormed') from the report might influence the reader.

1. Work with another student. Think about the following word choices made by the two writers. For each one, draw a diagram showing what the choice of the underlined words suggests to you.

   a <u>battled bravely</u>
   b <u>officers</u> <u>of the law</u>
   c <u>valiantly</u> occupied
   d <u>savage</u> pay cuts
   e <u>armed with</u> batons and pepper spray

2. Read one student's response to one of the writer's language choices:

   The writer uses the word 'stormed' to describe how the protestors went into the council buildings. This verb suggests that they were angry and were almost like an army. It also makes me think of a weather storm, which can be dangerous.

   Choose **two** examples of the writer's use of language that you have examined. For each example, use your diagram to help you write a comment explaining:

   a how the word(s) have been used
   b what the word(s) suggest.

3. Swap your comments with a partner. Tick where your partner has:

   a identified how the word(s) have been used
   b explained what the word(s) suggest.

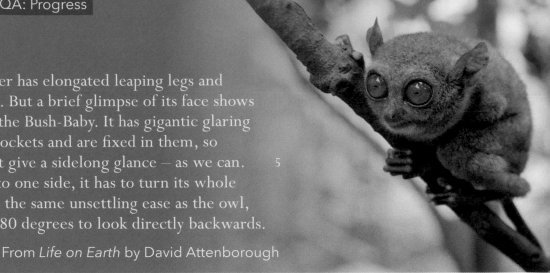

Source C

Like the Bush-Baby, the Tarsier has elongated leaping legs and long-fingered grasping hands. But a brief glimpse of its face shows that it is very different from the Bush-Baby. It has gigantic glaring eyes. They bulge from their sockets and are fixed in them, so that the little creature cannot give a sidelong glance — as we can. 5
If it wants to see something to one side, it has to turn its whole head, something it does with the same unsettling ease as the owl, swivelling its head through 180 degrees to look directly backwards.

From *Life on Earth* by David Attenborough

 Assess your progress

In this unit, you have:

- identified writers' purposes and audiences
- understood that writers choose detail to suit their purpose and audience
- examined how detail and words influence readers
- developed comments on uses of language.

Read Source C, an extract from a non-fiction book about the natural world.

1 Which of the following best describes the writer's purpose:

   a   to frighten and explain

   b   to inform, describe and interest

   c   to advise and instruct?

2 Who do you think is the intended audience?

3 Why do you think the writer includes comparison with the Bush-Baby?

4 Why do you think the writer chooses the words 'little creature' to describe the tarsier?

5 What does the comparison with the owl help the reader to picture?

6 Think about the following descriptions:

   a   elongated leaping legs

   b   long-fingered grasping hands

   c   gigantic glaring eyes.

For each one, write a comment on:

- what the words suggest
- how they make you feel about the tarsier.

How did you do?

Ask another student to check that you have:

✔ identified purpose and audience

✔ understood use of detail and words

✔ commented on the writer's use of language.

 Complete this assignment on Cambridge Elevate.

FURTHER PROGRESS

In his next paragraph about the Tarsier, Attenborough describes what happens when it hears a beetle:

Then swiftly the Tarsier springs downward, grabs the beetle with both hands, and sinks its teeth into it with an expression of ferocious relish, shutting its huge eyes with each crunch of its jaws.

---

1 What impression of the Tarsier does Attenborough give the reader here?

2 How does he do this?

READING
Unit 5
Examine how writers create and use tone

Make progress (AO2)
- examine how writers use adjectives and adverbs
- examine how writers use noun phrases
- investigate how writers create and use tone
- look at how writers vary sentence forms.

USE YOUR SKILLS

You will have noticed that writers choose and use words for effect. In this unit, you will learn more about the different language techniques that writers use to influence readers.

ACTIVITY 1

Source A shows a petition against a planned development of Chiswell Greenbelt. Greenbelt land is usually protected so no one can build on it. The first part of the text appeals to residents to sign the petition. The second part is the petition itself. Read the text, then answer the following questions.

1 Work with another student. Look at the appeal to residents.

   a The writer uses the word 'destruction' to describe the Greenbelt development. Why do you think they chose this word?

   b What is the effect of the short sentence 'Sign now!'?

   c Which two **pronouns** does the writer use to directly engage residents?

Source A

Chiswell Green: Greenbelt destruction that affects you …

Sign now! Don't be afraid to be identified. It's your right to object.

I strongly object to any proposals for planning applications on the Greenbelt behind Long Fallow. 450 potential homes is a disproportionate increase in number of households, injuring the very fabric of the village. It would result in some additional 900 cars spilling out onto the Watford Bypass – a dangerously busy road, which in rush hour is like a clogged artery. The added air, noise and light pollution would be detrimental to local residents' health and their quality of life, not to mention the negative impact on wildlife.

From www.petitions24.com/chiswell_green-greenbelt_destruction_that_affects_all

2 Now look at the wording of the petition.

    a Why does the writer object to the proposal?

    b The writer uses the simile 'like a clogged artery' to describe the bypass. What does this image suggest to you?

    c Find two other examples where language is used to suggest that the proposal would be bad for residents of this area.

3 If you lived in Chiswell and you received this appeal, would you sign the petition? Discuss this in your pairs. Give reasons for your decision.

HOW WRITERS USE ADJECTIVES AND ADVERBS

Writers start out with a purpose. They choose their words carefully, and writers often redraft their text by changing words or adding new words to make sure they achieve their purpose.

ACTIVITY 2

Source B is an early draft of a story from the website of Shelter – a charity for homeless people. Source C is the text as it appears on the website.

Source B

Tom and his mum Andrea spent last Christmas in a B&B room.

Christmas dinner was a takeaway.

But when Andrea called Shelter's helpline, our advisers gave her the help she needed.

We helped them find a flat closer to their family. Thanks to Shelter, this Christmas will be different.

£33 could help a family find and keep a home. £25 could fund a helpline adviser for one hour. Please donate.

Source C

Tom and his mum Andrea spent last Christmas in a tiny B&B room.

Christmas dinner was a cheap takeaway.

But when Andrea called Shelter's helpline, our expert advisers gave her the help she so urgently needed.

We helped them find a flat closer to their family and friends.

Thanks to Shelter, this Christmas will be happy.

£33 could help a family find and keep a home. £25 could fund a helpline adviser for one hour.

Please donate now.

Adapted from
england.shelter.org.uk/stories/toms_story

1 Compare Source B and Source C. List the differences between them.

2 Now explore the reasons for some of these differences. You can choose more than one of the suggested answers.

   a The writer has added the **adjective** 'tiny' to 'B&B room'. This may be because:
- it is more accurate
- it makes the story more interesting
- it makes the reader more sympathetic towards Tom and his mother.

   b The writer uses the adjective 'cheap' to describe the takeaway they had for Christmas dinner. This may be because:
- it suggests that Andrea is not a generous person
- it suggests this was all they could afford
- readers are more likely to give money if they realise how little Andrea had to spare.

3 Why do you think the writer adds the **adverbs** 'so urgently'? How might this influence readers?

4 The writer adds the adverb 'now' to 'Please donate'. Why do you think they did this?

5 Use your answers to Questions 1 to 4 to help you write a paragraph in which you explain how the writer uses words to influence readers in Source C.

HOW WRITERS USE NOUN PHRASES

A **noun phrase** can be a single **noun** or pronoun, for example 'man', 'he'. Writers often add detail to these to increase their impact and influence the reader.

Read Source D. The writer is describing the scene he observes during a bus journey through London on a rainy evening. Try to identify the noun phrases he uses as you read it.

Source D

The illuminated shops pass like an endless window. Groups of people stare in at them in spite of the rain; ill-clad, half-starving people. The well-dressed commuters hurry   5 onwards; they have homes. At the bright and happy entrance to a theatre, there is a small crowd waiting, and among them two ladies, plump and rosy-cheeked. Their faces 10 glow in the light — merry coal-fire faces. They laugh, they chat; their shoulders are wrapped in warm expensive furs. The bus goes on, and they are lost to view.   15

Adapted from 'A Wet Night in London' by Richard Jefferies

Did you notice that the writer uses the noun phrase 'ill-clad, half-starving people'? Study the diagram below to see what this suggests about the people:

ill-clad, half-starving people

suggests → poorly dressed for the weather

suggests → so hungry they are almost starving

ACTIVITY 3

In pairs, create a similar diagram to show what is suggested by the underlined words in each of the following noun phrases.

a   two ladies, <u>plump</u> and <u>rosy-cheeked</u>
b   <u>warm</u> <u>expensive</u> furs.

2   The writer uses noun phrases to show a contrast in the people he sees from the window of his bus. Talk about the differences between the people he sees.

3   Read this explanation of the writer's use of noun phrases. Work out what should go in the spaces. Then copy the explanation and fill in the gaps. Remember to use quotation marks when you use evidence taken directly from the text.

> The writer is clearly trying to influence the reader's response. He wants them to realise the big difference between _____ on London's streets. His use of _____ shows this difference. He describes the poor as _____. This suggests _____. He describes the rich two ladies as being _____ and wearing _____. These noun phrases suggest _____.

HOW WRITERS CREATE AND USE TONE

The word **tone** is used to describe a writer's attitude. There are many possible tones – for example sarcastic, angry, disgusted, sad, excited, amused and so on. Writers create tone in different ways.

Read Source E, written in 1845, in which the writer describes an area of London. Think about the words you would use to describe his tone. Then investigate how the writer creates this tone in Activity 4.

Source E

The want and filth surpass description. The walls are crumbling, windows broken, broken doors hang open, or there are no doors at all, because no doors are needed, there being nothing to steal. Garbage rots everywhere, and foul liquids emptied before the   5
doors gather in stinking pools. Here live the poorest of the poor, the worst paid workers, with thieves and prostitutes — unwanted, unnoticed, despairing. Those who have not yet drowned in the whirlpool of moral ruin which surrounds them, sink daily deeper,   10
losing daily more and more of their power to resist the demoralising influence of want, filth, and evil.

From The Condition of the Working Class in England by Frederick Engels

ACTIVITY 4

1 What does the writer of Source E suggest about this area in his opening sentence?

2 Identify the list the writer uses in his second sentence. What does this list emphasise?

3 Find where the writer uses a **metaphor** of a whirlpool. What is a whirlpool? Is it easy to escape from one? What does this metaphor suggest about the people who live here?

4 Find the following lists in the passage. Explain the effects of each one.

   a 'unwanted, unnoticed, despairing'
   b 'want, filth, and evil'.

5 Which of the following best describes the writer's tone? Use evidence from the text to support your choice.

   a He observes the poverty but has no strong feelings about it.
   b He is angry at the poverty he sees, and knows people have little chance of escape.
   c He is unsympathetic and thinks the people who live there deserve what they get.

HOW WRITERS VARY SENTENCE FORMS

Writers vary their sentence forms to make their writing more interesting. Read Source F, which is about Manchester.

ACTIVITY 5

1 Identify each of the following sentence forms in Source F:

   a one-word question to make reader stop and think
   b short statement asserting point of view
   c developed **complex sentence** explaining why Mancunians can boast
   d short exclamation referring to question
   e conditional sentence that makes clear what Manchester needs to do
   f simple statement in response to question.

2 Copy the following explanation of the writer's use of sentence forms. Use your answer to Question 1 to help you fill in the blanks.

The writer opens with a _____ which _____. He follows this with a conditional sentence that makes clear _____. The single-word question 'Why?' makes the reader _____. He answers this question with the simple statement that _____. He then uses a _____ to explain in detail why Mancunians have a right to boast. He ends with the short exclamation _____ which _____.

Source F

Manchester matters. If it stopped banging on about football and bands and shops, the city has something it can be genuinely proud of. Why? It changed world politics. Mancunians can boast, because from vegetarianism to feminism to communism, every snotty street-fighter of a radical idea, was born brawling in the streets, mills, pubs, and debating halls of the city. That's why!

    5

Adapted from *Pies and Prejudice* by Stuart Maconie

Assess your progress

In this unit, you have examined how writers:

- use adjectives and adverbs to influence readers
- use noun phrases to influence readers
- create and use tone to influence readers
- vary sentence forms to influence readers.

Source G is an extract from a 2008 essay by the American writer Eula Biss. Read the source, then answer the following question.

1 What methods does Bliss use to influence the reader's view of Rogerstown? Write about:

- her attitude, feelings and tone
- how she uses words to influence the reader
- how she varies sentence forms to influence readers.

Remember to use quotations to support the points you make.

How did you do?

Ask another student or your teacher to give you feedback on how well you have:

✔ understood the writer's attitude, feelings and tone

✔ examined the writer's use of words and sentence forms

✔ used quotations to support the points you make.

Complete this assignment on Cambridge Elevate.

Source G

I was naïve. I didn't understand that the Rogerstown estates, derelict islands where the Ethnic poor survived amongst a tide of garbage and graffiti, were regarded by 'my kind' as places of   5
danger. I learned. One evening after I moved here, a troop of boys gathered across the street from my apartment. They stared at me. One boy shouted, 'Don't be afraid of us!' I wanted to   10
shout back, 'I'm not!', but I was afraid. I was afraid to draw attention to my smart shoes, my smart suit, my bag; suddenly ashamed of them. Suddenly my outfit seemed like the uniform of   15
an occupying force. I turned toward the tall, iron gate in front of my apartment ... eager to pass through and close it behind me.

Adapted from 'In the City' by Eula Biss

FURTHER PROGRESS

Read the following extract, which contains information about King Henry VIII.

Perhaps optimistically believing he could 'upgrade' from his last wife, Henry courted the attention of the young and pretty Catherine Howard, aged just about 18 when they married.   5
Unfortunately for the bloated, aging monarch the attraction wasn't mutual – Catherine didn't appear to be starry-eyed over the bad-tempered king, over 30 years older than her, who was   10
almost unable to walk properly due to a large, running ulcer on his leg.

1 How would you describe the tone of this extract?

2 How does the writer use language to influence his readers?

Unit 6

Explore how writers use language to describe

Make progress AO2

- explore how writers use descriptive language and imagery
- explain the effect of descriptive techniques
- consider how writers create setting and atmosphere.

USE YOUR SKILLS

In some texts, writers both inform and describe. They mix facts with descriptive language. Investigate how one writer does this in Activity 1.

ACTIVITY 1

Read Source A, which is from a website about London landmarks. It contains a mixture of facts and descriptive language.

 1 Work in pairs. What facts are you told about the London Eye?

2 Identify words or phrases which show that the writer is doing more than simply giving information.

Source A

The London Eye is a giant space-age observation wheel located in the Jubilee Gardens on the South Bank. The 135-metre (443-foot) tall structure was built as part of London's millennium celebrations.

Construction took more than a year and a half to   5
complete. The wheel turns at a snail's pace – slow enough for people to embark while it is moving. The futuristic-looking glass pods were transported all the way from France. Each egg-shaped capsule is 8 metres long and weighs 500 kilograms. Thanks to   10
the construction of the capsules passengers have a heart-stopping 360-degree view over London.

Adapted from www.aviewoncities.com/london/londoneye.htm

3 Copy the following table. Write the words and phrases you identified in the left-hand column. With your partner, discuss the effect of each phrase. Record your ideas in the right-hand column. An example has been done for you.

Descriptive phrase	Effect
'space-age'	makes it seem very advanced – like something from space – something not seen before or in sci-fi movies
'The wheel turns at a snail's pace'	

4 Use your answers from the right-hand column to continue the following paragraph, describing the ways in which the writer is trying to capture the reader's imagination:

The writer describes the London Eye as 'space age'; this makes it seem very advanced, like something from a sci-fi movie. The writer also …

EXPLORE USE OF ADJECTIVES

Writers use adjectives to add to the meaning and effect of nouns. Adjectives give extra information. For example:

A <u>small</u> figure approached the <u>crowded</u> house.

The meaning of this sentence would be altered if the writer selected different adjectives. For example:

A <u>tall</u> figure entered the <u>empty</u> house.

The writer could also choose adjectives that have similar meanings but different effects.

For example:

> suggests huge size and power

A <u>towering</u> figure entered the <u>deserted</u> house.

> suggests abandonment and creates a sense of mystery

ACTIVITY 2

1 Copy the following sentences. Annotate the underlined adjectives to explain their effect.

a A <u>ghostly</u> figure entered the <u>haunted</u> house.
b A <u>mysterious</u> figure entered the <u>silent</u> house.

Now read source B – an extract from a short story about people living in a nursing home.

2 Identify **three** adjectives that have a similar meaning to 'red-faced'. For each one, write a sentence explaining its effect.

Source B

The old woman turns through the pages of her album … sweet and painful memories of a fading past. Here she is as a young, slim-waisted girl, flushed, bearing a sporting trophy aloft; here a blushing graduate, on the steps of a college – smiling and holding a certificate; and here a mother, cradling a rosy infant in her arms.

EXPLORE USE OF NOUN PHRASES

The writer of Source B develops descriptions by combining adjectives. For example:

- 'sweet and painful memories'
- 'young, slim-waisted girl'

The adjectives in these noun phrases help the reader to understand the woman's feelings and to picture her when she was younger.

ACTIVITY 3

Read Source C – an extract from a short story. Some of the noun phrases are underlined.

Source C

He ran along the top of the first wood and finding no shelter but the thin, wind-stripped hedge, dipped below the crest and jogged along to the wood of oaks. In blinding rain he lunged through the barricade of savage brambles at the wood's edge. The poor crippled trees were not much shelter, but at a sudden fierce fusillade of rain he chose one and crouched under the gun-black trunk.

From 'The Rain Horse' by Ted Hughes

1 In pairs, discuss the ideas that are suggested by each of the underlined noun phrases. For example:

2 Now work on your own. Use your ideas to help you write a paragraph in response to the following question:

Explain how Hughes uses noun phrases to suggest the violence of nature.

3 Compare your response with a partner's. Give feedback on how well they have explained the effects of the noun phrases.

EXPLORE USE OF VERBS AND ADVERBS

In Source C, Hughes uses a range of verbs of movement: 'ran', 'dipped', 'jogged', 'lunged' and 'crouched'. This range helps the reader picture how the man tries to escape from the weather. It is important to be aware of a writer's choice of verbs. In the following sentence, the verb 'walked' does little more than provide the reader with information:

The soldier <u>walked</u> across the battlefield.

The addition of an adverb modifies the meaning of the verb. For example:

The soldier walked <u>slowly</u> across the battlefield.

However, changing the verb may have a similar impact:

The soldier <u>crept</u> across the battlefield.

The use of the verb 'crept' not only suggests that he moved slowly, it also suggests secrecy and, possibly, fear. It leads the reader to think about what could happen next.

ACTIVITY 4

1 Read the following two versions of an extract from a story. Identify the differences between the two versions. Pay particular attention to the use of verbs and adverbs.

Version 1

The stranger waited just inside the inn door, looking round the corner. Once I went out into the road, but he called me back. When I didn't respond straight away, his expression changed, and he told me to come back in such an angry voice it surprised me.

Version 2

The stranger skulked just inside the inn door, peering slyly round the corner, like a cat waiting for a mouse. Once, I ventured out into the road, but he hissed at me to come back. When I did not obey instantly, a horrible change disfigured his face, and he ordered me in so violently it made me jump.

Adapted from *Treasure Island* by Robert Louis Stevenson

2 With a partner, discuss the effect of the writer's choice of verbs and adverbs in Version 2. Then copy and complete the following table.

Basic meaning (Version 1)	Writer's choice (Version 2)	Effect
'waited'	'skulked'	gives the impression that he is behaving secretly, as though he is hiding or avoiding something
'looking'	'peering slyly'	
'went'		
'called me'		
'respond'		
'his expression changed'		
'he told me'		
'surprised me'		

3 Share your ideas with another pair. Add to your table if you need to.

EXPLORE USE OF IMAGERY

In Version 2, the writer uses a **simile** to describe the stranger's behaviour. Read one student's explanation of the writer's use of this simile:

The writer uses the simile 'like a cat waiting for a mouse'. This makes the stranger seem cunning and gives the impression of a dangerous creature waiting to pounce on someone. It may also have the effect of making the reader feel that he is evil and a villain.

comments on effect

identifies language feature

explores effect

ACTIVITY 5

1 Read the following extract from the same story. Write an explanation of the writer's use of a simile. Annotate where you have:

- identified the language feature
- commented on its effect
- explored its effect.

In the meantime, we had no idea what to do to help the captain [...] I got the rum, to be sure, and tried to put it down his throat, but his teeth were tightly shut and his jaws as strong as iron.

Adapted from *Treasure Island* by Robert Louis Stevenson

EXPLORE SETTING AND ATMOSPHERE

Setting is the aspect of a story that gives descriptive details about the time and place in which events occur:

As the sun set over San Francisco, bustling shoppers surged onto the busy streets, pushing through jostling crowds as, burdened with bags, they hurriedly scuttled from one department store to another.

Here, the writer uses adjectives such as 'bustling', 'busy' and 'jostling' to create an atmosphere of tension and excitement. Verbs such as 'surged' and 'scuttled' add to this by suggesting both the power and the speed of the shoppers.

ACTIVITY 6

Copy this extract. Highlight where the writer gives the time, the place and descriptive details.

Dawn … and the city stirred gently to life, the soft murmurings of pigeons on the sun-streaked ledges of skyscrapers blending with the warmth of the morning sun and the faint hum of early trams.

1 How would you describe the atmosphere? Is it: busy, tense, mysterious, calm, tranquil, eerie or peaceful?

2 Write a paragraph explaining how the writer creates this atmosphere through his use of descriptive detail.

✔ Assess your progress

In this unit, you have:

- explored how writers use descriptive language
- explained the effect of descriptive techniques
- considered how writers create setting and atmosphere.

Look back through this unit to remind yourself of the different features of descriptive writing.

1 Read Source D closely. Write an explanation of how the writer uses detail and descriptive language to create setting and atmosphere.

Remember to:

a examine the writer's choice of detail and descriptive language

b explain how the detail and description create atmosphere

c refer to the text to support the points you make.

How did you do?

Ask another student or your teacher to give you feedback on your answer.

✔ **Complete this assignment on Cambridge Elevate.**

Source D

Most of the amusements were closed at this time of year, but I liked to wander idly past the canvas shrouded dodgem cars and shuttered gift stalls, past blank lights and peeling paint. There was an open air swimming pool, drained for the winter, and sand and silt had been washed over the rim by the storm tides. Near to this was one amusement centre, called Gala Land. It was built underground in a sort of valley between two outcrops of rock, over which was a ribbed glass roof, like those Victorian railway stations and conservatories. The walls were covered in greenish moss and the whole place had a close, damp, musty smell. It was lit dimly with neon and fluorescent lights. Everything looked somehow dark, furtive and gone to seed.

5

10

15

From Mr Proudham and Mr Sleight by Susan Hill

FURTHER PROGRESS

Read the next two sentences of Source D.

Some of the booths were closed down here, too, and those which kept open must have lost money, except perhaps on the few days when parties of trippers came from inland, in the teeth of the weather, and dived for shelter to the underground palace of fun. Then, for a few hours, the fruit and try-your-strength and fortune card machines whirred, loud cracks echoed from the rifle ranges, and hurdy-gurdy music sounded out.

5

From Mr Proudham and Mr Sleight by Susan Hill

2 Explain how the writer uses detail and descriptive language to create a different impression of Gala Land.

READING
Unit 7
Explore how writers order and organise texts

Make progress AO2

- consider how writers choose and order their words
- examine how writers order and link ideas in paragraphs
- examine how writers structure whole texts
- explore how writers use structure to influence readers.

USE YOUR SKILLS

It is sometimes important to do things in a particular order: to put toothpaste on the brush before brushing your teeth; to look both ways before crossing the road.

ACTIVITY 1

1 Work in pairs. Look at the actions in the word bank. Make a note of which of these things you do and the order in which you do them. Compare your lists and discuss any differences.

wake up	eat breakfast	watch TV
put shoes on	text friends	listen to radio
wash	get dressed	check messages
get out of bed	check school bag	brush teeth

2 Work on your own. Think about a journey that you make regularly, where A is your starting point and B is your destination. Write clear directions explaining how to get from A to B.

3 Swap your directions with a partner. Can you follow their directions? If not, explain the problem to them.

CHANGE THE ORDER OF WORDS

The order of words is important. The phrase 'She is at school', for example, has a different meaning from 'Is she at school?', even though they use the same words.

ACTIVITY 2

1 Turn the following statements into questions by changing the word order:

   a   They have raised money for charity.
   b   The school governors have congratulated them.

2 Turn the following questions into statements by changing the word order:

   a   Have they seen the new stadium?
   b   Are the yoghurts in the fridge?

3 Change the meaning of the following statements by changing the word order:

   a   The superhero tackled the villain.
   b   The politician asked the people for help.

EXAMINE HOW WRITERS CHOOSE AND ORDER WORDS

Writers choose their words and decide on the word order to suit their purpose and audience. When giving advice to a child, for example, a writer might use short sentences and simple words. For adults, a writer may use a wider range of sentence types and more difficult vocabulary.

ACTIVITY 3

The government has a website about the safety of children on the roads. One part of it is written for children and another part for parents. In pairs, read Sources A and B, then answer the questions that follow.

Source A

1 Find a safe place to cross.
2 Stop just before you get to the kerb.
3 Look all around for traffic, and listen.
4 If traffic is coming, let it pass.
5 When it is safe, go straight across the road. Do not run. Keep looking and listening while you cross.

From thinkdirect.gov.uk

Source B

Around 1,400 children aged 0–11 are killed or seriously injured on Britain's roads every year. That's almost 27 children every week.

Your child is currently learning about road safety at school but as a parent or carer you also play a big part in helping   5
him or her to learn how to stay safe. Children copy adults' behaviour, so if they see you taking risks they will probably take risks too. One of the best ways that you can help your child to stay safe is to set a good example when using roads, on foot and in the car.   10

This booklet will also help you to teach your child how to be a safe pedestrian, about the importance of the Green Cross Code and how to stay safe when cycling and riding in a car. In addition, it contains guidance on how children can 'Be Bright, Be Seen' and the law relating to child car seats and   15
seat belts.

From thinkdirect.gov.uk

1 Which source is written for children and which one for parents? List **three** reasons that explain your answer.

2 What is the purpose of Source A? What is the purpose of Source B?

3 Look again at Source A. It uses a sequence of **imperatives** such as 'find' and 'stop':

   a   List **three** other imperatives in Source A.
   b   Why do you think the writer has used imperatives?

4 Look again at Source B. It addresses the reader directly by using the pronouns 'you' and 'your'.

   a   How many times are these words used in Source B?
   b   Why do you think the writer has used these pronouns?

5 The following sentence has been written for parents. Rewrite it for young children. Remember to use short sentences and simple vocabulary:

Children need to understand that using their eyes and ears all the time is essential to being safe near traffic: they should avoid distractions such as chatting to friends or listening to music players when crossing roads.

FOLLOW IDEAS IN A PARAGRAPH

Writers use words to influence their readers. The imperatives in Source A make the advice very direct, so children are more likely to take notice of it. The pronouns in Source B directly target the reader and will make parents feel that it is their own child who is in danger.

Writers also take care when organising their ideas into paragraphs. They order and link their ideas to help the reader follow them without difficulty, and to give them maximum impact.

ACTIVITY 4

1 Read Source C, an extract from an article about holiday brochures. Answer questions a to e.

Source C

The key to all holiday brochures is the picture of the hotel swimming-pool. What you see is it. There isn't any more. Although the water laps the edge of the photograph to give you the impression that there's twice as much pool if only they had the space to show it, a millimetre more and you would see dry land. That peculiar triangle shape is not a segment of a huge Olympic-sized pool. It is a complete, close-cropped representation of a peculiarly triangular-shaped pool.

From 'How to Speak Brochurese' by Keith Waterhouse, in *Travel Writing*

a What does the first sentence suggest the paragraph will be about?

b What same point is emphasised in the short second and third sentences?

c What explanation is given in the long fourth sentence?

d Why does the writer tell you what the pool is **not** before telling you what it **is**?

e What final image of the pool is the reader left with?

2 Look at the beginning of one student's response to this question:

How does the writer order and express his ideas to influence the reader?

The writer starts by talking about the picture of the swimming-pool in a hotel brochure. He then gives the reader his views on this in the rest of the paragraph. He uses two short sentences to repeat the idea that what you see is all there is: 'What you see is it. There isn't any more.' These emphasise the point that the pool is very small. These short sentences are explained in more detail in . . . .

Copy and then complete the answer. Use the annotations and your answers to Question 1 to help you.

3 Compare your answer with a partner. Share your ideas to help you both make improvements.

INVESTIGATE STRUCTURE

When planning an article, a writer has to decide:

- what ideas to include
- the order in which to write about them
- how to best influence the reader.

ACTIVITY 5

1 Read Source D, the next three paragraphs of the article about holiday brochures. Discuss questions a to f with another student to make sure you understand the article.

2 Use your skills in **inference** to decide which of the following statements best summarises what the article is about:

a   It describes hotel swimming pools.
b   It explains how photographers who take pictures should not be trusted.
c   It suggests that holiday brochures should not be trusted.
d   It claims that booking a holiday is like having heatstroke.

 Watch a video about inferring meaning on Cambridge Elevate.

Source D

The same goes for bedrooms, where the photograph likewise contrives to suggest that there is a lot more room to the east of the twin beds. There isn't. When the photographer took that picture, it was with his back pressed up against the wall, or from inside the wardrobe that is not shown.   5

The bird's eye view of the beach looks inviting. The reason it's a bird's eye view is that shooting from a few feet back on the hotel roof, the camera avoids the four-lane highway that your balcony overlooks.

But anyone booking a holiday solely on the recommendation of a   10 brochure, particularly a tour operator's brochure, must be suffering from heatstroke. The only real use of a brochure, apart from giving you a vague idea what a resort looks like with the abattoir obliterated (that's why the picture is L-shaped) is to convey the only solid information it contains, which is the price. This is one   15 area in which the brochure cannot lie — or anyway, not much.

From 'How to Speak Brochurese' by Keith Waterhouse,
in *Travel Writing*

a What is the focus of this paragraph?
b What is the writer implying?

c What is the focus of this paragraph?
d What is the writer implying?

e What is this paragraph about?

f Why has the writer added these words? What effect do they have?

> **Vocabulary**
>
> **abattoir:** a place where animals are slaughtered

ACTIVITY 6

You are now going to investigate how the writer has structured the **whole** text to have maximum impact on the reader. You need to consider Source C (the first paragraph) **and** Source D (the second, third and fourth paragraphs).

1. What words does the writer use to make a direct link between the second paragraph and the first?

2. In the first paragraph, the writer suggests that photographs of pools cannot be trusted. How does he suggest that the same is true of:

   a. photographs of bedrooms?
   b. photographs of beaches?

3. By the end of the third paragraph, what has the reader realised about photographs in holiday brochures?

4. What does the writer imply at the start of the fourth paragraph when he says that anyone who books a holiday because of the brochure 'must be suffering from heatstroke'? Now that you have read the first three paragraphs closely, do you agree?

5. In the first three paragraphs, the writer suggests that the pool and bedroom are smaller than you think and that there might be a 'four-lane highway' between your balcony and the beach.

   a. What possibility, even worse than these, does he suggest in the fourth paragraph?
   b. How do you react to this possibility?

6. What key word directly links the first and last sentences of the article?

7. What does the last sentence suggest to you?

Assess your progress

In this unit, you have:

- examined how writers choose and order their words
- looked at how they order and link ideas in paragraphs
- examined how writers structure whole texts
- examined how writers use structure to influence readers.

Read Source E, then answer the following questions.

1 How does the writer use repetition in the first paragraph to emphasise her statement in the first sentence?

2 How does the first sentence of the second paragraph link with the first paragraph?

3 What do you learn about Raymond and the narrator in the second paragraph?

4 The second paragraph ends with the words 'I run'. How does the writer develop these two words in the third paragraph?

5 Which sentence in the fourth paragraph repeats the idea that the writer is 'the fastest thing on two feet'?

6 Why do you think the writer ends the fourth paragraph with a question?

7 What exception is introduced in the fifth paragraph?

8 Why do you think she chose to use the single-word sentence 'Ridiculous'?

9 What effect does the final sentence have on you, the reader?

How did you do?

Compare your answers with those of another student. Discuss any differences. Make sure that you understand how a writer:

✔ chooses and orders words for effect

✔ orders and links ideas in paragraphs

✔ structures a text to influence the reader.

Complete this assignment on Cambridge Elevate.

FURTHER PROGRESS

Use what you have leant to help you write a detailed answer to this question:

Explain how Toni Cade Bambara structures her writing to interest and influence her readers.

Before writing your answer, think again about:

- what she focuses your attention on in the first two paragraphs
- when she introduces the idea of running and how she develops this
- how she ends her writing.

Source E

I don't have much to do around the house. My mother does that. And I don't have to earn my pocket money by running errands and selling Christmas cards. My brother George does that. And anything else that's got to be done, my father does. 5

All I have to do is mind my brother Raymond, which is enough. He's bigger and he's older too, but a lot of people call him my little brother because he's not quite right and needs looking after. And if any of these smart mouths try to pick on Raymond, they have to deal 10 with me, and I don't believe in just standing around talking. I'd much rather knock them down and take my chances, even if I am a girl with skinny arms and a squeaky voice. And if things get too tough, I run.

As anybody can tell you, I'm the fastest thing on two 15 feet. There is no track meet where I don't win the first-place medal. I used to win the 20-yard dash when I was a little kid. Nowadays it's the 100-yard dash.

I'm the swiftest thing in the neighbourhood. Everybody knows that except the two people who know better 20 my father and me. My father can beat me in a race with me giving him a head start and him running with his hands in his pocket and whistling. But can you imagine a thirty-five year-old man stuffing himself into a pair of shorts just to beat his kid in a race? 25

So, as far as everyone's concerned, I'm the fastest. Except for Gretchen, who has put out the story that she is going to win the first-place medal this year. Ridiculous. No one can beat me, and that's all there is to that. 30

From *Raymond's Run* by Toni Cade Bambara

Make progress (AO2)
- investigate the use of contrast in descriptions
- learn about the technique of 'zooming in'
- track links between paragraphs
- explore the effects of structure on the reader.

Writers structure their descriptions carefully. The choices they make depend on the effect they want to have on you, the reader. Techniques that writers use include contrasts, 'zooming in' and using links between paragraphs.

USE YOUR SKILLS

When you contrast two things, you show the differences between them. You might use opposites such as light and dark, but contrasts can also just be different, such as angry and sad.

 Watch a video on narrative structure on Cambridge Elevate.

ACTIVITY 1

1 There are four points of contrast in the two sentences below. Two of these are highlighted. Identify the third and fourth points of contrast.

Shell shocked and weary, the child huddled in the doorway, fearful of everyone who passed.

Afraid of nothing and nobody, the child ran though the fairground, confident and full of life.

2 The following six sentences are made up of three pairs of contrasting sentences. Identify the pairs by correctly matching the contrasting sentences.

a It was a dark winter's night with only a dim shaft of moonlight to guide the way.

b Soothing waves gently brushed the waiting sand, as families gathered to enjoy the beach.

c   It stood alone, neglected and ashamed, with windows smashed and blinded by weeds.

d   The warm sun shone brightly, casting its bright rays on the path ahead.

e   The house welcomed its visitors, its windows gleaming and lawns manicured.

f   The beach was deserted as the towering waves smashed the defenceless sand dunes.

3 Copy the pairs of contrasting sentences. Highlight the points of contrast as shown in the example in Question 1.

4 Compare your answers with a partner. Have you highlighted the same points of contrast? If not, discuss the differences and make changes if you need to.

INVESTIGATE USE OF CONTRAST

You are going to investigate how a writer uses contrast to introduce the two main characters in a story. Read Source A carefully, then complete Activity 2.

ACTIVITY 2

1 Look at these six elements of the description. Place them in the correct order.

a   one man walked behind the other
b   details of what they both wore
c   details about the man behind
d   details of what they both carried
e   two men emerged from the path
f   details about the man in front

2 Make two headings: 'The first man' and 'The second man'. Read the following details and decide which describe the first man and which describe the second man. Write the details under the correct heading. Some details can go under both headings.

denim trousers	small and quick	small, strong hands
walked heavily	shapeless of face	denim coat with brass buttons
slender arms	arms hung loosely	sharp, strong features
huge	black, shapeless hat	blanket roll over shoulder
restless eyes	large, pale eyes	wide, sloping shoulders

Source A

Two men emerged from the path and came into
the opening by the green pool. They had walked
in single file down the path, and even in the open
one stayed behind the other. Both were dressed
in denim trousers and in denim coats with brass   5
buttons. Both wore black, shapeless hats and
both carried tight blanket rolls slung over their
shoulders. The first man was small and quick,
dark of face, with restless eyes and sharp, strong
features. Every part of him was defined: small,   10
strong hands, slender arms, a thin and bony nose.
Behind him walked his opposite, a huge man,
shapeless of face, with large, pale eyes, with wide,
sloping shoulders; and he walked heavily, dragging
his feet a little, the way a bear drags his paws. His   15
arms did not swing at his sides, but hung loosely.

From *Of Mice and Men* by John Steinbeck

3 Which of the following students best describes the structure of the extract?
Explain your choice.

Student A He tells us about the two men and how they walk together and he
describes each one in detail and compares the second man to a bear.

Student B He introduces the two men together and then writes about the
similarities between them and then he describes each one in detail.

Student C He describes the two men by introducing them together and telling us
about the similarities between them, before describing each one in detail to show how
they contrast with each other.

4 Think again about what you learn about the two men from the description.
Why do you think the writer described the 'small and quick' man as being
in front?

5 Compare your answers with a partner. How well have you understood that
writers sometimes use contrast to structure a description? Give yourself a
mark out of five.

INVESTIGATE ZOOMING IN AND OUT

The technique of 'zooming in' is often used in photography and in television and cinema. The big picture is given first – perhaps a shot of a large crowd – then this is reduced to focus on a detail – for example one of the people in the crowd. What effect does this have on the viewer?

Sometimes the reverse technique, 'zooming out', is used. Here, the focus is first on the person and then gradually moves out to show the situation or place they are in. What different effect does this have?

ACTIVITY 3

1 Work with another student. Look at the following photographs.

    a In which order would you place them to zoom in and zoom out?
    b Which order do you think is most effective?

2 Look at these two sequences of details. For each one, decide which order you would describe them to zoom in and to have maximum impact.

Sequence 1	Sequence 2
a an expanse of sea	**a** a hospital
b a distant swimmer	**b** an empty bed
c waves hitting the shore	**c** a doctor and nurse talking
d the shadow of an approaching shark	**d** the waiting room
e a crowded beach	**e** a hospital corridor
f a close-up of the swimmer	**f** the reception desk

3 Compare and discuss your choices with other students.

ACTIVITY 4

The technique of zooming in or out is also used by writers. The two men in Source A live in a bunkhouse – a place where American ranch hands lived in the 1930s. Source B describes the bunkhouse. Read it closely.

Source B

The bunk house was a long, rectangular building. Inside, the walls were
whitewashed and the floor unpainted. In three walls there were small, square
windows, and, in the fourth, a solid door with a wooden latch. Against the
walls were eight bunks, five of them made up with blankets and the other three
showing their **burlap ticking**. Over each bunk there was nailed an apple box 5
with the opening forward so that it made two shelves for the personal belongings
of the occupant of the bunk. And these shelves were loaded with little articles,
soap and talcum powder, razors and those Western magazines ranch men love to
read and scoff at and secretly believe. And there were medicines on the shelves,
and little **vials**, combs; and from nails on the box sides, a few neckties. Near one 10
wall there was a black cast-iron stove, its stove-pipe going straight up through the
ceiling. In the middle of the room stood a big square table littered with playing
cards, and around it were grouped boxes for the players to sit on.

From *Of Mice and Men* by John Steinbeck

 Vocabulary

burlap ticking: coarse cloth case for a mattress
vials: small bottles for liquids; also known as 'phials'

---

1 The first sentence starts with a view of the bunkhouse from the outside. Which word in the second sentence tells you this?

2 Track how the writer has structured this description by answering these four questions:

   a   What is **in** the walls?
   b   What is **against** the walls?
   c   What is **near** one wall?
   d   What is **in the middle** of the room?

3 Re-read lines 7–10, in which the writer lists in detail the contents of the apple boxes. Look at the following three reasons why he might have done this. Which is most likely? Which is least likely?

    a to tell us what the men keep in their apple boxes

    b to show that this is the men's home, where they keep all their personal belongings

    c to show how few possessions the men have.

4 The following response explains the structure of Source B. Some words and explanations are missing. Copy the paragraph and fill in the gaps.

> The writer takes the reader from the _____ of the bunk house inside. He then describes the walls of the bunk house and then _____ what stands against them. Clear details are given about the _____ above each bunk and what they contain. He gives this detail because _____. Then the writer moves the reader inward, leaving the walls, to focus on _____, which is near but not against or on a wall. Finally, the reader is drawn to the _____ of the room and the table which is 'littered with playing cards' and has _____ for the players to sit on. By moving gradually from the outside to the middle of the room, the writer helps the reader to _____. He also leads the reader to expect that something is about to happen at this table. It's in the middle of the room and it's the last thing mentioned in the paragraph.

5 Compare your answers to Questions 1–4 with a partner. Talk about the reasons for any differences.

RECOGNISE LINKS

You have learnt how descriptions can be structured through contrast and zooming in. Source C is the opening of the final chapter of the same book. In it, the writer uses one of these techniques over the space of several paragraphs. Lennie is the second of the two men you read about earlier. Read the source, then complete Activity 5.

ACTIVITY 5

1 The writer uses the technique of 'zooming in' to structure this chapter opening. With a partner, discuss how he does this.

Source C

The deep green pool of the Salinas River was still in the late afternoon. Already the sun had left the valley to go climbing up the slopes of the Gabilan Mountains, and the hilltops were rosy in the sun. But by the pool among the 5
mottled sycamores, a pleasant shade had fallen.

A watersnake glided smoothly up the pool, twisting its periscope head from side to side; and it swam the length of the pool and came to the legs of a motionless heron that stood 10
in the shallows. A silent head and beak lanced down and plucked it out by the head, and the beak swallowed the little snake while its tail waved frantically.

A fair rush of wind sounded and a gust drove 15
through the tops of the trees like a wave. The sycamore leaves turned up their silver sides, the brown, dry leaves on the ground scudded a few feet. And row on row of the tiny wind waves flowed up the pool's green surface. 20

As quickly as it had come, the wind died, and the clearing was quiet again. The heron stood in the shallows, motionless and waiting. Another little watersnake swam up the pool, turning its periscope head from side to side. 25

Suddenly, Lennie appeared out of the brush, and he came as silently as a creeping bear moves. The heron pounded the air with its wings, jacked itself clear of the water and flew off down-river. The little snake slid in among 30
the reeds at the pool's side.

Lennie came quietly to the pool's edge. He knelt down and drank, barely touching his lips to the water. When a little bird skittered over the dry leaves behind him, his head jerked up 35
and he strained toward the sound with his eyes and ears until he saw the bird, and then he dropped his head and drank again.

From *Of Mice and Men* by John Steinbeck

2 The passage is carefully crafted. The writer not only 'zooms in' on Lennie, he also links ideas between the paragraphs by returning to particular features of the scene. Look again at the first two paragraphs. The highlights show how often he refers to the pool and the snake:

Highlight a copy of the passage on Cambridge Elevate.

The deep green pool of the Salinas River was still in the late afternoon. Already the sun had left the valley to go climbing up the slopes of the Gabilan Mountains, and the hilltops were rosy in the sun. But by the pool among the mottled sycamores, a pleasant shade had fallen.
A watersnake glided smoothly up the pool, twisting its periscope head from side to side; and it swam the length of the pool and came to the legs of a motionless heron that stood in the shallows. A silent head and beak lanced down and plucked it out by the head, and the beak swallowed the little snake while its tail waved frantically.

    a   On a copy of the passage, continue to highlight references to the pool and snakes.

    b   Highlight further references to the sycamores and their leaves.

    c   Highlight further references to the heron.

    d   Highlight references to the wind.

    e   Highlight references to Lennie – by name or by the pronouns 'he' or 'his'.

3 Work in pairs. Discuss each of the following statements. Do you agree with them? What other reasons might explain why Steinbeck has made these links?

    a   He builds the scene carefully, detail by detail, showing how things change very slightly, to help the reader to picture it.

    b   By keeping the focus on the pool, the heron and a snake, he is able to show the reader how the scene is disturbed when Lennie appears.

    c   He keeps the reader focused on the pool because this is where Lennie first appears.

4 Read the beginning of a student's answer to the question:

How has the writer structured this opening of a chapter to interest the reader?

The writer sets the scene in the opening paragraph, giving details of the place and the time of day. In the following paragraphs he develops this scene, describing in detail what can be seen, helping the reader to imagine it. It is not until the fifth paragraph that he 'zooms in' on Lennie, showing his actions and behaviour and making the reader wonder what he is up to.

Complete the answer by writing about how and why the writer makes links between the paragraphs. You could start:

In the first four paragraphs the writer keeps returning to particular features of the scene. He starts with the pool …

5 Compare your answer with a partner. Make improvements if you can.

Source D

He moved unseen, cloaked by the darkness of heavy clouds and a sulky moon. Hunched and weary, he shuffled and stumbled, body-dead except for the eyes, still wide and alert, looking, searching. He needed somewhere to sleep and he had to find it soon, before the pubs turned out their drunken contents, before the police stormed the streets. For now, though, all was quiet. The good folk of the town were shuttered in, warmed by fires, windows blind to the piercing cold night. It was not these he feared.

5

Warmth and light awoke him. Half-blinded by the sun's bright rays, he rubbed his heavy, tired eyes awake and memory flooded in. The park, gate left unlocked by carelessness and good fortune, had saved him. He'd found a place, hidden by bushes, to rest unseen. But he had stayed too long. He did not need the chirping birds to tell him this. Footsteps, voices, filled his waking moments. The drunks were in bed. The good folk were about. It was they he now feared.

10

Assess your progress

In this unit you have:

- investigated the use of contrast in descriptions
- learnt about the technique of 'zooming in'
- tracked links between paragraphs
- explored the effects of structure on the reader.

Now read Source D and answer the following questions.

1 Which technique does the writer use in this description?

2 Copy and complete the following table to show different things that the writer contrasts in the description.

First paragraph	Second paragraph
cloaked by darkness	light awoke him
heavy clouds and a sulky moon	
eyes, wide and alert	

3 What do you notice about the final sentence of each paragraph? What do they make you think and/or feel?

4 Write a response to this task:

Explain how the writer has structured this description to interest the reader.

You should:

✔ explain the writer's use of contrast
✔ point out the links that the writer makes between paragraphs
✔ show that you understand how the writer has structured the passage overall.

How did you do?

Share your response with another student. Discuss the different points you make. Decide which response is best and the reasons for this.

Complete this assignment on Cambridge Elevate.

FURTHER PROGRESS

The first three sources in this unit come from *Of Mice and Men* by the American author John Steinbeck. You may enjoy reading the whole story or some of his other short novels such as *The Red Pony or The Pearl*.

Unit 9
Write about structure

Make progress · AO2
- consider the impact of openings
- investigate the inverted pyramid structure
- explore the structure of a review
- write about the effect of structure on readers.

USE YOUR SKILLS

Non-fiction texts are based on real events. They are sometimes structured in similar ways to fiction texts. For example the writers may use contrast or zoom in or out. They can, however, be structured in other different ways.

 Watch a video about structure in non-fiction texts on Cambridge Elevate.

ACTIVITY 1

Opening sentences are important in both non-fiction and fiction texts.

1. In pairs, discuss why opening sentences are important in both non-fiction and fiction texts. List your two most important reasons.

2. Now read Sources A–C, the openings of three non-fiction accounts. Discuss the questions after each source. They focus on how the writers have structured their openings.

Source A

WOLVERHAMPTON, 5 APRIL 1988

Here I am, on my 13th birthday. I am running. I'm running from The Yobs.

'Boy!'

'Gyppo!'

'Boy!'

I'm running from The Yobs in the playground by our house.

From How to be a Woman by Caitlin Moran

a   Why do you think the writer uses the **first person** and the present tense?
b   Why do you think she includes **direct speech**?
c   Why do you think she writes 'The Yobs' rather than just 'some yobs'?

Source B

True story. Last winter, three men from a village in West Yorkshire went fishing off the coast near Scarborough, and hauled in an unexploded mine from the Second World War. A crowd gathered to look at the bomb, and a reporter from local television turned up to interview the men on the beach. When the reporter asked one of them if they'd been frightened, he said, 'No, we're alright, us'.

From All Points North by Simon Armitage

5

10

d   How does the writer emphasise that this event actually happened?
e   How would you expect people to feel if they had 'hauled in an unexploded mine'?
f   What does the use of direct speech show about the attitude of the three men?

Source C

Frank Lahiffe loved Mary O'Dwyer as well. It was an intolerable triangle. She probably loathed both of us, but, at the age of four, I was not in the least interested in her feelings.

From *Is That It?* by Bob Geldof

a   What does the author make you think he is writing about in the first two sentences?
b   How does he surprise the reader in the third sentence?
c   What is amusing about the fact that he was 'not in the least interested in her feelings'?

3 Read one student's good answer to the question:

How does the writer of Source A engage the reader's interest in the opening sentences?

Copy the response and add a comment on the use of capital letters for 'The Yobs'.

The writer starts with the place and date, almost as though it was a diary. She writes in the first person and uses the present tense to make it seem more real to the reader – as though it's happening now: 'Here I am … I'm running'. She calls the people she's running from 'The Yobs'. By giving then a title with capital letters, she _____ . She uses direct speech to show that they call her hurtful names. She makes the reader want to know if she will escape from them or if they will catch her.

---

4 Choose Source B or Source C. Write a paragraph explaining how the writer engages the reader's interest in their opening sentences.

EXPLORE THE USE OF THE INVERTED PYRAMID

Sometimes non-fiction texts are structured in a specific way. One device often used in newspaper reports is the inverted pyramid:

1 Essential information: Who? What? Where? When?

2 Important but not essential detail

3 General background information

This structure gives readers a clear understanding of what the report is about, even if they do not read it in full. It also allows an editor to cut the article from the bottom up if there is not enough space, as the main points have already been covered.

ACTIVITY 2

Read Source D, a newspaper report on elephants. Then answer the following questions:

1 Focus on the first and second paragraphs. What happened? Where did it happen?

2 When do you discover who might be responsible for the injury to the older elephant?

3 When do you learn about the injury to the second, younger elephant? Why do you think this is less important?

Source D

Speared elephants saved from death

Vets in Kenya have removed a 6in metal spear tip embedded in an elephant's **temple**, in a risky procedure that could have seen the animal bleed to death. 5

The injured bull was one of two male elephants that had been seriously wounded on the edge of the Masai Mara game park in the country's south.

The animal had survived an attack with traditional 10 weapons, and while the spear was not deep enough to damage his brain, he had been cutting his trunk trying to pull the protruding piece of metal out of the side of his head, conservationists said.

Marc Goss, director of the Mar Elephant Project, 15 said: 'He had definitely been speared intentionally and from close quarters. The fact that both of them were speared at the same time suggests it was **premeditated**.'

It was not clear if the bulls were the victims 20 of would-be poachers or an attack by farmers annoyed by elephants breaking down fences and feasting on their vegetables.

This can lead to farmers shooting, spearing or poisoning elephants. However, the area 25 where the pair were hurt, on the edge of the Masai Mara reserve, was close to where local herdsmen had been grazing their cattle at night, possibly providing cover for poachers.

The younger of the two elephants, thought to be 30 around 20 years old, had a wound on his leg. It was his older companion, aged around 30 and with much larger tusks, that had been struck on the right side of his head. The wooden shaft of the spear had broken off, but the sharp metal tip 35 was lodged in his skull.

From an article in *The Times* by Jerome Starkey

💬 **Vocabulary**

temple: the side of the head
premeditated: planned

4 Journalists often refer in their reports to what other people have said. Whose words does the journalist refer to in this report? What do they add to the reader's understanding of this attack?

5 Why does the writer return to the main story in the last sentence?

USE YOUR IDEAS TO WRITE ABOUT STRUCTURE

To write about structure, you need to put together the different things you have learnt from your close reading of the report.

ACTIVITY 3

1 List the details you would include in answer to this question:

How has the writer structured his report?

2 Here is one student's complete answer. Read it closely. The underlined words show where the student demonstrates an understanding of structure.

This report gives the main details of the story <u>in the first two paragraphs</u> by telling us what happened (vets removed a six-inch metal spear from an elephant's temple) and where it happened (Kenya). <u>It then develops</u> the reader's understanding of the story <u>in the rest of the report</u>. So, for example, we learn about the '6in metal spear tip' in the elephant's temple in the <u>first paragraph but we don't know how it may have got there until the fourth paragraph</u>. We also learn <u>early on</u> that two elephants were injured <u>but we don't find out what happened to the second elephant until the last paragraph</u>.

The writer refers to what has happened as an 'attack' <u>in the third paragraph. He then uses a quotation from Marc Goss which supports this</u> and says it was definitely premeditated. <u>The writer continues to build the reader's understanding</u> by then explaining who might have done this attack – poachers or farmers. <u>This is followed by</u> an explanation of why farmers might attack elephants.

<u>The writer keeps the explanation of what happened to the second elephant until the end to hold the reader's interest</u> but <u>in the last sentence he links back to the start and reminds us again of the most important injury – the one to the older elephant</u>.

3 Look again at the list you made. What points does this student make that you had not worked out?

EXAMINE REVIEWS

Reviews help readers decide whether they want to buy,
read or watch a particular thing. Read the review in Source E.
The annotations explain its structure.

Source E

Anita and Me by Meera Syal is the story of a young Punjabi girl growing up in the fictional English village of Tollington in the Midlands in the1970s.

[introduces the book and author]

The book follows Meena during her pre-teen years as she is desperate to fit in with the other children in her neighbourhood, while forever feeling like an outsider because she is 'different'. In a rebellious mood, Meena makes friends with Anita, a slightly older girl who is the self-proclaimed leader of a gang of outcasts and outsiders.

5

[introduces the main characters]

Meena's cultural heritage provides a colourful background. The story tells of exotic food, exquisite clothing and late night dinner parties where her parent's Punjabi friends swap stories of a life far more exciting than the daily humdrum life in Tollington. As the book progresses, Meena seems to fit in quite well and the family are certainly accepted, admired even, by the community. This all begins to fall apart though, as Meena encounters first-hand how hurtful life can be.

10

[gives more detail and hints at how the story develops]

This is a brilliant story of Meena's development, from a selfish, self-involved child seeking to reject everything about her culture and heritage, into a self-assured and confident young girl capable of making the decisions that count. Narrated in the first person, Meena uses flashbacks and snippets of overheard conversations to piece the story together. In the end, it is expertly woven together and the book itself is incredibly powerful.

15

[gives personal opinion on the story and the writer's craft]

We all have memories of summers that seemed to last forever and of the lifetimes we spent as young children. I'm sure you'll understand then when I say that, although it only covers a year or two out of the life of a pre-teen girl, this is an epic story that will creep under your skin and affect your viewpoint for a long time to come.

20

[suggests how the story will affect readers]

Adapted from www.addictedtomedia.net

ACTIVITY 4

1 Work in pairs. Answer these questions on the first and second paragraphs.

   a   The book is called *Anita and Me*. Who is the 'Me' in the title?
   b   What do you learn about her?
   c   Who is Anita? What do you learn about her?
   d   What does the word 'outsider' suggest?

2 Focus on the third paragraph.

   a   What aspects of Meena's culture provide a background to the story?
   b   What issues cause difficulties for Meena?
   c   Why doesn't the writer tell you the full story?

3 Focus on the fourth paragraph.

   a   What do you learn about the way the story is told?
   b   What words show the writer's opinion on the book?

4 Focus on the fifth paragraph.

   a   Why does the writer use the words 'We', 'you'll' and 'your'?
   b   What might the writer mean when she calls it an 'epic story'?
   c   What effect does she predict the book will have on the reader?

 Assess your progress

In this unit, you have:

- examined the opening of a non-fiction text
- investigated the 'pyramid structure'
- explored the structure of a review
- learnt how to write about structure.

1 Now write an answer to this question:

How has the writer structured her review of *Anita and Me* to influence readers?

Use your answers from Activity 4 to help you.

Remember to:

✔ explain how the writer has structured her review
✔ comment on how the writer tries to influence readers.

How well did you do?

Share your response with a partner. Decide which response gives the best answer to the question. If you need to, make improvements to your response.

 Find an answer to this question to compare with your own response on Cambridge Elevate.

 Complete this assignment on Cambridge Elevate.

FURTHER PROGRESS

Read reviews to help you understand how writers structure them to influence readers. Try empireonline.com for reviews of films and gamespot.com for reviews of computer games.

Unit 10
Test your progress 1

Complete this test to assess your progress in the skills covered by Units 1–9.

You have **1 hour**.

Route to success:

*   Spend 15 minutes reading the passage and the questions carefully.
*   Notice how many marks are awarded for each question. This will give you a clue to how much time you should spend on each answer.
*   Remember to refer to the text to support the points you make.

Complete this assignment on Cambridge Elevate.

Source A is from a short story set in Dominica in the Caribbean. In it, a woman returns to a place she once knew well.

1 Read the first part of the story in the first and second paragraphs. List **four** details about the place the woman has returned to.

4 marks

2 Focus on the second, third and fourth paragraphs. Identify which **four** of the following statements are true:

a The road is the same as it always used to be.
b The woman was feeling happy.
c The woman was annoyed that the work on the road had been done carelessly.
d The sky looks different.
e The old pavement had been taken up.
f The stone steps are warm in the sunlight.
g The summer house is the same as she remembered it.
h The house has been painted white.

4 marks

3 Focus on the first to fourth paragraphs. Summarise the ways in which the place is different from the woman's memory of it.

8 marks

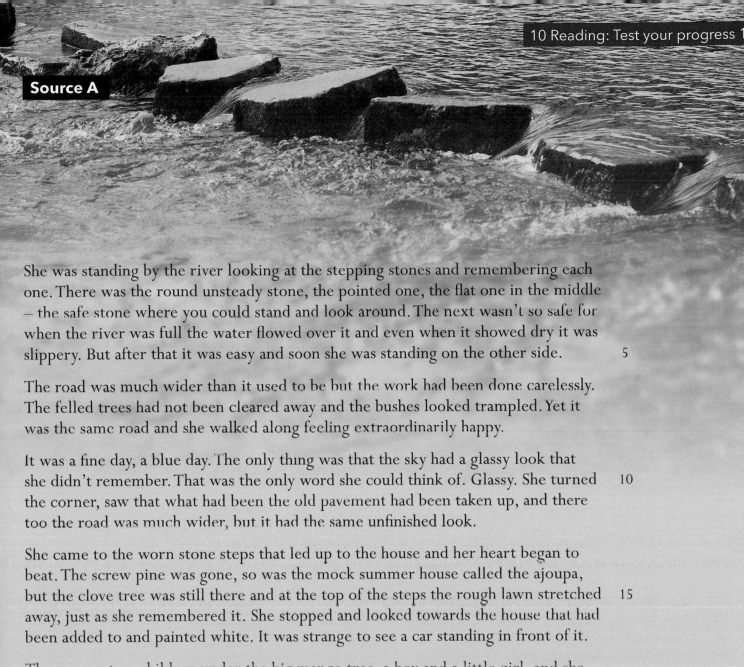

Source A

She was standing by the river looking at the stepping stones and remembering each
one. There was the round unsteady stone, the pointed one, the flat one in the middle
– the safe stone where you could stand and look around. The next wasn't so safe for
when the river was full the water flowed over it and even when it showed dry it was
slippery. But after that it was easy and soon she was standing on the other side.   5

The road was much wider than it used to be but the work had been done carelessly.
The felled trees had not been cleared away and the bushes looked trampled. Yet it
was the same road and she walked along feeling extraordinarily happy.

It was a fine day, a blue day. The only thing was that the sky had a glassy look that
she didn't remember. That was the only word she could think of. Glassy. She turned   10
the corner, saw that what had been the old pavement had been taken up, and there
too the road was much wider, but it had the same unfinished look.

She came to the worn stone steps that led up to the house and her heart began to
beat. The screw pine was gone, so was the mock summer house called the ajoupa,
but the clove tree was still there and at the top of the steps the rough lawn stretched   15
away, just as she remembered it. She stopped and looked towards the house that had
been added to and painted white. It was strange to see a car standing in front of it.

There were two children under the big mango tree, a boy and a little girl, and she
waved to them and called 'Hello', but they didn't answer her or turn their heads.
Very fair children, as Europeans born in the West Indies so often are: as if the white   20
blood is asserting itself against all the odds.

The grass was yellow in the hot sunlight as she walked towards them. When she was
quite close, she called again, shyly: 'Hello'. Then, 'I used to live here once,' she said.
Still they didn't answer. When she had said for the third time 'Hello' she was quite
near them. Her arms went out instinctively with the longing to touch them. It was   25
the boy who turned. His gray eyes looked straight into hers. His expression didn't
change. He said, 'Hasn't it gone cold all of a sudden. D'you notice? Let's go in.'

'Yes, let's,' said the girl.

Her arms fell to her sides as she watched them running across the grass to the
house. That was the first time she knew.   30

From 'I Used to Live Here Once' in *The Collected Short Stories* by Jean Rhys

4 Look in detail at this paragraph from the story:

The grass was yellow in the hot sunlight as she walked towards them. When she was quite close, she called again, shyly: 'Hello'. Then, 'I used to live here once,' she said. Still they didn't answer. When she had said for the third time 'Hello' she was quite near them. Her arms went out instinctively with the longing to touch them. It was the boy who turned. His gray eyes looked straight into hers. His expression didn't change. He said, 'Hasn't it gone cold all of a sudden. D'you notice? Let's go in.'

How does the writer use language here to help the reader picture the scene? You could write about the use of:

a words and phrases
b **dialogue**
c sentence forms.

8 marks

5 Think about the final sentence of the story: 'That was the first time she knew.' What does the woman know for the first time? Give evidence from the story to support your answer.

8 marks

6 You now need to think about the whole story. How has the writer structured the story to interest readers? You could write about:

a what the writer focuses your attention on at the beginning
b how and why the writer changes this focus as the story develops
c clues that the writer gives the reader
d how the writer ends the story.

8 marks

When you have finished your answers, look again at the marks that each question is worth. If you have time left over and you think you could add some detail to gain extra marks, do so.

READING

Unit 11
Understand viewpoint

Make progress
- understand viewpoint
- use the writer's ideas to identify viewpoint
- explore how writers use words to show viewpoint.

USE YOUR SKILLS

A viewpoint is a particular way of seeing something. Think of a TV programme or film, for example. You might love it; one friend might hate it; another friend might think it's just okay. If you spoke or wrote about it, you would make different points to support your point of view.

ACTIVITY 1

1 Work with another student. Read what two students have written about the Stealth ride at Thorpe Park. They have different viewpoints. Which of the following statements best matches the viewpoint of Student A and of Student B?

   a   Stealth is terrifying for anyone who hates heights and speed.
   b   Stealth can be great fun even if you hate heights and speed.
   c   Stealth is quite good but there are better rides around.
   d   Stealth is great if you like heights and speed.

Student A Stealth is really, really, really scary and you get loads of butterflies if you're the kind of person who hates fast rides and doesn't like heights (like me and my friend!). However, queuing and thinking about what's going to happen to you is by far the worst part. I found that once you start moving it's awesome and I loved it. The sad thing was that it just didn't last long enough. We spent ages queuing and then, suddenly, it was all over.

Student B   I enjoyed Stealth. It's quite fast and you go up high. Once. Twice? It was all over too fast for me to count properly. I love heights and speed so the more of that the better. Stealth only scores a 7 for me for that reason. My all-time top rollercoaster ride is Xcelerator. Once you have gone on that iconic ride, nothing else compares!

2 Write down any points that both the writers make. Are they used to support the same viewpoint in each text, or a different one?

LINK IDEAS AND VIEWPOINTS

You can work out more about viewpoint by identifying the writer's ideas. Read the following extract from an article on Glastonbury. The commentary boxes show you what you can work out from the points the writer makes.

Glastonbury is the greatest and largest festival in England. It attracts major names in the pop and rock worlds, as well as hundreds of other fantastic entertainers. Many of the staff are volunteers and every year millions of pounds are raised for good causes.

> This contains several facts that can be proved. The facts are all positive ones. Notice that it says nothing about the rain, the mud or the toilets!

> Words such as 'greatest' and 'fantastic' show the writer's opinion. They are also positive.

> So, using these clues, you can work out that the writer is a fan of Glastonbury.

ACTIVITY 2

A writer's ideas are often expressed in the facts and opinions they give. Read the newspaper report in Source A carefully, then answer the following questions.

1 The writer includes a number of facts and opinions in this article. Decide which of the following are facts and which are opinions:

  a   Kim Jong-un has ordered the country's 10 million men to have his haircut.
  b   Kim Jong-un has committed a crime against good taste.
  c   The decree was introduced in state-sanctioned guidelines.
  d   Women used to be allowed to choose from 18 styles and men from 10.
  e   North Korea produced a series on state TV called *Let Us Trim Our Hair In Accordance With Socialist Lifestyle*.
  f   His hairdo is never going to earn admirers.

2 The writer also quotes the opinions of others. Find and copy the quotations he uses.

3 Think about the quotations the writer has chosen to use. What does each one make you think about Kim Jong-un's order?

Source A

Make mine a Wrong-un: Kim Jong-un orders all men to have a haircut just like his

Wednesday 26 Mar 2014 10:49 pm

North Korea's dictator Kim Jong-un has committed a crime against good taste by ordering the country's 10 million men to get the same haircut as him. 5

The bizarre decree was introduced in state-sanctioned guidelines in the capital Pyongyang two weeks ago. 10

Barbers in Britain would probably call it the 'Wrong un'. In North Korea such talk can cost you dearly.

With its buzz-cut sides and slick centre parting, his hairdo is never going to earn admirers. 15

It is now being rolled out across the country and grumblings of discontent are surfacing.

One source told Radio Free Asia: 'Our leader's haircut is very particular, if you will. It doesn't always go with everyone since everyone 20 has different face and head shapes.'

Until the latest restrictive policy, women were allowed to choose from 18 styles and men could pick from ten.

In 2005, it emerged that North Korea 25 launched an offensive on the 'wrong' haircuts that included a series on state TV entitled: Let Us Trim Our Hair In Accordance With Socialist Lifestyle.

Mark Coray, of the National Hairdressers' 30 Federation, said Kim's haircut is 'not very fashionable.'

'It's not very nice but I'm sure he likes it,' he said. 'If the Queen said all women have to have the same hairstyle as her we would get 35 very bored.'

Adapted from an article in the *Metro* by Hayden Smith

4 Now think about the whole article. Which of the following statements best sum up the writer's viewpoint?

a   It's a good idea for North Koreans to have the same haircut as Kim Jong-un.
b   Kim Jong-un is hoping to make people more equal by ensuring that they have the same haircut.
c   Although it might be boring, the Queen should insist that all women copy her haircut.
d   It is ridiculous for Kim Jong-un to insist that his people have the same hairstyle as he does.

5 Compare your answers to Questions 1 to 4 with a partner. Talk about the reasons for any differences and change your answers if you think you need to.

EXPLORE VIEWPOINT AND LANGUAGE CHOICES

Did you work out from the facts and opinions in Question 4 that d best summed up the writer's viewpoint? There are other clues that reveal viewpoint. For example:

The <u>bizarre</u> decree was introduced in state-sanctioned guidelines in the capital Pyongyang two weeks ago.

Although this sentence contains a fact, the word 'bizarre' shows the writer's viewpoint. It reveals that the writer thinks the decree is very odd or strange and encourages the reader to think the same way.

ACTIVITY 3

1 Re-read the following sentences from the article. For each one, explain what the underlined word or words tell you about the writer's viewpoint.

    a 'With its <u>buzz-cut sides and slick centre parting</u>, his hairdo is never going to earn admirers.'

    b 'Until the latest <u>restrictive</u> policy, women were allowed to choose from 18 styles and men could pick from ten.'

2 Now think about the following two sentences:

Barbers in Britain would probably call it the 'Wrong-un'. In North Korea such talk can cost you dearly.

    a What **pun** or word-play does the writer use in the first sentence?
    b Which two words link the second sentence with the first sentence?
    c What does the writer suggest about life in North Korea?
    d Why do you think the writer has placed these two sentences next to each other?

USE THE FIRST AND THIRD PERSON

The news report in Source A is written in the **third person**. The writer is reporting on something that has happened. Whilst he clearly has strong views on this, he does not place himself directly in the story. He stands outside it. The third person is also used in more serious and formal reports. In more formal reports, the writer may not express a strong view on the subject.

Some writers choose to give their views more directly and write in the first person. This can make it easier to identify the writer's viewpoint.

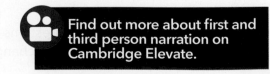

Find out more about first and third person narration on Cambridge Elevate.

ACTIVITY 4

Read Sources B and C, which are both about what students should or should not wear to school. Then work in pairs and discuss the questions that follow.

Source B

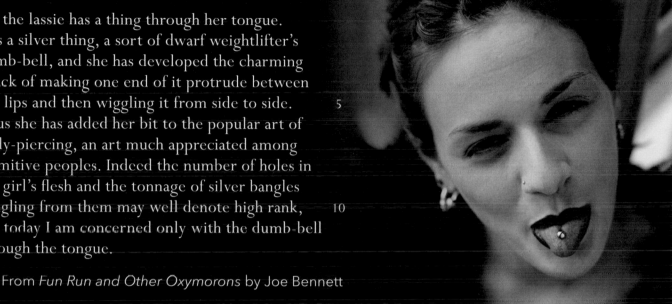

So, the lassie has a thing through her tongue. It is a silver thing, a sort of dwarf weightlifter's dumb-bell, and she has developed the charming knack of making one end of it protrude between her lips and then wiggling it from side to side. 5 Thus she has added her bit to the popular art of body-piercing, an art much appreciated among primitive peoples. Indeed the number of holes in the girl's flesh and the tonnage of silver bangles dangling from them may well denote high rank, 10 but today I am concerned only with the dumb-bell through the tongue.

From *Fun Run and Other Oxymorons* by Joe Bennett

Source C

More than 250 girls were taken out of lessons at a secondary school because their skirts were too short and the headmaster wants to prepare them for the 'world of work'.

Teachers at Ryde Academy on the Isle of Wight either sent home the 5 girls, aged between 11 and 18, or took them out of their classrooms to be placed in an isolated hall.

Others were sent home to change because their trousers were 'too tight' and did not fit with the school's strict new policy.

Boys at the academy were turned away if they arrived at lessons 10 without leather shoes.

From an article in *The Telegraph* by James Edgar

1   Which source is written in the first person and which is written in the third person?

2   Look at the following five statements about the sources. Which statements do you think best describe Source B, and which best describe Source C?

    a   The writer's view on the issue is not clear.
    b   The writer reports only the facts.
    c   The writer uses words and phrases to influence the reader.
    d   The writer gives his personal opinions.
    e   The writer uses words and phrases to inform the reader.

3   Now focus on Source B. The writer compares the tongue stud to 'a sort of dwarf weightlifter's dumb-bell'.

    a   What does this image suggest to you?
    b   What does it tell you about the writer's view on the stud?

4   Think about how the writer describes the way the girl moves the stud in her mouth. What impression does this give of the girl?

5   Where, according to the writer, might the girl have 'high rank'? What does this tell you about his viewpoint?

6   Which of the sources did you find most interesting to read? List the reasons for your choice.

7   Compare your answers to Questions 1–6 with a partner and add to your answers if you need to.

 Assess your progress

In this unit, you have:

- linked ideas with viewpoint
- linked language choices with viewpoints
- explored how writers reveal their viewpoints
- examined the use of the first and third person.

 Complete this assignment on Cambridge Elevate.

Now read Source D, an extract from Queen Victoria's journal. She wrote this extract in August 1832 when she was 13 years old. In it, she describes her travels through a coal-mining town in the Midlands.

1   Is the text written in the first or third person? Give one example to support your answer.

2   The word 'extraordinary' is used twice in the passage. Why might a princess who lived at Kensington Palace find this scene extraordinary?

Source D

It rains very hard. We just passed through a town where all coal mines are and you see the fire glimmer at a distance in the engines in many places. The men, women, children, country and houses are all black. But I can not by any description give an idea of its strange and extraordinary appearance. The country is very desolate   5
everywhere; there are coals about, and the grass is quite blasted and black. I just now see an extraordinary building flaming with fire. The country continues black, engines flaming, coals in abundance, every where, smoking and burning coal heaps, intermingled with wretched huts and carts and little ragged children.   10

3 Which colour is mentioned three times? What impression of the town does this give?

4 Think about the phrase 'with <u>wretched</u> huts and carts and <u>little ragged</u> children'. What do the underlined words suggest about Victoria's feelings?

5 The following three statements could describe Victoria's viewpoint. Find evidence to support each one:

   a She is fascinated by this town and has never seen anything like it before.

   b She doesn't seem to see anything good in this town – only the bad things.

   c She feels sorry for the people who live here.

6 Use your answers to Questions 1–5 to help you answer this question:

What different things does Victoria think and feel about the town and the people who live there?

Remember to:

✔ identify ideas that indicate the viewpoint

✔ examine language choices that indicate viewpoint

✔ explain the writer's viewpoint clearly.

How did you do?

Share your response with a partner. Identify the ideas and language choices you have examined. Decide which response gives the clearest explanation of the writer's viewpoint.

FURTHER PROGRESS

Find and read a magazine or newspaper article that interests you. Work out the writer's viewpoint and how they try to influence reader opinion by examining their:

- use of facts and opinions
- language choices
- use of first or third person.

Unit 12

Examine similarities and differences in viewpoint

Make progress
AO3

- recognise similarities and differences in viewpoint
- learn about subjectivity and objectivity
- consider how writers use language to show their viewpoint
- examine links between viewpoint and the time when something is written.

USE YOUR SKILLS

You make choices and judgements based on the information you are given. Suppose you and your friends are choosing between the two pizza restaurants in these photographs. The restaurants look very different. Their appearance might influence the choice you make.

ACTIVITY 1

1 Work with another student. Identify and list at least **four** differences between the two restaurants.

Pizza 4 You

Amazing value – always. Choose your base from thin, regular or thick. It's all the same price, and even if you want your thick crust stuffed with cheese, it's only £2 extra.

Keep it Simple
A delicious basil, garlic and tomato topping with mozzarella cheese
£7.50   Calories: 180

Meatfeast
Tomato, salami, crispy beef and tandoori chicken all topped with cheese
£10.75   Calories: 440

Spicy!
Fresh chillies, sliced sausage, garlic, basil, tomatoes, cheese
£8.00   Calories: 370

New 4 U
Artichokes, mushrooms, peppers, tomato, spinach and cheese
£9.00   Calories: 210

Pink Pizza!

Our hand-made crispy bases have to be tasted to be believed. Pizzas start with a 7-inch diameter. After that, simply add another £1 for every delicious extra inch.

Margherita: juicy tomato, fresh basil, garlic and mozzarella
£8.00   Calories: 168

Pepperoni: pepperoni, tomato and mozzarella
£9.50   Calories: 360

Catch of the day: anchovies, tuna, prawns, capers, tomato and mozzarella
£11.00   Calories: 503

In the pink: goat's cheese, grated beetroot, onion and tomato
£10.00   Calories: 200

2 Read the two menus carefully. There are similarities and differences in what they offer. Which is:

a the cheapest pizza
b the pizza with the least calories
c the pizza with the most toppings?

3 Find two pizzas that have the same ingredients but different names. What is each one called?

4 Jess does not eat fish and Sami is vegetarian. Which restaurant gives them the most choice?

5 Which restaurant appeals most to you? Explain the reasons for your point of view.

RECOGNISE DIFFERENCES IN VIEWPOINT

People can have very different points of view on the same subject. Look at the following two reviews of the Pink Pizza restaurant. The reviews contain some similar details, but the writers have very different viewpoints.

Source A

I wanted to try Pink Pizza because I had heard that 'it does what it says on the tin'. I wasn't disappointed. Everything was stunning and in my favourite colour, pink: the walls, the chairs, the drinks, puddings ... even the pizzas. We ordered pink lemonade, delicious pink smoothies and shocking pink milkshakes flavoured with strawberries and raspberries. I was brave enough to try a Pink Perfection Pizza, which is topped with grated beetroot to stain the cheese, and I really liked it, though my favourite is still pepperoni. I finished off my meal with a sensational raspberry cheesecake, while everyone else tucked into strawberry ice creams. I'll definitely be going back!

Source B

The only reason I went into Pink Pizza was for a dare. I decided I could just about cope with sitting inside a giant pink marshmallow if the food was good. But it wasn't. My milkshake was far too sweet and I don't like soft, milky puddings like cheesecake and ice creams. I prefer cake or pies but there was none left and the raspberry cheesecake was really soggy. One big surprise though was trying the Pink Perfection Pizza. I didn't think I would like cooked beetroot, but the pizza was delicious and I'm now a beetroot fan. Even so, I don't think I'll be visiting Pink Pizza again anytime soon.

ACTIVITY 2

1. Copy and complete the following table to help you identify the similarities and differences in the reviewers' viewpoints.

Question	A	B
Why did they go to Pink Pizza?		
How do they describe the surroundings?		
What did they eat?		
What did they think about the pizza?		
What did they think about the pudding?		
Would they go there again?		

2. On your completed table, highlight similarities in one colour and differences in another.

3. Write a sentence explaining each similarity and each difference. For example:

Reviewer A went because she wanted to try Pink Pizza and had heard good things about it, but Reviewer B went for a dare.

UNDERSTAND SUBJECTIVITY AND OBJECTIVITY

In Activity 2, you examined two viewpoints on a similar event – a visit to the same pizza restaurant. Both viewpoints are examples of **subjective** writing, where the writer tries to influence the reader by including personal opinions.

Good readers learn how to distinguish subjective writing from **objective** writing. In objective writing, the writer aims to present information without trying to influence the reader's opinion. Objective writing presents a fair and balanced viewpoint and allows readers to make up their own minds.

ACTIVITY 3

The reports in Sources C and D both concern the use of rickshaws to transport passengers in London. They are both written in the third person.

1 Work with another student. Read the reports carefully and decide which one is subjective and which one is objective.

Source C

It is time that the chaotic operation of rickshaws in London is properly controlled before someone dies. These pedal-powered taxis are nothing but a dangerous menace. A recent report highlighted the need for rip-off rickshaw drivers to have a proper licence, but nothing has been done about it. Urgent action is needed now to tackle this diabolical curse on London's streets. Innocent passengers put their lives in danger the minute they step into one. Only a few months ago a dodgy rickshaw flipped on its side in Westminster. That time the passengers escaped with only minor injuries. Next time they might not be so lucky.

Source D

Both businesses and tourists benefit from the return of the rickshaw to capital cities across the world. Tourists clearly enjoy the novelty of taking in the sights of London in a rickshaw, and businesses make a lot of money from their eagerness to do so. Rickshaw businesses pay more tax and tourists spend more money. This helps both the local and the national economy. However, not everyone wants to see rickshaws on London's streets. Some people claim they are dangerous and not licensed. Taxi drivers, delivery-van drivers and even commuters are often delayed by traffic jams created by a line of rickshaws. Many would prefer these tourists to take a taxi, train or bus.

Did you work out that C is subjective and D is objective? You are now going to focus on the detail of the reports which help you recognise this.

2 Source C contains fewer facts than Source D. Identify the facts used in each report.

3 Source D contains fewer opinions than Source C. Identify how many opinions are given in each report.

4 Source C says nothing positive about rickshaws. What positive points are made in Source D?

5 Source C uses language to influence the reader's attitude to rickshaws. Find two examples of this and explain their effects.

UNDERSTAND HOW WORD CHOICES REVEAL ATTITUDE

By looking closely at a writer's choice of words, you can work out more about their attitude.

In Source C the writer uses the noun phrase 'chaotic operation'. The adjective 'chaotic' suggests disorder and confusion. It shows that the writer disapproves of the operation of rickshaws in London.

Sometimes the writer of source C combines an adjective and a noun to create an even stronger impression. In the noun phrase 'dangerous menace', the noun reinforces the idea of danger and of threat. It shows the reader how strongly the writer feels about the problem.

ACTIVITY 4

1 What do the adjectives in the following noun phrase tell you about the writer's attitude?

a   innocent passengers
b   dodgy rickshaw.

2 Think about the noun phrase 'diabolical curse'. What does the noun 'curse' tell us about the meaning of the adjective 'diabolical'? What does this noun phrase show you about the writer's attitude?

ACTIVITY 5

1 Read Source E and find evidence in the text to support each of the following statements about the writer's perspective.

a   The noise of the trains is new to him.
b   He hates the sound of the trains.
c   He misses the silence of the Temple at night.
d   He feels that worse is to come.
e   He regrets that children will not know a world without railways.

2 Think about each of the following extracts from Source E. Explain how the underlined words reveal the writer's attitude.

a   <u>dull wearing</u> hum
b   the bitter shriek of some <u>accursed</u> engine
c   the <u>torture</u> of this new noise

3 Compare your answers to Questions 1 and 2 with a partner. If you need to, add to your answers.

Last night and tonight I have observed for the first time the noise of the new Charing Cross Railway. Even as I write the dull wearing hum of trains upon the Surrey side is going on: it goes on far into the night, with every now & then the bitter shriek of some accursed engine. 5

I almost welcome the loss, which I had been groaning over, of my view of the Thames; hoping that the new building when it rises may keep out those sounds. No one who has not tasted the pure & exquisite silence of the Temple at night can conceive of the horror that it 10 is gone for ever. Here at least was a respite from the roar of the streets by day; but now, silence and peace are fast going out of the world. It is not merely the torture of this new noise in a quiet place: but one knows that these are only the beginnings of such sorrows. 15

Our children will not know what it is to be free of railways.

From the diary of Arthur F. Munsby, 22 January 1862

Source E

 Vocabulary

Temple: an area of central London

Source F

On the one hand, HS2 supporters promise HS2 will offer punctual, speedy, and comfortable train journeys. For weary commuters who need to zip from London to Manchester regularly for meetings that is an attractive prospect. HS2 supporters also argue it could mean people from the north 5 can take southern jobs meaning a better economy for everyone. And of course there will be all those new jobs created by building and running HS2.

However, HS2's opponents claim that HS2 threatens 350 unique habitats, 67 irreplaceable ancient woods, 30 river corridors, 10 24 Sites of Special Scientific Interest plus hundreds of other sensitive areas' (*source: Stop HS2 website*) and, they say, it is going be very expensive to set up: £50 billion they estimate. Both the cost to the environment and money have to be balanced against those 30 minutes saved on the journey time from London to 15 Birmingham. And how many more jobs will it really create if other rail networks lose those customers?

That's a lot to think about before anyone starts laying the track.

Assess your progress

In this unit, you have:

- recognised similarities and differences in viewpoints
- learnt about subjectivity and objectivity
- considered how writers use language to show their viewpoint
- examined links between viewpoint and the time when something is written.

Source F was written in the 21st century. In it, the writer discusses the consequences of a proposed new train line called High Speed 2 (HS2). Read Source F, then answer the following questions.

1 What advantages might HS2 bring?

2 What might the disadvantages be?

3 Sources E and F were both written in response to a new train line, but they present different ideas and perspectives. Complete sentences **a** to **g** by filling in the spaces to correctly identify the differences between the two sources.

    a Source E was written in the … , whereas source F was written in the … .

    b Source … is subjective, whereas source F is … .

    c Source … is written in the … , whereas Source … is written in the third person.

    d Source … presents a negative viewpoint, for example … .

    e Source … presents positive and negative points, for example … .

    f The writer of Source … tries to influence his reader against the train line through his use of language, for example … .

    g The writer of Source … presents the points and lets readers make up their own minds.

How did you do?

Ask for feedback on how well you have:

✔ identified the advantages and disadvantages of HS2

✔ identified the differences in the writers' perspectives

✔ used examples to support points made.

 **Complete this assignment on Cambridge Elevate.**

FURTHER PROGRESS

Read the following opening of another article about HS2. What do you learn about the writer's viewpoint from the points he makes and his language choices?

Maddest waste of money since Concorde: HS2 will destroy our countryside and cost up to £100 billion

- List of HS2's critics would fill a page and quite rightly

- The huge project is expected to destroy 135 acres of ancient woodland

- Last week Government admitted another hike in HS2 cost to £43 billion

Nobody seems to love HS2, and with good reason. It is by far the largest, and possibly the craziest, infrastructure project in British history. It is not green. It will destroy town and country the length of the land. It is presented as a much-needed boost for the economy, but the boost will likely come during the next boom, when such reckless public spending will seem foolish.

From an article in the *Mail Online* by Simon Jenkins

Unit 13

Compare writers' viewpoints

Make progress (AO3)
- examine similarities and differences in ideas and perspectives
- compare writers' ideas and viewpoints in two texts
- compare how writers convey their ideas and viewpoints
- develop your skills in writing a comparison.

USE YOUR SKILLS

You already know how to read a text and work out the writer's ideas and viewpoints. You can also recognise similarities and differences between the ideas and viewpoints of two writers.

ACTIVITY 1

In Sources A and B, two journalists – writing for national newspapers – respond to the news that the 15-year-old son of two millionaires is working in a coffee shop.

Source A

I always groan inside when someone tells me: 'I want my kids to have everything I didn't have.'

But, why would you want your kids to be 'given' a life? A life that you've decided they should have; a life you think is better than the hard-working one you had. How is a child supposed to work toward 5 achieving their own goals if you've already scored them all for them?

Victoria and David Beckham clearly think along the same sort of lines as me. I think it's absolutely brilliant that Brooklyn Beckham is doing a weekend job in a coffee shop. Believe me, when my son turns 15 on Wednesday I'm pushing him out of the door. I've 10 already eyed some kitchen porter and washer-upper jobs at the local pub. In fact I've been nagging the newsagent down the road since my son was 11 to see if he could do a paper round.

From an article in *The Mirror* by Fiona Phillips

Source B

There have been the expected songs of praise from columnists directed at David and Victoria's splendid down-to-earthness in making sure their progeny learned a few of life's harsher lessons in a real workplace 5 environment before he gets old enough to spend their hard-earned squillions on models, shiny motor cars and fizzy champagne.

Although, given the work ethic displayed by his mum and dad over the 10 past 20 years or so, it's unlikely that their sharp-dressing offspring will be anything other than diligent, ambitious and beyond-his-years savvy in business. Let's face it: he was never going to fail, 15 was he?

From an article in *The Independent* by Donald MacInnes

1 Five students were asked to write about the similarities and differences between these two articles. Look at the following responses. Some of the words are missing. Rewrite the sentences using the correct words from the word bank.

her own son	good	third person
Source B	sarcastic	genuine
identify	personal	Source A
support	rhetorical questions	
readers of newspapers		
'he was never going to fail, was he?'		

a Both writers are writing for .... Source A is written in the first person. The writer makes it ... by writing as a mother who has a son the same age as Brooklyn Beckham. In contrast to this, Source B is written in the ....

b The writer of Source B comments on the Beckhams and their decision but does not ... with them. Both writers appear to ... with the Beckham's decision. The writer of ... calls it 'splendid down-to-earthness' whilst the writer of ... says it is 'absolutely brilliant'.

c The writer of Source A uses ... to engage the reader, for example: 'But, why would you want your kids to be "given" a life?' The writer of Source B also uses a **rhetorical question** at the end: ....

d Both writers seem to think that it's ... for young people to work. The writer of Source A wants ... to get a job and the writer of Source B thinks it is good to learn 'a few of life's harsher lessons in a real workplace environment'.

e However, I think the writer of Source B is being a bit ... about Brooklyn Beckham, whereas the writer of Source A seems totally ... .

2 Compare your rewritten sentences with a partner. Do you agree? If not, look again to check who is correct.

3 To write about the similarities and differences, the students had to compare the two texts. Here are some words and phrases they used to draw comparisons:

- both writers
- in contrast to this
- but
- whilst
- also
- however
- whereas

Copy these words and phrases. They will help you when you write your own comparisons.

COMPARE VIEWPOINTS

When you compare writers' viewpoints, you need to think about:

- their ideas and viewpoints
- how they convey these to the reader.

Spend 10 minutes reading and thinking about Sources C and D, then do Activity 2.

Source C

This source was written in 2001. The writer had spent his childhood in Botswana, Africa, where his mother studied lions.

A gun is fired. Startled antelopes look up from their grazing as the noise echoes across the savanna. As the reverberation fades, one of Africa's most incredible animals struggles to take his last breath through his punctured lungs. All is quiet apart from the sound of the hunter's footsteps on the brittle grass. He squats by the bloodstained carcass, still holding his gun, and smiles as his picture is taken. Victory shots are fired into the air as the proud $\quad$ 5 hunter gets into the car, driven by his guide, and goes back to the hunting camp where he is served a meal and a stiff drink. The skinners then get to work carefully removing the tawny coat from the carcass. Vultures circle above the mass of meat and, as the last car leaves, they descend and finish off what the hunter has left behind.

One of the most magnificent male lions in our study area has been killed. Armagnac $\quad$ 10 will soon be flown halfway across the world, where on arrival his head will be stuffed and mounted on the hunter's wall, along with the photograph. His skin will be used as a carpet, and the hunter will tell his friends about his trip to Africa, with a few embellishments. Above him Armagnac will stare into oblivion with his new glass eyes.

From *The Lion Children* by Angus, Maisie and Travers McNeice

Vocabulary

savannah: open grassland scattered with trees
reverberation: an echoing sound
embellishments: added details to make something more interesting
oblivion: the state of being forgotten or mentally blank

Source D

This text was written in 1908. The writer was a game hunter. In 1908, she went to Somaliland in Africa with the intention of shooting lions. At the time, this was a widely accepted sport for wealthy people, although it was less usual for a woman to go hunting.

In one tense second I realized I had seen two monstrous moving beasts, yellowish and majestic. They were very close, and moved at a slow pace. I remember that though the great moment for which we had planned and longed was really at hand, all my excitement left me, and there was nothing but a cold tingling sensation running about my veins. How mighty they looked. They hardly seemed related to   5
their cousins at the Zoo. The mane of the wild lion is very much shorter. And yet the wild beast is much the more beautiful in his suggestion of enormous power.

The lions being located, we crept on warily towards the bush, a typical bit of jungle cover. The men went round the lair and shouted and beat at the back. Whether the cats were driven forward or not with the din, I cannot tell, but I saw from thirty-   10
five yards off, as I stood with my finger on the trigger, ferocious gleaming eyes, and heard ugly short snarls, breaking into throaty suppressed roars every two or three seconds. The jungle cover parted, and with lithe stretched shoulders a lioness shook herself half free of the density, then crouched low again. Down, down, until only the flat of her skull showed, and her small twitching ears. In one more moment   15
she would be on us. I heard Cecily say something. I think it may have been 'Fire!' Sighting for as low as I could see on that half arc of yellow, I pulled the trigger.

From *Two Dianas in Somaliland* by Agnes Herbert

ACTIVITY 2

1 Work in groups of three. Take it in turn to explain what you thought about Source C.
You could include:

a thoughts about the killing of the lion   **c** ideas about the writer

b impressions of the hunter   **d** anything you did not understand.

2 In the same groups, take it in turn to explain what you thought about Source D.
You could include:

a impressions of the lions   **c** what you were thinking at the end

b thoughts about the writer's feelings   **d** anything you did not understand.

3 By now you will have started to recognise some of the similarities and differences
between the texts. Complete the following table to record these points and any new
ones you discover. You should each keep a copy of the table. Some points have been
made to get you started.

	Source C	Source D
What do you know about the writer? (the introduction to each source will help)	Writing in 2001. Spent his childhood in Botswana where his mother studied lions.	
What words do the writers use to describe the lions?		'monstrous moving beasts, yellowish and majestic'; 'mighty'; 'beautiful'; 'ferocious gleaming eyes'; 'ugly short snarls'
What can you work out about the writers' attitudes to lions?	Knew the lion by name – Armagnac – personal attachment – thinks they're incredible animals	
What can you work out about the writers' attitudes to hunting?		Thinks it's fine to hunt lions – has wanted to kill one for a long time doesn't seem to see anything wrong with this
What can you work out about the writers' feelings?		Excited at first and then a bit frightened – 'cold tingling sensation'
Other similarities and differences?		
At what point in the extract is a gun fired?		

WRITE A COMPARISON

When you write a comparison, you should show that you can:

- recognise similarities and differences between two texts
- make comparisons between two texts
- refer to the texts to support the points you make.

Read the following extracts from students' writing. The annotation with each one shows you what the students have achieved. The highlights show you the words the students have used to make comparisons.

Student A The mother of the writer of Source C studied lions so they were important to him. The writer of Source D was a visitor to Africa.

— no comparison made

Student B They were both interested in lions but they treated them differently.

— begins to compare

Student C The writer of Source C spent his childhood with lions in Africa, whereas the writer of Source D is a visitor. They are both interested in lions but they treat them differently. The writer of Source C is against the hunting and killing of lions but the writer of Source D enjoys hunting and wants to kill a lion.

— develops comparison

Student D The writer of Source C spent his childhood in Africa where his mother studied lions. He knows and loves the lion that was killed - he even had a name for it, Armagnac. He clearly dislikes the hunter who shot him and calls him 'proud'. In contrast, the writer of Source D is a visitor to Africa. Although she also admires lions, she sees lion hunting as a sport and wants to kill a lion and had 'planned and longed' for the 'great moment' when she would be able to.

— develops comparison and refers to the text to support points

ACTIVITY 3

1 Read the following three examples of students' writing. Match the annotations to the student response:

a   no comparison made   **b**   begins to compare   **c**   develops comparison.

Student A *Source C starts with a gun being fired whereas, in contrast, Source D ends with a gun being fired.*

Student B *Source C is written by someone who spent his childhood with lions. Source D is about lions being hunted. The lion Armagnac is killed and the writer is unhappy about it. He says that the lion would be flown halfway across the world and that his head would be put on the hunter's wall so that the hunter could tell his friends stories about it.*

Student C *Source C starts with a gun being fired, whereas Source D ends with this. The writer of Source C describes what happens to the body of the dead lion. We can tell that he is sad about what has happened and thinks it is a waste. In contrast, Source D is about the hunt itself and the focus is on live lions rather than a dead one, and the writer is fascinated by the hunt rather than being saddened and disgusted by it.*

2 List evidence from the text that Student C could have used to support their points and improve their answer.

Assess your progress

In this unit, you have:
- examined similarities and differences in ideas and perspectives
- compared writers' ideas and viewpoints
- compared how writers convey their ideas and viewpoints
- developed your skills in writing a comparison.

1 Write a detailed answer to the question:

> **Compare how the two writers show their attitudes to lions and hunting.**

Remember to:
- ✔ compare the writers' attitudes
- ✔ compare how they show their attitudes through what they say and how they say it
- ✔ refer to the text to support the points you make.

How did you do?

Ask another student or your teacher to give you feedback on how well you have developed your comparison.

✔ **Complete this assignment on Cambridge Elevate.**

FURTHER PROGRESS

Look on the internet and find two opposing views on a subject. For example, you could look at two views on reducing the voting age to 16 on the Children England website.

1 Compare the writers' ideas and viewpoints. Which argument do you find most persuasive? Give your reasons.

Unit 14
Judge for yourself

Make progress (AO4)
- identify and evaluate a writer's views
- evaluate a writer's use of language
- evaluate a writer's use of facts
- express and support your opinion.

USE YOUR SKILLS

When you **evaluate**, you use the evidence you have to make a judgement on something. One of the first steps in evaluating a text is to consider the writer's viewpoint.

Read Source A – an extract from an online newspaper article.

Source A

Chilling truth about the video games your children got for Christmas

… a crowded shop. A man saunters in. He produces a hand-gun and fires bullets at a security guard. An assistant looks up. He shoots her. A customer tries to hide. He shoots her too. No mercy, no emotion. Anyone who gets   5 in the way is assassinated – 11 people in two minutes. CCTV footage of a massacre on a news broadcast? No, this is a video game – and the choice of who to shoot is in the hands of the player. And the player could be your child … .

When I was young, entertainment at Christmas revolved around families playing board   10 games. But this year, violent video games were probably among the most popular presents received by children. It seems many parents don't realise the levels of sex and violence in such games, and the damage they may do to the vulnerable minds of children.

This week, I reviewed some of these games. I was not prepared for the extreme realism, or the fact that players take such an active role in murdering, maiming and torturing   15 others. As an adult, I found the lingering attention to every detail of death disturbing. As a mother I found imagining this through the eyes of a child terrifying.

Adapted from an article in the *Daily Mail* by Tanith Carey

ACTIVITY 1

1 In pairs, decide:

    a who is the intended audience of this article

    b what the writer is hoping to achieve.

2 Which view do you think is expressed in each paragraph of the article from the suggestions. Find evidence to support your decisions.

Paragraph 1:
- The writer expresses horror at the content of news broadcasts.
- The writer expresses horror that violent video games are available to children.

Paragraph 2:
- The writer suggests that parents are unaware of the damage they are doing to their children by giving them these games.
- The writer suggests that parents do not care about the damage done to their children.

Paragraph 3:
- The writer suggests that these games are shocking for an adult, and even more shocking for a mother.
- The writer suggests that only adults should play these games.

3 What does the journalist reveal about herself in the final sentence? How might this perspective have affected her viewpoint?

EVALUATE A WRITER'S USE OF LANGUAGE

Writers often use language to arouse emotions in the reader. This is known as **emotive language**. For example the headline of Source A begins with the phrase 'chilling truth'. This suggests that the article contains facts that are frightening, and that the writer's intention is to shock the reader.

 Find out more about assessing evidence on Cambridge Elevate.

 Watch a video about inluencing the reader on Cambridge Elevate.

ACTIVITY 2

In the following table, the first column contains examples of emotive language from Source A.

Emotive language	Intended effect
'… the choice of who to shoot is in the hands of the player. And the player could be your child.'	The writer is trying to horrify the reader with the idea of their own child being an assassin.
'… parents don't realise the levels of sex and violence in such games, and the damage they may do to the vulnerable minds of children.'	
'… players take such an active role in murdering, maiming and torturing others.'	
'As a mother I found imagining this through the eyes of a child terrifying.'	

1 Work in small groups. Copy the table onto a large piece of paper.
For each example, discuss how the writer is trying to influence the reader.
Record your ideas in the second column.

2 Here are some examples of students' writing about the use of emotive
language in Source A. Match the comments with the student responses.

> **Student A** The writer uses emotive language in Source A.

> Student understands why the writer uses emotive language and comments on its possible effect.

> **Student B** The writer uses emotive language to make the reader respond personally to her views. An example of this is when she says 'the player could be your child'. This could shock the reader by making them think of their own child shooting and killing people.

> Student shows some awareness of the writer's purpose in using emotive language.

> Student makes a simple statement.

> **Student C** The writer uses emotive language to provoke a response from the reader.

3 Choose two examples from the table you completed in Question 1. For each
one, show that you understand the writer's use of emotive language by:

a explaining its purpose
b commenting on its possible effect.

SUPPORT YOUR EVALUATION

Student B used a quotation from the text as evidence to support their opinion. You should always aim to do this. Here is another example to help you:

It is not certain these games were the most popular presents children received at Christmas, because the writer says they were 'probably among the most popular'. The word 'probably' indicates that she doesn't know for sure.

statement of opinion

reference supporting this opinion

explanation of how the reference supports the opinion

ACTIVITY 3

Look at the following diagram. The red boxes (A) contain responses from students discussing the article. The yellow boxes (B) contain supporting references. The green boxes (C) contain explanations of how each reference supports a particular response.

A Response to the article	**B** Supporting reference	**C** How the reference supports the response
A1 It is not certain that these games were the most popular presents children received at Christmas.	**B1** 'It seems many parents don't realise the levels of sex and violence in such games.'	**C1** Indicates that she is only expressing her own feelings as a parent.
A2 There is no proof that parents do not know what these games are like.	**B2** 'they were probably among the most popular'	**C2** Implies she is guessing how little parents know about the games.
A3 There is no proof that these games damage the minds of children.	**B3** 'As a mother I found imagining this through the eyes of a child terrifying.'	**C3** The word 'probably' indicates that she doesn't know for sure.
A4 There is no evidence that all parents feel the same way as the writer.	**B4** 'the damage they may do to the under-developed minds of children'	**C4** Suggests that these games may have no harmful effect.

1 Identify the appropriate yellow and green boxes to match with A2, A3 and A4.

2 Write **four** evaluative comments. Use the red statements as your starting point for each one. Then develop the comments using the appropriate yellow reference and green explanation.

3 Write a paragraph using the opening sentence below. Remember to use quotations and develop explanations.

Tanith Carey's article on the danger of video games is dominated by opinion and lacks factual evidence.

Source C

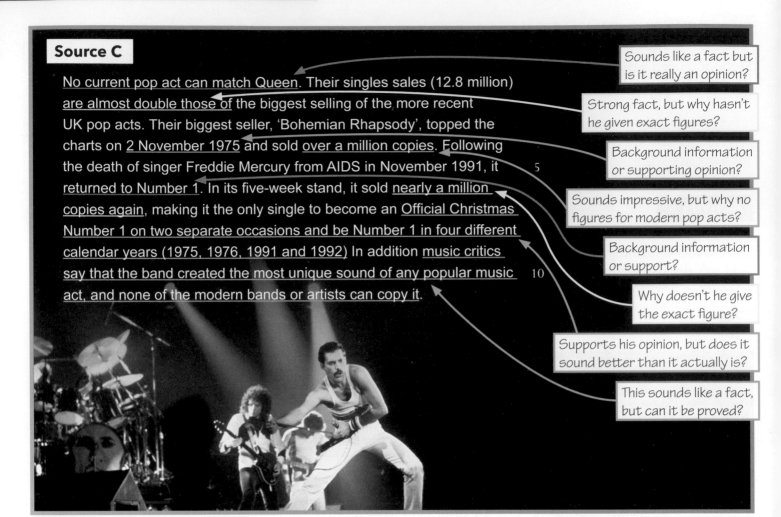

No current pop act can match Queen. Their singles sales (12.8 million) are almost double those of the biggest selling of the more recent UK pop acts. Their biggest seller, 'Bohemian Rhapsody', topped the charts on 2 November 1975 and sold over a million copies. Following the death of singer Freddie Mercury from AIDS in November 1991, it returned to Number 1. In its five-week stand, it sold nearly a million copies again, making it the only single to become an Official Christmas Number 1 on two separate occasions and be Number 1 in four different calendar years (1975, 1976, 1991 and 1992) In addition music critics say that the band created the most unique sound of any popular music act, and none of the modern bands or artists can copy it.

5

10

Annotations:
- Sounds like a fact but is it really an opinion?
- Strong fact, but why hasn't he given exact figures?
- Background information or supporting opinion?
- Sounds impressive, but why no figures for modern pop acts?
- Background information or support?
- Why doesn't he give the exact figure?
- Supports his opinion, but does it sound better than it actually is?
- This sounds like a fact, but can it be proved?

EVALUATE A WRITER'S USE OF FACTS

Writers often choose facts to support their opinions and to influence the reader. You need to:

- distinguish fact from opinion
- question how far the facts support the view.

Source C is a blog written by a middle-aged music fan. It has been annotated to show how you might question the writer's use of 'facts'.

ACTIVITY 4

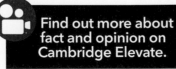
Find out more about fact and opinion on Cambridge Elevate.

1 Read the opening paragraph of one student's answer to the question:

How convincing is this writer's viewpoint?

Identify where the student:

a identifies the writer's view
b uses textual reference
c evaluates the evidence
d supports his or her opinion
e evaluates the language.

The writer expresses the view that Queen is better than modern pop acts. He supports this with some strong factual evidence about their singles sales, saying they have sold '12.8 million' singles. However, his claim that 'sales are almost double those of modern UK pop acts' is not completely convincing. He uses the phrase 'almost double'. The world 'almost' is quite vague and makes me wonder why he has not given an exact figure.

2 Read the question again. Write **two** further evaluative comments that you would include in an answer to it.

Assess your progress

In this unit, you have learned how to:

- identify and evaluate a writer's views
- evaluate their use of language
- express and support your opinion
- evaluate a writer's use of facts.

Remember: when you evaluate, you use the evidence you have to make a judgement on something. Read Source D – an extract from a newspaper article.

1 To what extent do you think the writer presents a convincing argument?

Complete this assignment on Cambridge Elevate.

In your answer you should:

- show that you understand the writer's point of view
- evaluate how he uses emotive language to persuade the reader
- evaluate how he uses facts to support his argument.

Remember to refer to the text to support the points you make.

How did you do?

Ask another student or your teacher to give you feedback on how well you have expressed and supported your opinion.

FURTHER PROGRESS

Being able to evaluate what a writer says is an important skill. Without it, you would simply believe everything you read. Most newspapers have a 'Letters' page. Read some of these letters in newspapers or online at:

- www.telegraph.co.uk/comment/letters
- www.theguardian.com/tone/letters
- www.independent.co.uk/voices/letters

Work out how the writers use facts, opinions and language to influence readers. Decide how far you agree or disagree with the writers' views.

Source D

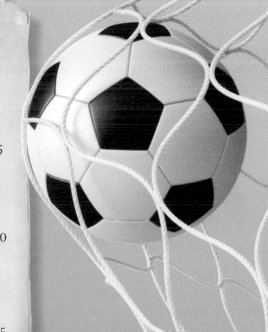

In the latest bank-busting deal, Sky/TV have paid over £5 billion to retain its stranglehold on Premier League TV from 2016 to 2019. This works out at over £10 million a game and, no doubt, more 'superstar' players on over £300,000 a week.

So, who wins? Well the shareholders certainly do and the players destined for ever greater pay-outs. But what about the supporters? It's unlikely that any of this money will seep through to reduced season ticket prices. In fact, it's more likely that faithful fans will be asked to fork out even more next season - and every season after that. For fans like these, it's a double-whammy as the cost of their Sky Sports package will no doubt fly through the ceiling too.

And while the mighty rake in their zillions, staff at the bottom of these same organisations don't even earn a 'living wage' (currently set at £7.85 an hour or £9.15 in London). They scrape by on the minimum wage of £6.50 an hour.

Something has gone sadly wrong with our beautiful game.

Unit 15

Evaluate texts and support the points you make

Make progress (AO4)

- identify and evaluate a writer's views
- evaluate a writer's use of language
- evaluate a writer's use of facts
- express and support your opinion.

USE YOUR SKILLS

When you evaluate a piece of writing, you act as a judge. You should take into account:

- the impact the writing has on you
- the way the writing might influence others
- the evidence that supports your opinion.

A question might ask you to evaluate a single aspect of a text, such as:

How effective is the writer's attempt to build atmosphere?

ACTIVITY 1

 1 The atmosphere is the feeling or mood created by the writer. In pairs, read Source A. Which words would you choose from the word bank to describe the atmosphere created by the writer? Give your reasons for your choices.

dangerous	peaceful	forbidding
friendly	threatening	chilling
lonely	dreary	

Source A

The boy crept cautiously up to the fence and looked around. There was the familiar sign… KEEP OUT! PRIVATE PROPERTY. TRESPASSERS WILL BE SHOT. And hanging next to it, just to make sure that the message was clearly understood, were the bodies of several dead animals, strung up like criminals, wire twisted round their broken necks.

From *SilverFin* by Charlie Higson

A writer creates atmosphere through:

- choice of details
- the words used to describe those details.

2 Which details does the writer focus on in the extract? How do they build the atmosphere?

    a How does the writer describe the boy's movement?
    b What do these words suggest?
    c What image does the writer use to describe the dead animals?
    d How does this help to build atmosphere?

EVALUATE ATMOSPHERE

So far you have identified how the writer has used detail, words and **imagery** to build atmosphere. To write an evaluation of it, you need to:

- identify the atmosphere
- explain how it is created
- comment on its effectiveness.

ACTIVITY 2

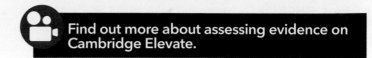

Find out more about assessing evidence on Cambridge Elevate.

Read two responses to the question:

How effective is the writer's attempt to build atmosphere?

Student A Higson creates an atmosphere in this passage. He does this in lots of different ways. He says that the boy 'crept cautiously'. He also writes about the sign and tells us about the animals 'strung up like criminals'.

Student B The writer creates a dangerous and threatening atmosphere in this passage. He tells us that the boy 'crept cautiously' and mentions the sign which warns that trespassers 'will be shot'. This suggests that the boy is in danger and needs to be careful. This sense of danger is increased by the image of 'dead animals'. The fact that they are described as 'strung up like criminals' with 'wire twisted around their broken necks' makes the threat seem very real and frightening.

1 Which of the following teacher's comments goes with which student response?

   a 'You identify the atmosphere of the passage and explain how several details are used to create this atmosphere. You comment on the writer's use of description and suggest how these descriptions affect the reader.'
   b 'You mention that the writer creates atmosphere but have not identified it. You use examples from the text but need to explain how they create atmosphere and the effect they have on the reader.'

2 Copy Student B's response. Annotate it to show where the student has:

   a identified atmosphere
   b explained how it is created
   c commented on effect.

EVALUATE STRUCTURE

You are now going to evaluate the structure of Source A together with Source B – the next three paragraphs of the story. When you evaluate structure, you need to:

* identify and explain how the writer organises and links ideas
* comment on the effects achieved through the structure.

Source B

He knew them so well; they were almost like old
friends. There were rabbits with their eyes pecked out,
tattered black crows with broken wings, a couple of
foxes, a few rats, even a wildcat and a pine marten. In
all the days he'd been coming here the boy had watched   5
them slowly rotting away. But there were a couple of
fresh ones since yesterday, a squirrel and another fox.

Which meant that someone had been back.

In his thick brown poacher's jacket and heavy green
cotton trousers the boy was fairly well camouflaged,   10
but he knew he had to be on his guard. The signs
and the fifteen-foot-high fence entwined with rusted
barbed wire were enough to keep most people away,
but there were the men as well. The estate workers.
A couple of times he'd spotted a pair of them walking   15
the perimeter, shotguns cradled in their elbows, and
although it was a few days since he'd seen anyone up
here, he knew they were never far away.

From *SilverFin* by Charlie Higson

ACTIVITY 3

Read one student's response to this question:

Higson uses structure to build an increasing sense of danger. To what extent do you agree?

Higson sets the scene in the opening paragraph (**1**). He introduces (**2**) the boy and the
sign and creates an atmosphere of danger. The first paragraph ends with (**3**) a description
of the dead animals which adds to the sense of danger. (**4**)

The second paragraph starts with an explanation of the link (**5**) between the boy and the
dead animals. We are told that 'He knew them so well'. The second sentence gives (**6**) a
detailed list of the types of animals, emphasising how many have been brutally killed. (**7**)
The writer then reveals at the end of the paragraph (**8**)that there are a 'couple of fresh
ones' making the reader wonder how they got there. (**9**)

The reader's question is answered in the next single-sentence paragraph: (**10**)
'Someone had been back'. This sentence is quite dramatic. (**11**) It is set on its own (**12**)
and increases the sense of danger by suggesting the boy might not be alone. (**13**)

1 The highlighted sections show you features of the response. Which highlighted sections:

a   identify and explain structure?

b   comment on the effects?

2 Re-read the final paragraph of Source B. Write a short piece to explain:

a   how the paragraph links with the rest of the passage

b   how the ideas in the paragraph are organised

c   how the writer continues to build a sense of danger.

EVALUATE PRESENTATION OF CHARACTER

To evaluate how a character is presented, you need to:

- consider how the writer presents the character's appearance, actions, thoughts and feelings
- comment on the effectiveness of how the writer presents the character.

ACTIVITY 4

Read Source C. The author is describing a woman called Bertha Flowers. She recalls an afternoon when Mrs Flowers stops at the store run by her mother.

Source C

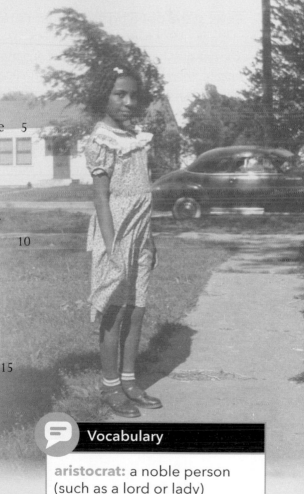

Mrs Bertha Flowers was the aristocrat of the Black Community. Her voile dresses and flowered hats were as right for her as denim overalls for a farmer. Her skin was a rich black that would have peeled like a plum if snagged, but then no one would have thought of getting close enough to Mrs Flowers to ruffle her dress, let alone snag her skin. Mrs Flowers never laughed, but she smiled often. The action seemed so graceful and kind. When she chose to smile on me I always wanted to thank her.   5

One afternoon, she stopped at the store to buy provisions. Another woman of her age would have been expected to carry the paper   10
sacks home, but Momma said 'Sister Flowers I'll send Bailey to your house with these things'.

'Thank you Mrs Henderson. I'd prefer Marguerite.'

[Young Maya changes for the journey. On her return, Mrs Flowers compliments her dress.]   15

'Mrs Henderson you make most of the children's clothes don't you?'

'Yes Ma'am, sure do. Store bought clothes ain't hardly worth the thread it takes to stitch them.'

'I'll say you do a lovely job. That dress looks professional.'   20

Adapted from *I Know Why the Caged Bird Sings* by Maya Angelou

> **Vocabulary**
>
> **aristocrat:** a noble person (such as a lord or lady)
> **voile:** a fine fabric
> **Bailey:** the writer's brother

103

1 Work in pairs.

a What does the writer's use of detail in the description of Mrs Flowers' appearance (lines 1–3) suggest about her character?

b What does the writer's description of the way others react to Mrs Flowers (lines 4–6) suggest about the way people think of her?

c What does the writer's description of Mrs Flowers' behaviour (line 6) suggest about her character?

d What does the writer's description of the way she responded to Mrs Flowers (lines 7–8) add to this impression?

e What does the dialogue add to the reader's impression of her character?

Consider the following question:

Mrs Flowers is presented as an aristocratic and kindly figure. To what extent do you agree?

Look at the opening to a student's response to this question.

The details the writer uses in her description of Mrs Flowers' appearance help to show her character. The references to 'voile dresses' and 'flowered hats' suggest that she looks aristocratic. In addition, the adjective 'rich' is used to describe her skin. This suggests something luxurious, and almost makes it seem as if her skin is untouchable. The writer uses a simile to tell us that her skin would have 'peeled like a plum if snagged'. This emphasises how delicate her skin is. It also makes me think that there is something sweet and tempting about it.

identifies element of characterisation

uses quotations from the text

comments on effect

personal opinion

supports opinion

begins to explore effect

2 Write **three** more paragraphs continuing this response. Use the notes from your discussion to help you.

3 Swap your work with a partner. Give feedback on how successfully they have:

a identified elements of characterisation

b commented on their effect

c supported their opinions.

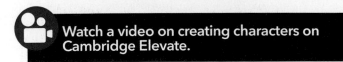

Watch a video on creating characters on Cambridge Elevate.

Assess your progress

In this unit, you have learnt:

- how writers create atmosphere
- how writers use structure for effect
- how writers present character
- how to develop skills in writing evaluation.

You are now going to write a detailed evaluation.

1 Read Source D, a description of life on board a slave ship. As you read, think about and make notes on:

a the point of view from which the description is given

b the words the writer uses to create the scene for the reader

c the effect of the words used.

2 Write a detailed response to the following question. Aim to:

✔ identify how the writer shows the reality of life on a slave ship

✔ comment on the effectiveness of the writer's choices

✔ support your views with evidence.

The writer effectively shows the reality of life on a slave ship. To what extent do you agree?

How did you do?

Ask another student or your teacher to give you feedback on how well you have evaluated.

Complete this assignment on Cambridge Elevate.

Source D

Kunta woke on his back in a pitch darkness full of nightmarish shrieking, weeping and praying. He closed his eyes, beseeching Allah's forgiveness. Only the rasping of the hatch being opened told Kunta if it was day or night. Hearing it he would jerk his head up – the only free movement his chains and shackles would allow. Four shadowy figures would descend, two of them with lights. They moved along the narrow aisleway shoving a tub of food. They would thrust tin pans of the stuff up onto the filth between each two shacklemates. So far, each time the food had come, Kunta had clamped his jaws shut, preferring to starve to death.

From *Roots* by Alex Haley

5

10

FURTHER PROGRESS

As your skills in evaluation improve, you should progress from personal comments to comments that take account of the way in which other readers may respond to a text.

1 Work in groups of four or five.

a Compare your response to Source D with the responses of other group members.

b Talk about any differences of opinion and the reasons for these.

c Think about how you could improve your own response to show awareness of other readers' possible responses.

d Write an improved version of your response.

READING

Unit 16
Test your progress 2

Complete this test to assess your progress in your reading skills.

The test is in two parts. You have **30 minutes** for Part 1 and **45 minutes** for Part 2. You are told which reading skill you are being tested on in each question.

Route to success:

- Read the texts closely.
- Notice how many marks are awarded for each question. This will give you a clue to how much time you should spend on each one.
- Remember to refer to the text(s) to support the points you make.

PART 1

Source A is the opening of a natural history book. Spend 30 minutes reading the source closely and answering Questions 1 to 3.

Identify information and ideas

1   According to the text, which **four** of the following statements are true?

    a   Forests of fir and spruce can be found in the Arctic.
    b   The sun disappears below the horizon after 18 hours of daylight.
    c   Amphibians and reptiles cannot survive the extreme cold of the Arctic.
    d   Collared lemmings live a foot beneath the surface of the snow.
    e   Lemmings are twice the size of a pet hamster.
    f   A small seed would feed a family of lemmings.
    g   The lemmings pay a lot of money to live there.
    h   Collared lemmings can conserve heat because of their fur.

4 marks

Explain and comment on the writer's use of language

2   Look again at lines 1 to 8. How has the writer used language to create an effective image of winter in the Arctic?

8 marks

Source A

Winter in the Arctic. The forests of fir and spruce are half buried in snow. Their
sloping branches are burdened with it. It lies several feet deep all over the ground.
The sun, when it comes, appears for only a few brief hours each day, hanging red
and sullen just above the horizon before sinking down and disappearing for another
eighteen hours or so. And as it vanishes, the bitter cold tightens its grip. There is   5
no sound except for the distant muffled thud as a raft of snow slides off one of the
slanting branches to explode in a cloud of white powder on the snowdrift beneath.
Few places are more hostile to animal life. Amphibians would freeze solid here.
Nor can reptiles tolerate such extreme and continuous cold. Further south, frogs
and salamanders, lizards and snakes take shelter beneath the ground and relapse into   10
torpor, their bodily processes suspended until the arrival of spring months later.
But here the winter cold is so intense that they would die.

Yet there are animals here. A foot down beneath the surface of the snow a small
entirely white creature the size of a pet hamster scurries along a tunnel. It is a
collared lemming. It and other members of its family have excavated a complex home   15
within this snow field. It has different kinds of accommodation. Some are sleeping
chambers. Others are dining rooms where the sparse leaves of half-frozen grass still
rooted in the earth are exposed and can be cropped. Some of the passage-ways that
connect these chambers run along the ground beneath a roof of snow. Others tunnel
their way through the snow itself and lead up to the outside world where one of the   20
family may occasionally go to prospect for any vegetable foot – a small seed perhaps –
that might have recently arrived on the upper surface of the snow.

It costs the lemmings a great deal to survive here. They pay by using some of their
precious food to generate heat within their bodies. In order to keep their fuel costs
to a minimum, they have to conserve as much heat as they can. And they do that by   25
insulating their bodies with fur. It is dense and fine and covers them entirely except
for their eyes.

From *The Life of Mammals* by David Attenborough

Explain and comment on the writer's use of structure

3 Source A is from the opening of a book about animals. How has the writer structured
this opening to capture the interest of the reader? You could write about:

   a   what the writer focuses your attention on in the opening paragraph
   b   how the writer develops his ideas in the second and third paragraphs
   c   how the writer links paragraphs
   d   how the writer frequently reminds the reader of the cold weather
   e   the effect of the final sentence.

8 marks

PART 2

Source B is an extract from a diary. Spend 45 minutes reading the source closely and answering Questions 4 to 7.

Identify information and ideas

4 According to the source, which **four** of the following statements are true?

   a   The weather is always clear and bright.
   b   Saxifrage does not upset the men's stomachs.
   c   Fredericks is the first person to see the bear.
   d   Fredericks and Long had hoped to shoot the bear.
   e   Ellis died because of scurvy.
   f   The writer went to the shrimping grounds on the Sunday.
   g   They buried Whistler during the storm.
   h   They plan to build a new shelter.

4 marks

Select and synthesise evidence from two sources

5 Using details from Source A **and** Source B, summarise the difficulties faced by animals and man in the Arctic winter.

8 marks

Compare writers' ideas and perspectives

6 Compare how the two writers reveal their ideas and perspectives on life in an Arctic winter. Before you answer, think about:

   a   whether they write in the first or third person
   b   whether they are personally affected by the Arctic winter
   c   why and what they are writing
   d   how the writers use language to show their viewpoint.

10 marks

Evaluate texts critically

7 Which of the two sources (A or B) do you think is most effective in showing the hardship of the Arctic winter? Explain the reasons for your choice.

8 marks

Source B

May 17th

A clear, beautiful day. Every bright day we lie on a pile of old clothing and sleeping bags outside and bask in the sunlight.

I caught sixteen pounds of shrimps and four pounds of vegetation. Extremely tired and weak afterward. The hunters and myself receive a double ration of the thin shrimp stew.

A portion of a can of lard, which had been used as ointment for Elison's wounds, was 5
today issued in equal portions to all. The green buds of saxifrage have been introduced by some in their stews. It has not upset their stomachs and appears to be nutritious.

May 19th

Fredericks went out at 4 a.m. to cut ice for breakfast. In a moment he returned greatly excited, with the welcome information, 'Bear outside.' He and Long immediately started in pursuit with their rifles. 10

Fredericks returned at 10 a.m. and Long came in about an hour later. Neither had been able to get within range of the animal. They were thoroughly exhausted by their arduous journey, and had turned back while they had strength enough to reach Camp Clay.

The large English sledge was cut up for fuel today. Ellis quietly breathed his last at 10:30 a.m. No symptoms of scurvy were apparent. Death was due solely to starvation. 15

Sunday, May 25th

Southeasterly wind began blowing at 10 a.m. and continued all day. In the evening it blew a moderate gale. In the heavy drift I was unable to make the customary trip to the shrimping grounds, although the demand for them is great.

We buried Whistler after dinner when the storm was at its height.

Four of us still sleep in the old shanty and are but poorly protected against the storms. 20
But there is no remedy for the matter. Our strength is not equal to the task of getting out the canvas necessary to build a shelter.

My God! This life is horrible; will it never change?

From *Six Came Back* by David L. Brainard

Unit 17
Investigate story openings

In this unit, you will read and explore a range of story openings.

1 Know the correct terms

When you talk and write about story openings, you should use the correct terminology.

- Make sure you know the following by matching the terms on the left to their correct meanings on the right.

setting	the use of spoken words to convey ideas and character
character	the narrator is an observer, not a character, and is able to see everything that happens
first person	the person or people in the story
third person	the narrator is a character in the story and gives a personal viewpoint
description	the organisation of the detail to influence the reader
dialogue	the place in which the story starts
structure	the use of words to create a visual image for the reader

2 Think while you read

A good reader never simply reads the words on a page. They are thinking all the time about the words, their meaning and what the writer is suggesting.

- Read the opening paragraphs of *Alicia* in Source A. The annotations show you some of the thoughts and questions a good reader might have while reading. Are there any you would add?

Source A

Sanderford is a yellow cat with yellow eyes and he is never allowed in the attic. But Elizabeth Ann had seen him go up, so she went after him.

She stopped five steps from the top of the stairs. The step that put her eyes just above the attic-floor level. She stood quietly for a moment and looked along between boxes and bureau legs for a patch of yellow fur. 'Here, Sandy; here, Sandy,' she called softly.

The attic door had been standing open a little. That's strange, she thought. She had seen Sandy's tail disappearing into the darkness, so she knew he was here. 'Here, Sandy; here, Sandy.'

He wasn't allowed in the attic. Ever.

'Here, Sandy; here, Sandy.'

'Here, dear. He's over here, dear Alicia,' a sweet, soft voice answered. Elizabeth Ann froze. Her mouth dropped open slightly and her eyes grew wide with astonishment as they turned in the direction of the gentle but terrifyingly unexpected voice.

In the chair. In the dainty great-great-grandmother rocker. A pale, pretty, white-haired woman in a delicate blue dress. Right next to the chair sat Sanderford with his tail curled neatly around him. Both of them were looking at her.

From *Alicia* by Louise Francke

5

10

15

Sounds creepy.

I wonder why not?

She can't be vey tall – must be a child.

Something's not quite right here.

Makes it sound important.

Why does she call her Alicia?

She wasn't expecting an answer.

What's in the chair?

She sounds harmless but what's she doing there?

Why are they looking at her?

3 **What can you work out?**

Work in pairs.

- Is the story in Source A told in the first or third person? How did you work this out?
- Who do you think is the intended audience for this story? Explain why you think this.
- What do you think might happen in this story? Explain why you think this.

4 **Be a good reader**

Work on your own. Read Source B.

- Annotate a copy of the source to show your thoughts and questions about it. If you cannot annotate a copy, list your thoughts and questions.

5 **How well did you read?**

Work in pairs. Answer the following questions:

- Is the story in Source B told in the first or the third person?
- What is the effect of the narrator's use of the words 'us' and 'we' in the first paragraph?
- What place is the setting for the opening of this story?
- What hint does the narrator give in the first paragraph about what might happen in the story?
- What different things have you worked out about Adam Kindred?
- The writer structures the opening carefully. Place the following details in the correct order:

predicts that young man will appear

description of young man

young man appears

explains what young man is doing

predicts that young man's life will change

explains what young man has been doing

places reader on same side as narrator

name of young man is given

- Why might the last sentence make the reader want to read on?

Source B

Let us start with the river – all things begin with the river and we shall probably end there, no doubt – but let's wait and see how we go. Soon, in a minute or two, a young man will come and stand by the river's edge, here at Chelsea Bridge, in London.

There he is – look – stepping hesitantly down from a taxi, paying the driver, gazing around him, unthinkingly, glancing over at the bright water (it's a flood tide and the river is unusually high). He's a tall, pale-faced young man, early thirties, even-featured with tired eyes, his short dark hair neatly cut and edged as if fresh from the barber. He is new to the city, a stranger, and his name is Adam Kindred. He has just been interviewed for a job and feels like seeing the river (the interview having been the usual tense encounter, with a lot at stake), answering a vague desire to 'get some air'. The recent interview explains why, beneath his expensive trenchcoat, he is wearing a charcoal-grey suit, a maroon tie with a new white shirt and why he's carrying a glossy solid-looking black briefcase with heavy brass locks and corner trim. He crosses the road, having no idea how his life is about to change in the next few hours – massively, irrevocably – no idea at all.

5

10

15

From *Ordinary Thunderstorms* by William Boyd

 Annotate a copy of the opening to *Ordinary Thunderstorms* on Cambridge Elevate.

6 **Which opening most appeals to you?**

Not all readers are the same. They like to read about different things and they like different styles of writing.

Work on your own. Read Sources C, D and E.

- List **three** reasons why each opening might make a reader want to read on.
- Choose the opening that most appeals to you. List your reasons.

Work in small groups.

- Explain the reasons for your choice to the other members of your group. Try to use some of the terms listed in the last activity correctly. You could also explain why you did not choose the other openings. Remember, there is no 'correct' choice!

Source C

The death warrant arrived that morning, packaged in a large white envelope marked confidential and addressed to Tab Mason, Superintendent, Oregon State penitentiary. Mason had been warned the order might be coming. A couple of weeks earlier, the Crook County DA had let the word slip that after nineteen years on death row, condemned murderer Daniel Joseph Robbin had stopped his appeals.   5

Mason dropped the envelope on his desk, along with a file about as thick as his fist, then ran his hand over the top of his cleanly shaved skull. He'd been in corrections for twenty years – Illinois, Louisiana, Florida – and on execution detail a half-dozen occasions, but he'd never been in charge of the actual procedure. Those other times he'd simply walked the guy into the room, strapped him down, opened the blinds on   10 the witness booth, then stood back and waited. He'd worked with one guy in Florida who's done the job fifty times. 'It becomes routine,' the officer told Mason, who was busy puking into a trash can after witnessing his first execution.

From *The Crying Tree* by Naseem Rakha

Source D

It is a relatively little-known fact that, over the course of a single year, about twenty million letters are delivered to the dead. People forget to stop the mail — those grieving widows and prospective heirs — and so magazine subscriptions remain uncancelled; distant friends unnotified; library fines unpaid. That's twenty million circulars, bank statements, credit cards, love letters, junk mail, greetings, gossip and bills, dropping daily on to doormats or parquet floors, thrust casually through railings, wedged into letter-boxes, accumulating in stairwells, left unwanted on porches and steps, never to reach their addressee. The dead don't care. More importantly, neither do the living. The living just follow their petty concerns, quite unaware that very close by, a miracle is taking place. The dead are coming back to life.

It doesn't take much to raise the dead. A couple of bills; a name; a postcode; nothing that can't be found in any old domestic bin-bag, torn apart (perhaps by foxes) and left on the doorstep like a gift. You can learn a lot from abandoned mail: names, bank details, passwords, e-mail addresses, security codes. With the right combination of personal details you can open up a bank account; hire a car; even apply for a new passport. The dead don't need such things any more. A gift, as I said, just waiting for collection.

From *The Lollipop Shoes* by Joanne Harris

Source E

Three things happened when I was seven years old.

In the spring I learnt how to spell my full name. It took weeks but when I'd finally grasped all fifteen letters I wrote them wherever I could — in books, on furniture, on my plate in ketchup, on my arms in biro, in spit on windowpanes. Once I etched my name above the skirting board in the downstairs loo. My mother never found it, but I knew it was there. I'd sit, swing my legs, and eye my handiwork under the sink. It shone out in blue wax crayon.

Then in the summer I burned. I'd spent the day in the garden, digging for worms. The paving slabs were too hot to walk on and the shed roof softened. By evening I was scarlet. She lowered me into a cool bath and dabbed on calamine lotion, but still I wailed. For three days I couldn't sleep. I was feverish, grizzly, and the bed sheets stuck to my blisters. Two weeks later more freckles appeared.

And ten days before Christmas I lost her.

From *Eve Green* by Susan Fletcher

7 **Read closely**

Work in pairs. Read Source F.

- What detail in the first paragraph suggests that Sam and Terry are very young?
- Focus on the first paragraph only. Which of the following words would you use to describe the setting: dangerous, idyllic, peaceful, beautiful, threatening?
- What images does the writer use to describe the pike in the second paragraph?
- What does the pike do?
- Focus on the third paragraph. How does the writer help you understand Terry's reaction to what has happened?
- The scene changes very quickly in these opening paragraphs. Explain how.

Source F

Clive was on the far side of the green pond, torturing a
king-crested newt. Sam and Terry languished under a vast oak,
offering their chubby white feet to the dark water. The sprawling
oak leaned out across the mirroring pond, dappling the water's
surface with clear reflections of leaf and branch and of acorns   5
ripening slowly in verdant cups.

It was high summer. Pigeons cooed softly in the trees, and
Clive's family picnicked nearby. Two older boys fished for perch
about thirty yards away. Sam saw the pike briefly. At first he
though he was looking at a submerged log. It hung inches below   10
the surface, utterly still, like something suspended in ice.

Green and gold, it was a phantom, a spirit from another world.
Sam tied to utter a warning, but the apparition of the pike had
him mesmerized. It flashed at the surface of the water as it came
up to take away, in a single bite, the two smallest toes of Terry's   15
left foot.

The thing was gone before Terry understood what had happened.
He withdrew his foot slowly from the water. Two tiny crimson
beads glistened where his toes had been. One of the beads
plumped and dripped into the water. Terry turned to Sam with   20
a puzzled smile, as if some joke was being played. As the wound
began to sting, his smile vanished and he began to scream.

From *The Tooth Fairy* by Graham Joyce

8 **Evaluate effectiveness**

When you evaluate, you assess and judge the worth of something. When you evaluate the effectiveness of a story opening, you assess and judge its qualities and the effect of these on the reader. To evaluate you need to:

- give your opinion
- explain your opinion
- support your opinion by referring to the text.

Work on your own. The following questions ask you to evaluate different aspects of the opening of *The Tooth Fairy* in Source F. Remember to give evidence to support your opinion.

- 'The writer starts by creating an idyllic summer scene.' To what extent do you agree with this statement?
- How effective is the writer's description of the pike?
- 'The writer makes the reader believe that Sam and Terry are both very young.' Do you agree? Give your reasons.
- 'The opening reminds the reader of the uncertainty of life and how things can quickly change forever.' To what extent do you agree with this statement?
- Look again at your evaluations. Highlight where you have given or explained your opinion. Underline where you have referred to the text.

FURTHER PROGRESS

You have read the openings of six stories in this unit. Remember – to be a good reader you need to be constantly thinking and asking questions about what you are reading.

Choose another story opening. Read it and then write down at least **five** questions that it raises.

Unit 18

Reading sources from different genres

In this section, you will read and write about three texts, from the 19th, 20th and 21st centuries. These texts cover a range of genres: fiction, literary non-fiction and non-fiction. They are linked by a focus on man-made or natural disasters.

The tasks will help you to:

- identify and interpret information and ideas
- select and synthesise evidence from different texts
- explain how writers use language and structure for effect
- compare writers' viewpoints and how these are conveyed
- evaluate texts critically
- support your points with reference to the text.

Source A is fiction and was written in the 20th century.

Work in pairs.

- What damage has the hurricane caused? List the details.
- What comments can you make about the structure of the passage?
  Focus on:

  - what each paragraph is about
  - the contrast between night and day in the opening paragraph
  - how the opening sentences of the second and third paragraphs tell you what the paragraph will be about
  - what the final phrase 'you could not tell' emphasises.

- Compare your answers with those of another pair. Have you missed any details in your list? Can you add to your comments on how the description is structured?

Source A

The narrator describes the scene after a fierce hurricane in Jamaica.

All night the water poured through the house floor onto the people sheltering below: but it did them no harm. Shortly after the second bout of blowing, however, the rain stopped; and when dawn came Mr Thornton crept out to assess the damage.

The country was quite unrecognisable, as if it had been swept by a spate. You could hardly tell, geographically speaking, where you were. It is vegetation which 5 gives the character to a tropic landscape, not the shape of the ground: and all the vegetation, for miles, was now pulp. The ground itself ploughed up by instantaneous rivers, biting deep into the red earth. The only living thing in sight was a cow: and she had lost both her horns.

The wooden part of the house was nearly all gone. After they had succeeded 10 in reaching shelter, one wall after another had blown down. The furniture was splintered into matchwood. Even the heavy mahogany dining-table, which they loved, and had always kept with its legs in little glass baths of oil to defeat the ants, was spirited right away. There were some fragments which might be part of it, or they might not: you could not tell. 15

From *A High Wind in Jamaica* by Richard Hughes

Source B is fiction and written in the 21st century.

Work in pairs.

- The following comments all help to describe this extract. Support each comment with reference to details in the text.
  - The storm is shown to be both terrifying and destructive.
  - The writer creates a vivid picture of how dangerous the storm can be for ordinary people.
  - There is some humour in this description of the storm.

- Examine the following extracts. What can you say about the use of language in each one?

Once in the kitchen Samad flashed his torch around: kettle, oven hob, teacup, curtain and then a surreal glimpse of the shed sitting happy like a treehouse in next door's horsechestnut.

… when the wind reasserted itself, knocking him sideways and continuing along its path to the double glazing, which it cracked and exploded effortlessly, blowing glass inside, regurgitating everything from the kitchen out into the open air.'

- Which do you think is the most effective - Source A or Source B? Support your choice with reference to the text.
- Compare your answers with those of another pair. Add to your answers if you feel they could be improved.

Source B

Samad takes a final look around his home before leaving it to find safety from a severe storm.

Once in the kitchen Samad flashed his torch around: kettle, oven hob, teacup, curtain and then a surreal glimpse of the shed sitting happy like a treehouse in next door's horsechestnut. He picked up the Swiss army knife he remembered leaving under the sink, collected his gold-plated, velvet-fringed Qu'rãn from the living room and was about to leave when the temptation to feel the gale, to see a little   5 of the formidable destruction, came over him. He waited for a lull in the wind and opened the kitchen door, moving tentatively into the garden, where a sheet of lightning lit up a scene of suburban apocalypse: oaks, cedars, sycamores, elms felled in garden after garden, fences down, garden furniture demolished. It was only his own garden, often ridiculed for its corrugated-iron surround, treeless interior and   10 bed after bed of sickly smelling herbs, that had remained relatively intact.

He was just in the process of happily formulating some allegory regarding the bending Eastern reed versus the stubborn Western oak, when the wind reasserted itself, knocking him sideways and continuing along its path to the double glazing, which it cracked and exploded effortlessly, blowing glass inside, regurgitating   15 everything from the kitchen out into the open air. Samad, a recently airborne colander resting on his ear, held his book tight to his chest and hurried to the car.

From *White Teeth* by Zadie Smith

Source C is literary non-fiction and was written in the 21st century.

Work in pairs.

- Which of the following statements are true according to Source C?

  - The sun had set by the time the coach arrived.
  - Many types of birds can be heard.
  - It is raining.
  - The writer is upset by what she sees.
  - The nuclear power plant is still standing.
  - The landscape is radioactive.
  - The writer is crazy to be there.
  - Sheep farms in Cumbria are no longer tested for radiation.

- What comments can you make about the structure of the passage?
  Focus on:

  - how the writer sets the tone in the first paragraph
  - how the writer guides the reader through what she observes in the next three paragraphs
  - the contrast between the first and final paragraphs.

- Examine each of the following extracts. Explain how the writer uses language to describe what she sees.

  Below us, fish leap at mosquitoes. The air rising from the water is damp and cool; the familiar smell of pond life doing its thing. Another movement, less distinct, draws us to the gentle wake of a beaver, paddling back to its lodge.'

  Upstream, the silhouette of the infamous power plant, site of the world's worst nuclear disaster, in 1986, is darkening against the flamboyant sky.

- How does the writer help the reader to understand her thoughts and feelings on seeing Chernobyl?
- This passage is the opening of a longer article. Is it likely to make readers want to read on? Explain the reasons for your answer and refer to the text to support them.

Source C

In 1986 the effects of an explosion at the Chernobyl Nuclear Power Plant in the Ukraine were felt as far away as the Lake District. The writer describes what Chernobyl is like today.

The coach stops haphazardly on an empty two-lane bridge, high over the Pripyat River. It's going to be a spectacular sunset. Clumps of yellow stonecrop and wild carnations are pushing up through cracks in the tarmac. 5 In the gathering dusk we lean on rusting railings, looking out over the softly flowing water, and listen.

From the willow brush on either side of the broad river float the soothing sounds of reed 10 bunting, yellowhammer, blackcap, thrush, nightingale, hoopoe, woodlark, tree pippet and an intermittent cuckoo. Paul Goriup, a birding expert, concentrates as he sits through all the notes. 'Thought so!' The 15 fishing-reel whirr of a Savi's warbler, 'Hear that squeaking sound? There's a woodcock out there somewhere too.'

Below us, fish leap at mosquitoes. The air rising from the water is damp and cool; the 20 familiar smell of pond life doing its thing. Another movement, less distinct, draws us to the gentle wake of a beaver, paddling back to its lodge. I feel tears welling in my eyes. This is Chernobyl in northern Ukraine. The 25 fact that there is wildlife here at all – let alone in such profusion – is deeply moving, a miracle that once seemed beyond all hope of realization.

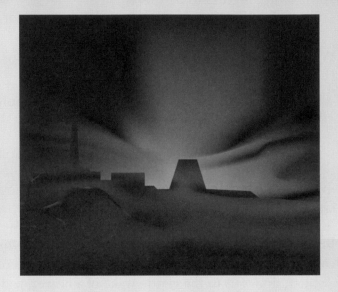

Upstream, the silhouette of the infamous 30 power plant, site of the world's worst nuclear disaster, in 1986, is darkening against the flamboyant sky; a reminder that the landscape and everything in it – the scrub, the mosquitoes, this bridge – is radioactive. 35

It's hard not to feel we're crazy to be here, It is, after all, only 10 months or so since the last sheep farms in Cumbria were removed from radiation testing, contaminated after toxic rain fell from the cloud that drifted 40 over Europe when a reactor here exploded. Chernobyl is still a dirty word, a skull and crossbones in our collective memory, a place of no return.

From an article in the *Sunday Times* by Isabella Tree

Source D is non-fiction and was written in the 19th century.

Work in pairs.

- Focus on the first two paragraphs only. Identify and list **four** facts about the 1815 volcanic eruption.
- How does the writer convey the power of the eruption in the following extract? Think about the detail he includes and his language choices.

Violent whirlwinds carried up men, horses, cattle, and whatever else came within their influence, into the air; tore up the largest trees by the roots, and covered the whole sea with floating timber. Great tracts of land were covered by lava, several streams of which, issuing from the crater of the Tomboro mountain, reached the sea.

- Copy and complete the table to help you identify similarities and differences between Sources C and D. Some details have been given to help you:

	Source C	Source D
Subject of source		eruption of Tomboro
Writer's purpose	to describe /explain/inform/interest	
Intended audience		
Writer's perspective (first or third person)		third person – written 35 years after the eruption
Use of fact and opinion		
Use of descriptive detail	detailed description of wildlife	
Tone		impartial/formal
Other relevant things?		19th century

- Work on your own. Use your completed table to help you write a detailed answer to the following question:

Compare the two writers' ideas and viewpoints and how these are conveyed to the reader.

FURTHER PROGRESS

1 In pairs, list the information you could include from sources A and D to help you complete this task.

Explain the damage that can be caused by natural disasters.

2 Now think about all four sources. Talk about which sources you found most and least interesting. Give reasons for your choices.

Source D

In April, 1815, one of the most frightful eruptions recorded in history occurred in the province of Tomboro, in the island of Sumbawa, about 200 miles from the eastern extremity of Java. In the April of the year preceding, the volcano had been observed in a state of considerable activity, ashes having fallen upon the decks of vessels which sailed past   5
the coast. The eruption of 1815 began on the 5th of April, but was most violent on the 11th and 12th, and did not entirely cease till July.

The sound of the explosions was heard in Sumatra, at the distance of 970 geographical miles in a direct line; and at Ternate, in an opposite direction, at the distance of 720 miles. Out of a population of 12,000, in the province   10
of Tomboro, only twenty-six individuals survived.

Violent whirlwinds carried up men, horses, cattle, and whatever else came within their influence, into the air; tore up the largest trees by the roots, and covered the whole sea with floating timber. Great tracts of land were covered by lava, several streams of which, issuing from the crater of the   15
Tomboro mountain, reached the sea.

So heavy was the fall of ashes, that they broke into the Resident's house at Bima, forty miles east of the volcano, and rendered it, as well as many other dwellings in the town, uninhabitable. On the side of Java the ashes were carried to the distance of 300 miles, and 217 towards Celebes, in   20
sufficient quantity to darken the air. The floating cinders to the westward of Sumatra formed, on the 12th of April, a mass two feet thick, and several miles in extent, through which ships with difficulty forced their way.

The darkness occasioned in the daytime by the ashes in Java was so profound, that nothing equal to it was ever witnessed in the darkest night.   25

From The History of Java by Sir Thomas Raffles

SPOKEN LANGUAGE
Unit 19
Prepare and give a presentation

USE YOUR SKILLS

How important is it to speak clearly and listen carefully? Are speaking and listening skills as important as reading and writing skills? Is it as important to be good at speaking as to be good at maths? If you never listen carefully, do you ever really learn?

ACTIVITY 1

1 Work in small groups. Discuss the following things that people have said about speaking. Use the questions next to each one to help you.

> 'We've got to dispel the myth of the grunting teenager, the monosyllabic teenager that makes employers say "I've got this person who I know on paper is quite good but they can't string a sentence together".'
>
> Peter Hyman, headteacher

What do you think he means by 'the myth of the grunting teenager'? Do you think it's important to speak well in interviews?

> 'If young people are silent, it doesn't mean they don't have anything to say … it can be that no-one has ever asked them for their opinions before.'
>
> Janine Ryman, English-Speaking Union

Do you think young people 'are silent'? Do adults ask you for your opinions?

> Sometimes not speaking says more than all the words in the world.
>
> From *Ugly Love* by Colleen Hoover

Do you agree? Do people sometimes talk too much? How important is it to listen?

2 Peter Hyman says that employers are concerned about young people's ability to speak well. Think about the following occupations. Why are speaking and listening skills important in each of them?

a	shop assistant	**e**	lawyer
b	police officer	**f**	plumber
c	soldier	**g**	driving instructor
d	nurse	**h**	personal trainer.

3 Look back at the questions above Activity 1. Discuss the reasons for your answers.

4 How well did you speak to and listen to the other people in your group during this discussion? Award yourself a mark between 1 and 5 for each of these skills, where 5 is excellent. Ask another student in your group if they agree with your self-assessment.

 Watch a video about real-life presentations on Cambridge Elevate.

SPOKEN LANGUAGE IN YOUR GCSE

As part of your GCSE in English Language you will be assessed on your skills in presenting information and ideas. You will also need to listen carefully to questions from your audience and respond to these questions.

The most important starting point for any presentation is to have something worth saying. If you are interested in your subject and believe in what you say, you are more likely to interest and convince your listeners.

 Discover what makes a good presentation on Cambridge Elevate.

ACTIVITY 2

1 Work in small groups. Look at the following suggestions for presentations that should last for between three and five minutes. Discuss the possibilities each one offers and then choose the one that most interests you.

a Give a talk to your class on a subject that is of interest to teenagers in general (for example social networking, the right to vote at 16, being successful in life).

b Many schools choose charities to support. Present the case for the charity of your choice to your school governors.

c Give a talk to your class on a subject that you think will entertain them. It could be a subject of personal interest (e.g. comedians of the 21st century) or focus on an extreme and potentially amusing point of view (e.g. close schools on Mondays).

DECIDE ON CONTENT

Once you have made your choice you need to decide on the content of your presentation. You will probably need to research your subject. Three minutes is a long time to fill and you must avoid running out of ideas.

1 Make notes on what you want to say. Remember, it is the details that will help to make your presentation interesting, so research your subject thoroughly. If, for example, you have chosen to talk about the right to vote at 16, your research could help you to include relevant, interesting facts and refer to expert opinion.

2 Think about your aims. Are you hoping to interest, inform, argue, discuss, entertain or persuade? You may want to do more than one of these things. Will your material enable you to achieve your aims? If not, do further research.

3 Effective presentations are well planned. Think about how best to order the points you want to make to achieve maximum impact. If you have chosen to talk about a charity, for example, you could keep the most disturbing example of the need for help until last.

4 Make a plan for your presentation. This should show the main areas you want to speak about and the detail you will include in each main area. Your plan could be similar to the following partly completed example.

Main areas	Detail to include
explain how Help for Heroes started	launched October 2007 – Bryn & Emma Parry – war – Injured servicemen and women – Selly Oak Hospital – aims to improve lives
what you might know about H4H	sporting events – X Factor single – Tedworth House opened by William & Harry – Pathways – physical and psychological help
examine one case of help given	Martin Beaney – Basra 2007 – roadside bomb – injuries – Hedley Court – golf – Snow Warrior Expedition
examine second case of help given	Annie Devine
explain why more money is needed	
reveal personal reason – injured uncle	

ENGAGE YOUR AUDIENCE

You have planned your content. You now need to think about how you can capture and keep the interest of your audience. As in your writing, you will need to use a range of vocabulary, images and sentence structures to engage your listeners.

ACTIVITY 4

Read the following presentation openings. Both are about global warming.

Learn more about engaging your audience on Cambridge Elevate.

Student A

Today I'm going to talk about global warming. In my presentation I will tell you about how global warming is affecting us all. I will also tell you about the dangers of global warming and what we need to do to stop global warming.

Student B

When you got out of bed this morning, did you notice how warm it was for February? Did you think 'Great!', or did you pause to ask 'What's going on here?' Because [pause] you should. High temperatures in February are not great. High temperatures in February mean something's going on.

1 Work with a partner. Talk about which opening is better. Which one makes you want to hear more? Give reasons for your choice.

2 Write the first four or five sentences of your presentation. Aim to engage your audience right from the start.

3 Join up with your partner again. Decide how each of you could further improve your opening sentences.

THINK ABOUT USING VISUAL AIDS

You may decide to use a visual aid such as PowerPoint. When used well with slides containing key words, clear diagrams and striking photographs, PowerPoint can greatly enhance a presentation.

However, you need to be careful. There is nothing worse than a presenter turning his or her back on the audience in order to read directly from an overloaded PowerPoint slide. Consider using other visual aids, such as a map or globe, posters or items linked directly to your subject.

ACTIVITY 5

1 Look at the plan you made in Activity 3. List items that might be useful to include on PowerPoint slides. These might be:

- key words and logos
- short bullet points that sum up detail
- diagrams
- photographs.

Aim to have no fewer than five and no more than ten. Decide whether these slides would enhance your presentation. If you think they would, then plan their content in more detail.

VARY PACE AND INTONATION

You may know someone who speaks in monotone – with little variety in **pace** or **intonation**. And yet it is pace and intonation that make speech sound interesting and convey meaning and emotion. Effective speakers:

- control the pace at which they speak
- pause for effect
- vary their intonation to convey meaning and emotion.

To be an effective speaker, you need to develop these skills. This takes practice.

 Watch a video about pace and intonation to engage your audience on Cambridge Elevate.

ACTIVITY 6

1 How often do you listen to yourself speak? By listening to how you say something, you can work out how to vary your pace and your tone for maximum effect. Look at the sentences you wrote in Activity 4 to open your presentation. Practise saying these and then, if you can, record yourself.

Listen to the recording critically and practise it until you are happy with the result. If you cannot record your presentation opening, practise it with a partner and ask for feedback.

2 Now think about how you could end your presentation. It is always a good idea to leave your listeners with a dramatic point or something new to think about. Write two or three sentences to end your presentation and practise saying them using pace and intonation for effect.

BE AWARE OF YOUR BODY LANGUAGE

Your eye contact, posture, facial expressions and gestures all have an impact on your audience. A smile at the beginning and end of your presentation will create a positive impression, for example.

ACTIVITY 7

1 Take it in turns to create exaggerated poses to suit the following situations. Remember to consider posture and facial expressions.

a sitting – appearing interested in what the teacher is saying
b sitting – appearing bored by what the teacher is saying
c standing – meeting someone for the first time who you want to impress
d standing – not paying attention to someone who is talking to you.

2 Now modify your poses so that they are no longer exaggerated but still reflect the situation described. Discuss the effect this body language might have on other people.

3 You will often have seen your teacher giving presentations, and perhaps you have seen some by visiting speakers. Using this experience, what aspects of body language would you adopt when making a presentation? Make a list.

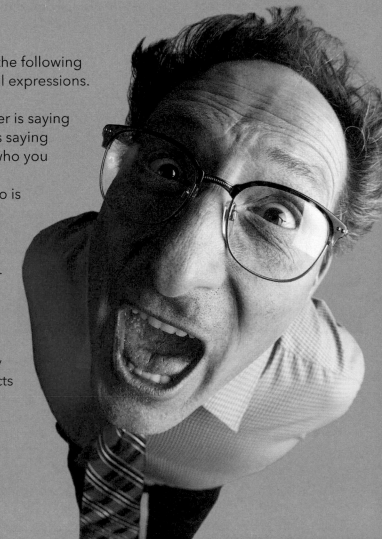

SPEAK IN STANDARD ENGLISH

The way we speak often depends on where we come from and how well we know the person or people we are talking to. Many of our day-to-day conversations are informal and the language we use reflects this. We might, for example, speak in local dialect or use slang or shortened words.

The setting for your presentation is 'formal'. This means that you must speak in **Standard English**. This is the form of spoken English most commonly used in formal and public situations. It is the form that you are taught to use in school. Do not confuse Standard English with 'posh' ways of speaking. Standard English can be spoken with any accent.

ACTIVITY 8

1 Work in pairs or small groups. Check your understanding of Standard English by speaking the standard form of the following non-standard sentences:

    a He couldn't of done it 'cause he was with all the other lads.
    b We was just about to go there.
    c Look at them cars over there.
    d When he came in he sees it like 'n and he says it was brill.
    e Are yous lot goin' out?

2 Talk together about the way you speak and identify examples of non-standard language in your own speech. They might be non-standard because they are slang or part of your local dialect. Decide what the standard version of these is.

> I ain't goin'. I'd've really liked to but we've gotta go 'n see Nanna on Sunday, 'cause it's her birthday. Soz mate.

ASK AND ANSWER QUESTIONS

Think about the following questions:

Was this an important event in your life?

Can you explain the importance of this event in your life?

The first question requires a simple 'yes' or 'no' answer. Questions like this, which require very short, specific answers are called **closed questions**. They are appropriate when you want to know specific details, such as a person's date of birth or address.

The second question invites a fuller, more detailed answer. This is called an **open question**. Open questions are better when you want to learn more about a subject or a person's ideas, thoughts and feelings. A good listener can help a presenter by asking questions that will prompt the presenter to give more information. This can also be achieved by linking a closed and an open question:

'Was this an important event in your life and, if so, can you explain why?'

ACTIVITY 9

1 Work in pairs. Start by each writing **four** questions designed to find out as much as possible about your partner's views on school and the reasons for these. Aim to write open questions.

2 Take it in turn to interview each other. You may need to change your questions in light of the responses you get.

3 Discuss together how successful your questions were in prompting detailed responses. Talk about how they could have been improved.

GIVE YOUR PRESENTATION

Look again at the plan you made for your presentation and for your opening and ending. Before you proceed, you may want to make changes to this. You may also need to do further research and/or prepare a PowerPoint or other visual aids.

Read the points in the following checklist carefully. They will help you to give a good presentation.

 Watch a video about preparing a presentation on Cambridge Elevate.

CHECKLIST

☐ Make sure that you have something interesting to say, and do your research.

☐ Use simple prompt cards to help you remember points. Do not read from a script.

☐ Speak in Standard English.

☐ Vary your vocabulary and sentence structures.

☐ Use pace and intonation to give colour and variety to what you say.

☐ Show confidence in your body language. Look directly at your audience.

☐ Make sure that any visual aids are clear, relevant and well presented.

☐ Time your presentation carefully. It should last for no less that three minutes and no more than five minutes.

☐ Practise your presentation. Ask a friend to record you and to give you feedback on your performance.

☐ Practise again before giving your presentation.

✔ **Fill in the checklist on Cambridge Elevate.**

 Assess your progress

The following list shows the main elements of an effective presentation. Consider each one carefully and decide how well you did on it. Give yourself a mark from one to five for each. Then write a short commentary on your presentation. Start with what you did well. End with comments on the areas where you feel you were weakest and give suggestions for how you could improve.

✔ interesting, well researched content
✔ effective use of prompt cards
✔ sustained use of Standard English
✔ variety in vocabulary and sentence structures
✔ use of pace and intonation
✔ confident body language
✔ relevant, well presented visual aids
✔ efficient timing.

Unit 20

Write for purpose and audience

Make progress (AO5)
- use your ideas to tell an interesting story
- link purpose and audience with control and craft
- order your ideas to interest your reader
- choose words to help the reader understand your feelings.

USE YOUR SKILLS

You probably write almost every day and have already developed many good writing skills.

ACTIVITY 1

1. List the different kinds of texts you have written in the last 24 hours. These might be notes in your science exercise book, a text message, a letter of complaint, comments on Facebook, and so on.

2. Beside each type of text on your list, write a short explanation for why you wrote it – for example:

   Text message: to tell a friend what I'm doing.

3. Now consider how much effort you put into writing each of these texts. Rank them, with the one that took the most effort at number 1.

4. Put a star by the two pieces of writing that you think were most successful. Compare your list with a partner. Explain why you chose your 'successful' entries. For example: 'I wrote a funny story in English which my teacher liked' or 'One of my tweets was re-tweeted lots of times'.

 Watch a video about the features of descriptive writing on Cambridge Elevate.

Source A

Well it was once when I was a kid. I was at Junior school, I think, or
somewhere like that, and went down to Fowlers Pond, me and this other kid.
Anyway it was Spring, tadpole time, and it's swarming with tadpoles down
there in Spring. So this kid, Reggie, says, 'Take thi wellingtons off and put
some in there, they'll be all right 'til tha gets home.' So I took 'em off and   5
we put some water in 'em and then we started to put taddies in 'em.

We kept ladling 'em in and I says to this kid, 'Let's have a competition, thee
have one welli' and I'll have t'other, and we'll see who can get most in!'

You ought to have seen 'em, all black and shiny, right up to t'top. When we'd
finished we kept dipping us fingers into 'em and whipping 'em up at each   10
other, all shouting and excited like.

Then this kid says to me, 'I bet tha daren't put one on.'

So I took my socks off, and I kept looking at this welli' full of taddies, and
this kid kept saying, 'Go on then, tha frightened, tha frightened.' I was an' all.
Anyway I shut my eyes and started to put my foot in. Oooo. It was just like   15
putting your feet into live jelly. They were frozen. And when my foot went
down, they all came over t'top of my wellington, and when I got my foot to
t'bottom, I could feel 'em all squashing about between my toes.

Anyway I'd done it, and I says to this kid, 'Thee put thine on now.' But he
wouldn't, he was dead scared, so I put it on instead. I'd got used to it then, it   20
was all right after a bit; it sent your legs all excited and tingling like. When I'd
got 'em both on I started to walk up to this kid, waving my arms and making
spook noises; and as I walked they all came squelching over t'tops again and
ran down t'sides. This kid looked frightened to death, he kept looking down at
my wellies so I tried to run at him and they all spurted up my legs. You ought   25
to have seen him. He just screamed out and ran home roaring.

It was a funny feeling though when he'd gone; all quiet, with nobody there,
and up to t'knees in tadpoles.

From *A Kestrel for a Knave* by Barry Hines

ABC XYZ **S1 tadpoles:** find out how to form plurals in Unit 31.

HAVE SOMETHING TO SAY

You write and speak because you have something to say – you have a **purpose**.

 Watch a video about writing for a particular purpose on Cambridge Elevate.

ACTIVITY 2

Read Source A, an extract from a novel. Anderson is in an English lesson and his teacher asks him to tell the class about something interesting that happened to him when he was a child. This is Anderson's story.

1 Work in groups of three or four. Discuss the following comments made by students about Anderson's story. Which ones do you agree with?

  a 'It's a good choice for a story: it's both believable and funny.'
  b 'I loved the way he described the tadpoles. I could just imagine how it would feel to put your foot into a welly-full of them – the idea of "live jelly" – ugh!'
  c 'The ending works well. You get all the noise of the kid screaming and roaring and then it's "all quiet". It's a good contrast. It made me wonder what Anderson really felt like.'
  d 'I'm not sure I liked what he did, but it did make me laugh.'
  e 'When I read it, I felt as though I could actually hear Anderson telling the story.'

2 On your own, prepare to tell your group a story about something amusing or interesting that you did when you were younger (but would not do now!). Plan your story and practise telling it in your head.

Take it in turn to tell your stories. Give feedback to each student on:

  a what you liked about their story
  b what they could have done to make it even better.

USE CONTROL AND CRAFT

In Activity 2, you told a story to suit:

* your purpose – to interest your listeners with a story about your childhood
* your audience – the other students in your group.

When you write, you also need to think about your purpose and audience. These factors will affect the content of your writing, as well as how much you control and craft it.

ACTIVITY 3

1 Some kinds of writing require very little control or crafting. Others require a lot. Read the following table. Decide which kind of writing:

   a   needs the best control and crafting
   b   is expected to be controlled and crafted
   c   does not need to be controlled and crafted
   d   needs some control and crafting.

Kind of writing	Examples
writing that is personal and not meant for others to read	diaries, notes
writing that is social and for an audience	texting, blogging, tweeting
writing that is for a known or unknown audience	letters, official documents, work emails
writing that is assessed on its craft and control by a teacher or examiner	an essay in an English exam, an entry for a creative writing competition

2 Look at these ten tips for writing successful controlled and crafted texts. Decide how important each tip is and rank them, with 1 being the most important and 10 the least.

   a   Use different types of sentences for effect.
   b   Organise your text so it has a clear beginning, middle and end.
   c   Make your handwriting neat and tidy.
   d   Write in paragraphs.
   e   Spell correctly.
   f   Use a wide range of words to influence your reader.
   g   Use a range of punctuation to make your meaning clear.
   h   Interest your reader.
   i   Write in Standard English (the form you are taught at school).
   j   Use techniques such as repetition for effect.

3 If Anderson was writing his story for a teacher, he would need to show control and craft. He might write the opening sentences like this:

One time, when I was a child at junior school, I went with a friend called Reggie down to Fowlers Pond. It was springtime and the pond was always swarming with tadpoles at that time of year.

Write the first two sentences of the story you told in Activity 2. Aim to control and craft your sentences.

WRITE FOR YOUR AUDIENCE

When you write a story, you want to interest your reader. Whatever subject you choose, you can tell it in an interesting way to 'hook' your reader and keep their attention. You can:

- make your readers wonder what will happen next
- use detail to build suspense
- choose words to help the reader understand your feelings
- create a surprise ending.

ACTIVITY 4

1 Read Source B. Work with a partner to answer the questions in the margin.

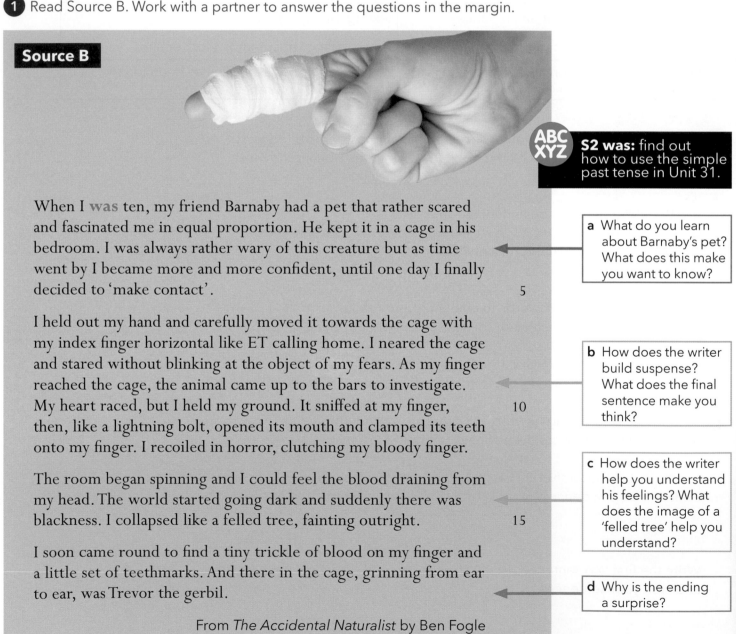

Source B

S2 **was:** find out how to use the simple past tense in Unit 31.

When I **was** ten, my friend Barnaby had a pet that rather scared and fascinated me in equal proportion. He kept it in a cage in his bedroom. I was always rather wary of this creature but as time went by I became more and more confident, until one day I finally decided to 'make contact'. 5

a What do you learn about Barnaby's pet? What does this make you want to know?

I held out my hand and carefully moved it towards the cage with my index finger horizontal like ET calling home. I neared the cage and stared without blinking at the object of my fears. As my finger reached the cage, the animal came up to the bars to investigate. My heart raced, but I held my ground. It sniffed at my finger, 10 then, like a lightning bolt, opened its mouth and clamped its teeth onto my finger. I recoiled in horror, clutching my bloody finger.

b How does the writer build suspense? What does the final sentence make you think?

The room began spinning and I could feel the blood draining from my head. The world started going dark and suddenly there was blackness. I collapsed like a felled tree, fainting outright. 15

c How does the writer help you understand his feelings? What does the image of a 'felled tree' help you understand?

I soon came round to find a tiny trickle of blood on my finger and a little set of teethmarks. And there in the cage, grinning from ear to ear, was Trevor the gerbil.

d Why is the ending a surprise?

From *The Accidental Naturalist* by Ben Fogle

2 In Source B, the writer keeps back some information until the end to surprise his audience. Work in pairs. Look at one student's notes for a story below. Decide how the detail could best be ordered to lead to a surprise ending.

My aunt's TV was broken
My team was in the final
Cousin Sami arrived with tickets
I'm a keen football fan
We were staying at my aunt's
The final was on TV

3 In Source B, the writer uses detail to build suspense. Develop some of the following details to write a paragraph for the story in Question 2. Aim to build suspense:

TV on wall	nothing happened	tried controls on TV
reached for remote	tried again	blank fuzzy screen
pressed buttons	nothing happened	

4 In Source B, the writer chooses words to help the reader understand his feelings. Write **three** sentences in which you choose words to show the reader your feelings when you realised that you would not be able to watch the match on TV.

PROGRESS PUNCTUATION

Punctuation guides your reader through your writing. It is very difficult to make sense of writing that is not punctuated.

Remind yourself of these rules:

- Every sentence must start with a capital letter.
- Every sentence must end with a full stop, a question mark or an exclamation mark.
- Capital letters are used to show the names of months of the year and people.

ACTIVITY 5

Look at the following opening of one student's story. The writing is good, but the punctuation has been removed:

it was one day in late december i had been to visit my granny eveline in hospital and was heading home when the snow began to fall it was very gentle at first but then swirling flakes started to descend within minutes i was making my way through a blizzard it was impossible to see in front of me and the pavement had all but disappeared before long i knew i was hopelessly lost what was i to do

1 Rewrite the paragraph using the correct punctuation.

Assess your progress

In this unit, you have:

- learnt that you write to suit your purpose and audience
- thought about how to make a story interesting for your readers
- revised the use of capital letters and punctuation to end sentences.

1 You are going to write a story based on something amusing or interesting that you did when you were younger. Your audience is your teacher. Follow these steps:

a **Plan** the order of your story. Aim to create a surprise ending. List your planned order.

b **Think** about how to use details to build suspense. List details you could include.

c **Think** about words you could use to show your feelings. List these.

d **Write** your story. Remember you need to show your teacher that you can craft and control your writing.

e **Read through** your story. **Check** that your meaning is clear and that you have used capital letters and end-of-sentence punctuation correctly.

How did you do?

Swap your story with another student. Give feedback on how well they have:

✔ ordered the story and created a surprise ending

✔ used detail to build suspense

✔ chosen words to help the reader understand feelings.

 Complete this assignment on Cambridge Elevate.

FURTHER PROGRESS

The more stories you read, the better you will become at writing them. Here are a few collections of short stories that you might enjoy:

- *Tales of the Unexpected* by Roald Dahl
- *The Crystal Fountain and Other Stories* by Malchi Whitaker
- *Bradbury Stories* by Ray Bradbury.

Unit 21
Write effective sentences

Make progress (AO6)

- use your skills to assess writing
- learn about simple, compound and complex sentences
- add descriptive detail to sentences for effect
- vary your sentence structures to interest your reader.

USE YOUR SKILLS

When you write a text, you make your writing suitable for your purpose and audience. This involves making choices about:

- the content of your writing
- the sentence structures you use
- the vocabulary you choose.

ACTIVITY 1

Read Source A, a text written for young children who are learning to read. Floppy is a dog.

1 Work with another student. Discuss whether you think the content is suitable for young children. Explain why.

2 Each beat in a word is a syllable. For example:

/	/ /	/ /	/ / /
bat	bat+ter	bat+tered	bat+ter+ing
1	**2**	**2**	**3**

Count the syllables in the words in Source A. What do you discover about choosing words for young readers?

3 Which words and phrases are repeated in the text? How might repetition help young readers?

Source A

Floppy was dreaming about dragons. Floppy saw a baby dragon with its mother. The mother dragon saw Floppy.

'Go away,' she roared.

The dragon roared again and flapped her wings. She flew at Floppy.

'Oh help!' he said.

Whoosh! Flames came out of the dragon's mouth. Floppy hid but the dragon saw him.

Floppy ran onto the bridge.

Whoosh! Flames came out of the dragon's mouth again.

'Help!' said Floppy. 'The bridge is on fire.'

 S1 flew: find out about the irregular past tense in Unit 31.

From *Dragon Danger* by Cynthia Rider

CHOOSE SENTENCES TO SUIT YOUR AUDIENCE

Stories for young readers are often short with a simple storyline. In Source A, the writer mainly uses **simple sentences**.

A simple sentence has one **main clause**. A main clause always makes sense on its own. It needs:

- a subject – the person or thing that does something
- a verb – the action that takes place.

Floppy was dreaming about dragons.

The writer also uses some **compound sentences**. A compound sentence contains two or more main clauses. The main clauses are joined together by a **co-ordinating conjunction**. There are three co-ordinating conjunctions: 'but', 'and', 'or'.

Floppy hid but the dragon saw him.

In this sentence, 'but' creates suspense. It shows that Floppy's efforts to hide haven't worked and makes the reader wonder what will come next. Sometimes, the subject of the second main clause is left out to avoid repetition. For example:

The dragon roared again and (the dragon) flapped her wings.

The use of 'and' allows the writer to show that the roaring and flapping happened at the same time.

ACTIVITY 2

1 Write the next part of the story, in which Floppy escapes from the fire on the bridge and then saves the baby dragon from being crushed by a rock. Model your writing on the extract in Activity 1. Remember to:

a use only simple and compound sentences.
b choose your vocabulary to suit young readers.
c use repetition to reinforce learning.

DEVELOP SIMPLE AND COMPOUND SENTENCES

Simple and compound sentences can be developed to include more descriptive detail. For example:

Floppy was dreaming about dragons.

Floppy, <u>the mischievous mongrel</u>, was dreaming about <u>dangerous, diabolical</u> dragons.

The descriptive detail tells us more about Floppy and the dragon. The use of **alliteration** adds an element of fun to the story.

The dragon roared again and flapped her wings.

The <u>diabolical</u> dragon roared again <u>loudly</u> and flapped her <u>powerful, muscular</u> wings <u>above the head of the defenceless Floppy</u>.

Here, descriptive detail emphasises the power and threat that the dragon presents. The word 'defenceless' suggests that Floppy is at the dragon's mercy.

Floppy hid but the dragon saw him.

The defenceless Floppy hid in a small crevice beneath the bridge, <u>but</u> the diabolical dragon saw him <u>and</u> turned her glowing nostrils on him <u>and</u> breathed out flames of fiery red and orange.

Here, the writer links four main clauses to create a clear picture of the sequence of events, with one thing leading directly to another. This extended compound sentence would be suitable for an older child with better reading skills.

ACTIVITY 3

1 Look again at the part of the story you wrote in Activity 2. Rewrite your sentences to make them suitable for an older child. Aim to:

a include descriptive detail
b use alliteration to add an element of fun
c extend one of your compound sentences to show a linked sequence of events.

2 Underline the detail you have added to each sentence.

USE COMPLEX SENTENCES

Writers use simple, compound and complex sentences when writing for older readers.

A complex sentence contains at least one main clause and one **subordinate clause**. The subordinate clause has a subject and a verb, but it cannot stand as a sentence in its own right. It depends on the main clause to give it complete meaning:

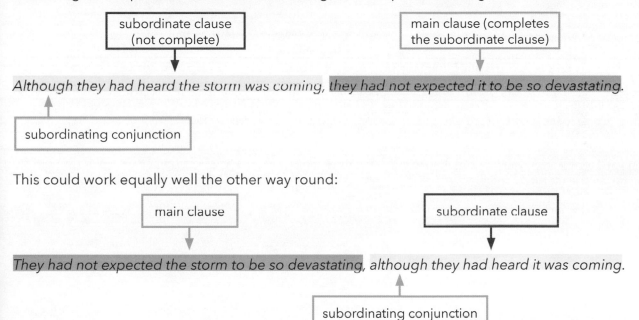

This could work equally well the other way round:

In these examples, the two clauses are linked by the **subordinating conjunction** 'although'. The subordinating conjunction is usually placed before the subordinate clause. Words often used as subordinating conjunctions are: 'although', 'if', 'while', 'when', 'since', 'until', 'after'.

ACTIVITY 4

Look at the main and subordinate clauses of the following complex sentences.
Choose the best matches to form the sentences. An example is given for you.

a	They had not expected the storm to be so devastating	the pet dog shuddered in the corner.
b	The rain lashed the roof	several trees crashed to the ground.
c	As thunder pounded the air	they would have been swept away.
d	After the lightening struck	since records were started.
e	If the children had not stayed inside	although they had heard it was coming.
f	There had never been such a powerful storm	until the gutters overflowed.

1 Writers can make subtle changes to the meaning and emphasis of a
sentence by changing the position of the subordinate clause. In pairs, look
at the following pairs of sentences. Discuss how they suggest or emphasise
different things:

   a   The rain lashed the roof until the gutters overflowed.
       While the gutters overflowed, the rain lashed the roof.
   b   As **thunder** pounded the air, the pet dog shuddered in the corner.
       The pet dog shuddered in the corner as thunder pounded the air.

2 Write **three** complex sentences describing the morning after a storm.
For each sentence:

   a   highlight the main clause
   b   highlight the subordinate clause
   c   underline the subordinating conjunction.

 S2 thunder: find out more about syllables
in Unit 31.

USE A RANGE OF SENTENCE STRUCTURES

Different sentence structures can help you choose the best way of saying what you want to say and influencing your readers. The use of a range of sentence structures is part of your control and craft.

ACTIVITY 5

Read these extracts from two students' responses to this question:

Describe your ideal home.

Student A My ideal home would be by the sea. There would be a long beach and lots of waves. I would like it to be in a busy town as well. There would be a shop over the road from my house and lots of houses nearby so I would have a lot of neighbours. It would also be near to a main road. There would be lots of shops on the main road. The beach would also be busy but there would not be any tourists there. There would only be the local people. They would go there almost every day.

Student B When you walk through the door, the house is warm and cosy. The first thing that greets you is the kitchen with its welcoming smells of baking. In the centre of the kitchen is a large wooden table, where the family sit every weekend and share stories of their lives and enjoy Mum's amazing Sunday roast. Under the table, snoring lightly, lies the family pet. His name is Goofy. Look through the window and you see a garden, colourful flowers, a bright red slide and a matching swing. It used to be my playground.

1 Work with another student. Look at the following comments used by examiners to assess students' writing. Decide which comments apply to Student A and which to Student B. Some comments apply to both.

Comments	A	B
Use of capital letters and full stops is correct.		
Standard English has been used throughout.		
Commas are used to guide the reader through sentences.		
There is some variety of sentence structures.		
Sentence structures are used for effect.		
There is an attempt to describe.		
Descriptive detail is effective.		

Did you work out that Student B was awarded a higher mark than Student A because they:

- used a variety of sentence structures for effect
- made effective descriptive detail
- used commas to guide the reader through the sentences?

PROGRESS PUNCTUATION

Commas are used to help the reader by separating parts of a sentence. Commas separate items in a list (but not usually before 'and'):

Look through the window and you see a garden, colourful flowers, a bright red slide and a matching swing.

Commas mark off extra information:

Under the table, snoring lightly, lies the family pet.

Commas are used after a subordinate clause that begins a sentence:

When you walk through the door, the house is warm and cosy.

Rewrite the next paragraph of Student B's description. Put in the commas.

If you step out of the kitchen and turn left you will enter the lounge. This is where the family spend much of their free time. A large television sits in the corner whilst the wall facing you has a glowing electric fire surrounded by books CDs smiling photographs and scenic pictures. Your eye travels around the room. You spot something unexpected. Standing against the wall by the window is a glowing full-sized classic jukebox.

✔ Assess your progress

In this unit, you have:

- used simple, compound and complex sentences
- added descriptive detail for effect
- varied your sentence structures to interest your reader
- uses commas to guide your reader through your sentences.

1 Now think of your ideal bedroom. What does it look like? Spend a few minutes jotting down ideas about:

   a   what is in the room

   b   how you could describe it to impress your teacher with your writing skills.

2 Write one or two paragraphs describing your ideal bedroom.

Complete this assignment on Cambridge Elevate.

How did you do?

Read the writing of two other students. Give feedback on how well they have:

✔ varied sentence structures to interest the reader
✔ included descriptive detail
✔ used commas to guide the reader though your sentences.

Use the feedback you get to help you improve your paragraph.

FURTHER PROGRESS

1 Look around your classroom. Choose three things to describe – they could be:

   a   books in a bookcase
   b   the view from the window
   c   another student
   d   the floor
   e   a wall display
   f   the paintwork.

2 Write two or three sentences describing each of your three choices.

WRITING

Unit 22
Use effective vocabulary

USE YOUR SKILLS

There are hundreds of thousands of words in the English language, yet people often use only a small number of these when they write. The wider your vocabulary, the easier you will find it to express your ideas clearly, precisely and effectively.

ACTIVITY 1

One word that is over-used is 'said'. For example:

'You have to give me that now,' she said.

The verb 'said' tells us very little about how she spoke the words.

1 Work with a partner. What do the following replacement verbs suggest about how she said the words?

a 'You have to give me that now,' she <u>mumbled</u>.
b 'You have to give me that now,' she <u>screamed</u>.
c 'You have to give me that now,' she <u>insisted</u>.

2 There are ten further replacement verbs for 'said' in the word bank. What does each of these suggest about how the words are spoken?

whispered	exclaimed	bellowed
roared	stammered	yelled wailed
grunted	muttered	screamed

3 There are many verbs that describe movement. Copy the following table and put the verbs from the word bank on the following page into the correct column.

Move quickly	Move slowly	Move gracefully	Move awkwardly	Move downwards	Move upwards	Move round

lurch	bolt	whirl	sway	falter	dart	stagger	raise	dash	drop
race	stumble	run	shoot	spin	stampede	amble	crawl	stroll	
glide	slide	fly	gallop	shuffle	trip	descend	fall	sink	circulate
soar	zoom	turn	twist	rush	rotate	dawdle			

4 Did you know all these verbs? How many of them do you use in your writing? Compare your table with that of another student. Discuss any differences.

 USE VERBS AND ADVERBS TO ENHANCE MEANING

You can describe movement more clearly if you choose your verbs carefully. Take the simple sentence:

The man walked down the path.

Notice how the way the man walked is made clear by the choice of verbs in the following sentences:

The man <u>staggered</u> down the path.

The man <u>strolled</u> down the path.

Adverbs can help you develop your descriptions even more. Adverbs generally answer the questions:

* **How?** slowly, hesitantly, deliberately
* **When?** yesterday, soon, earlier
* **Where?** outside, there, away
* **How often?** never, sometimes, regularly.

Notice how the adverbs add to the meaning of the following sentences:

The man staggered drunkenly down the path.

The man frequently strolled down the path.

 S1 adverbs: find out how to change adjectives to adverbs in Unit 31.

ACTIVITY 2

1 Use the following table to help you make new sentences by replacing the verb 'saw' with a different verb and a suitable adverb.

Verb		Adverb
glimpsed		steadily
noticed		quietly
watched	The girl saw the rising sun.	suddenly
observed		patiently
spotted		determinedly
viewed		fearfully

2 Replace the underlined verbs in the following sentences with a different verb and adverb.

  a The woman <u>walked</u> to the shops.
  b He <u>put</u> the letter on the kitchen table.
  c The boy <u>said</u> that he had taken it.
  d The child <u>fell</u> into the mud.
  e It <u>shone</u> in the sky.

3 Compare your sentences with those of another student. Decide which one are most effective.

 **UNDERSTAND SUFFIXES**

Most people have a wider vocabulary than they realise. The trick is to make sure you know how to use **suffixes**.

A suffix is a letter or group of letters added to the end of a root word, which changes the meaning of the word. Take, for example, the word 'shadow':

When describing this picture you could write:

There was a <u>shadow</u> of a tree on the path.

> The noun tells you what is on the path.

However, you can write more effective sentences by using suffixes to create a different form of the word 'shadow'. For example:

The <u>shadowy</u> path reached into the distance.

> The adjective makes the path sound mysterious.

Trees <u>shadowed</u> the path as I hurried along.

> The verb makes the trees seem alive and perhaps threatening.

<u>Shadowing</u> the path, giant trees lined the pavement.

> The use of the present participle shows that this is happening now and adds to the creepiness of the scene.

Here are some frequently used suffixes:

You can extend your vocabulary further by combining suffixes. For example:

fright   fright+en   fright+en+ed   fright+en+ing

ACTIVITY 3

1 Create different meaning by adding suffixes to the following words:

a	wonder	**e**	happy
b	play	**f**	agree
c	dread	**g**	light.
d	sense		

> ly   able   ible   ed   en   ful   ing   ment   ness
> ation   er   est

2 Compare your words with those of another student. Add to your list if you can.

THINK ABOUT WORD CHOICE

To be a good writer, you need to show that you have a developed vocabulary. The following student is describing a trip to the seaside:

Last Tuesday a whole load of us went to the beach. It was really hot. The sand was so hot you couldn't walk down to the sea without flip-flops but when you got in the sea it was lovely and cold. We aren't great swimmers so we just spent ages just lying on the edge of the sea.

The student writes in clear sentences, but there is not much sign of a developed vocabulary. With a little extra thought, the student could have written something like this:

Last Tuesday a large group of us descended on the beach. The sun was shining brightly and it was extremely hot. The sand scorched our toes and we couldn't walk to the sea without flip-flops, but when we dipped our feet in the icy waves it was lovely. We aren't brilliant swimmers. Consequently, we just paddled and lay by the water's edge.

ACTIVITY 4

Look at the next paragraph from the student's writing:

We must have looked really funny all lined up in a row like that. It was nice just chatting and lying in the sea and everyone getting on. We were wondering what to do next when we heard the tune of an ice-cream van. We got up and ran over to it. There was a bit of a queue but we decided to wait. After a few minutes we were all walking back to the sea holding giant ice-cream cones.

1 Rewrite the paragraph to show that you have a developed vocabulary. You can also change the sentence structures if you want to.

2 Ask another student for feedback on the effectiveness of your writing. Use their feedback to make further improvements.

DEVELOP IMAGES

You can improve your writing through the occasional use of effective images. The most common images are similes and metaphors.

In a simile, something is compared with something else using the words 'as' or 'like'. For example:

… we just paddled and lay by the water's edge …

…we just paddled and lay by the water's edge <u>like seals glistening in the sunshine</u>.

In a metaphor, something is described as actually being something else. For example:

We must have looked really funny all lined up in a row like that.

We must have looked really funny all lined up — <u>a platoon of soldiers ready for action</u>.

ACTIVITY 5

1 Work with a partner. Develop effective similes or metaphors to create vivid images for the following sentences:

  a The water crashed onto the beach.
  b We heard the tune of an ice-cream van.
  c There was a bit of a queue.
  d We were holding giant ice-cream cones.

2 Work on your own. Write an effective paragraph describing a trip you made with friends. It could be to town, to a park, to a match or something else. Aim to:

  a use a developed vocabulary
  b create one or two vivid images.

3 Read the work of other people in your class. Then give your similes and metaphors a mark of between 1 and 3, where 1 = a little effective and 3 = very effective.

INVESTIGATE DESCRIPTIVE WRITING

Writers choose details, vocabulary and images to build a clear picture for their readers. Source A is written in the first person. It is the start of a full-length story. Read it closely before completing Activity 6.

ACTIVITY 6

1 Work in pairs. Investigate the writer's use of verbs by discussing:

  a the choice of the following verbs: 'clasp', 'leached', 'clenched'
  b the writer's listing of these verbs: 'get', 'move', 'work', 'sit'.

2 What is the effect of the adverb in the phrase: 'I can only watch helplessly'?

3 Identify the simile the writer uses. What image does it create for the reader?

4 What impression of the narrator's situation does the writer create in this opening paragraph?

Source A

I clasp the flask between my hands even though the warmth from the tea has long since leached into the frozen air. My muscles are clenched tight against the cold. If a pack of wild dogs were to appear at this moment, the odds of   5
scaling a tree before they attacked are not in my favour. I should get up, move around, and work the stiffness from my limbs. But instead I sit, as motionless as the rock beneath me, while the dawn begins to lighten the woods. I can't fight   10
the sun. I can only watch helplessly as it drags me into a day that I've been dreading for months.

From *Catching Fire* by Suzanne Collins

ABC XYZ **S2 muscles:** find out more about the letter sequence 'sc' in Unit 31.

151

PROGRESS PUNCTUATION

In Activity 1 you chose verbs to indicate how something is spoken. When you write spoken words, it is important to punctuate correctly. The basic rules of punctuating direct speech are:

- Each piece of speech begins and ends with inverted commas ('…'). These are sometimes called speech marks or quotation marks.
- Each new piece of speech starts with a capital letter.
- Every piece of speech ends with a punctuation mark.

ACTIVITY 7

1 Copy and correctly punctuate the following sentences:

   a   have you seen them she asked
   b   they're playing in the park he replied
   c   let's go and check they're alright she insisted

FURTHER PROGRESS

1 Examine the writer's use of verbs, adverbs and imagery in Source B.

2 Write a paragraph in which you effectively describe the appearance of a strange or unexpected creature.

Assess your progress

In this unit, you have:

- used a developed vocabulary for effect
- chosen verbs and adverbs to enhance meaning
- understood suffixes
- created effective images
- crafted your writing.

1 Write the first paragraph of a frightening story. Someone is trapped in a dark room and scared about what will happen next. You can write in the first or the third person.

Remember to:

- use a developed vocabulary
- choose verbs, adverbs and imagery to enhance meaning
- create an effective opening for a frightening story.

2 Read through your paragraph carefully. Can you improve it further? Make any changes you think necessary.

How did you do?

Ask another student or your teacher to give you feedback on the effectiveness of your opening paragraph.

Complete this assignment on Cambridge Elevate.

Source B

I saw it in an instant. It quite startled me. A huge dark shape was lumbering slowly out of the white water, and was heading, inching, up the beach. First one emerged, then another, and another — until there were maybe fifteen of them, moving slowly and almost painfully up the sloping sand, like wounded soldiers of an invasion force. One of them approached within two metres of us — and once so close, I could see exactly what it was.

A green turtle.

From an article in *National Geographic* by Simon Winchester

WRITING

Unit 23
Control your writing

Make progress　**AO5**
- plan your writing
- write coherent paragraphs
- link paragraphs.

USE YOUR SKILLS

You use planning skills in almost every aspect of your life. You have to plan:

- what to take to school to make sure you have everything you need
- what to do at the weekend and who you are going to do it with
- what train or bus you are going to catch to get to a place on time.

ACTIVITY 1

Work in groups of three or four. You are going to plan a leavers' party that the majority of your year group would enjoy attending. You will need a few big sheets of paper on which to jot down ideas.

Follow these steps.

1 **Gather ideas:** collect as many ideas as possible about the kind of party you could have. Listen carefully to everyone's suggestions. Agree to consider two or three suggestions in more detail. Use the following prompts to help you think about each suggestion more carefully.

Where will it be? Does it need to be booked in advance?

When will it be? What day of week? Month? Time?

Will the weather affect its success? If so, what precautions are needed?

What should people wear? How will they get there?

Who will be invited? Will invitations be sent? Should there be a Facebook ban?

What could go wrong? How would you deal with things going wrong?

What will it cost? Will everyone be able to afford it? What if they can't?

Will there be entertainment, food and drink? What will they be?

2 **Plan:** Now decide which suggestion will best suit your audience – the students in your year group. Use the following headings to give details about your party. Change the headings if you need to.

- Type of party
- Time and place
- Dress code
- Transport
- Outline of what will happen
- Food, drink and entertainment
- Estimated cost
- Why people will enjoy it

3 **Present:** Present your ideas to your class. Be prepared to answer questions. Take a vote on the best-planned party.

GENERATE IDEAS

To produce a good piece of writing, you need to plan it carefully. Firstly, you need to identify your audience and purpose. You then need to generate a range of ideas. Here are two methods that you could use to help you.

> **Task:** Your local council is running a competition. They are asking for an effective description of the best places to visit in your area. Write your description.
>
> **Purpose:** describe the best places in the area
>
> **Audience:** members of the local council

Watch a video about generating ideas on Cambridge Elevate.

Method 1

Brainstorm by placing the subject in the centre and jotting down ideas connected with it. Extend some ideas with further detail.

Important: you can invent places that are not in your area if you like.

Method 2

Use a sequence of simple questions to help you develop ideas and build detail. For example:

Write a story to be read by other students in your class which begins or ends with: 'He had never been so frightened.'

154

Who? Arjun – 16

What? saw a violent attack

Where? city – by the river – dark/dangerous

When? late evening – November – misty/cold

~~How?~~

Why? walking home after seeing girlfriend

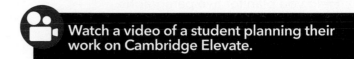

Watch a video of a student planning their work on Cambridge Elevate.

Purpose: write a story – interest? entertain? shock?
Audience: other students

Important: only make notes on the questions that help you build your ideas.

ACTIVITY 2

1 Read this task and identify the purpose and audience.

Write a story for students which begins or ends with: 'The door slammed shut behind her.'

Use Method 1 or Method 2 to help you generate ideas.

2 Talk through your ideas with one or two other students. Ask for feedback on how well you have generated ideas and for further suggestions. Add any suggestions that you like.

PLAN FOR PARAGRAPHS

Now that you have generated ideas, you need to impose order on them. One way to do this is to plan for **paragraphs**. It is a good idea to plan for five paragraphs.

Look again at the ideas generated under Method 2. Study the paragraph plan below and track the ideas which have been used to help form it:

Para 1: set the scene – walking by river – misty November night – just been to see girlfriend

Para 2: hears noises – stops – sees two men approaching – arguing

Para 3: start to fight – Arjun watches – knife?

Para 4: Arjun races home – starts to rain – can hear footsteps – thinks about girlfriend

Para 5: arrives home – breathing heavily – no footsteps – mother asks what's wrong – end: He had never been so frightened

S1 paragraph: find out more about 'f' sounds in Unit 31.

155

ACTIVITY 3

1 Use the ideas you generated in Activity 2 to help you plan for five paragraphs.

2 Talk through your paragraph plan with one or two other students. Ask for feedback on how well you have sequenced your ideas and for further suggestions. If you can, improve your plan.

3 Do you feel confident that you now have a clear plan for your writing? Assess your confidence with a mark from 1 to 5.

USE YOUR PARAGRAPH PLAN

You do not have to follow your paragraph plan exactly. It should be a guide to take you from the start to the end of your writing.

ACTIVITY 4

1 Look again at the plan for paragraphs. Read Source A – the first page of a story based on this plan. Talk about how the writer has used and developed the plan.

Source A

There were no stars in the sky. The night was dark and misty and a bitter November wind blew through the air. But Arjun didn't mind. He had spent the evening with Riya, his girlfriend of eight months, and was feeling very happy as he walked home alone. There were not many people about and the bridge over the river was deserted. He could hear his footsteps echoing in the cold night air. As he crossed the bridge, the silence was disturbed by the sounds of angry shouting. He glanced down at the path by the side of the river and stopped to watch what was happening there. 5

Two men were standing facing each other. They were clearly angry and were arguing about something. Fragments of their conversation reached Arjun on the bridge.

'Hey, I've already told you I don't have it,' the smaller of the two figures shouted. 10

'It's not good enough,' replied the other. 'You've had as many warnings as I'm going to give.'

They carried on arguing for some time before the smaller man started to walk away. He did not get far. Arjun watched as the larger man pushed him to the ground and soon they were fighting seriously. He wanted to stop them or to call for help but 15 there was no one around. Then, without warning, the smaller man pulled out a knife and, swift as lightning, plunged it into the other man's stomach. The big man crashed to the ground while the other one looked around to see if he had been seen. It was then he looked up at the bridge and saw Arjun gazing down.

For a moment Arjun caught the gleam in the murderer's eye and then he ran 20

156

2 Look again at the plan you made in Activity 3. Now write your first paragraph.

WRITE COHERENT PARAGRAPHS

The sentences in a paragraph should:

- follow a logical sequence
- develop the ideas.

ACTIVITY 5

1 Ask a partner to read your first paragraph and give you feedback on:

   a whether you have followed a logical sequence
   b how well you have developed the ideas
   c ways you could improve your paragraph.

2 Use the feedback to redraft your first paragraph.

USE PARAGRAPHS FOR DIALOGUE

Dialogue can add interest to a story, but you should not overuse it. You should start a new paragraph for each new piece of speech. For example:

'Hey, I've already told you I don't have it,' the smaller of the two figures shouted.

'It's not good enough,' replied the other. 'You've had as many warnings as I'm going to give.'

ACTIVITY 6

1 Look again at your plan. Write a few lines of dialogue to include in your story. Remember to punctuate your direct speech correctly.

 Listen to how writers use dialogue on Cambridge Elevate.

LINK PARAGRAPHS

Each paragraph should move the writing forward with a shift in focus. Look back to Source A. The writer ends the first paragraph with Arjun looking down to see what is happening. The second paragraph shifts the focus to the two men. It ends with a reference to 'fragments of their conversation'. The third and fourth paragraphs reveal what the two men are saying.

ACTIVITY 7

1 Answer these questions to track the links between paragraphs:

   a How does the start of the fifth paragraph link with the fourth paragraph?
   b How does the fifth paragraph end?
   c How does the start of the sixth paragraph link with the end of the fifth?

2 Write the first sentence of your second paragraph. Make sure it links with your first paragraph and marks a shift in focus.

PROGRESS PUNCTUATION

Paragraphing is a feature of punctuation as well as organisation. There is no 'correct' length for a paragraph. You use paragraphs:

- to indicate to your reader a shift in focus
- to indicate to your reader a change of speaker in a dialogue.

ACTIVITY 8

1 Read Source B. Decide where you would place paragraphs.

157

Source B

The sun was gently disappearing below the horizon, its muted ruby rays glancing against the soft clouds. 'It's time to go,' she murmured softly. Slowly, they gathered the remnants of their last day together. They drifted aimlessly across the now-deserted beach, the imprints of their feet marking the sand before quickly fading. They moved in silence, uncertain of what to say, both knowing there was no more time to put things right. Darkness fell quietly.

 S2 disappearing/uncertain: find out more about the prefixes 'dis-' and 'un-' in Unit 31.

 Assess your progress

In this unit, you have:

- generated ideas
- planned for paragraphs
- learnt how to write coherent paragraphs
- learnt how to link paragraphs.

✔ sequence your ideas
✔ use dialogue effectively
✔ write coherent, linked paragraphs.

Remind yourself of the title of your writing task:

Write a story for students that begins or ends with: 'The door slammed shut behind her.'

1 Use your paragraph plan to help you continue and complete your story. Aim to write between 300 and 500 words. Remember to:

2 Read through your story. Check that your meaning is clear and that you have used paragraphs and dialogue appropriately. Make improvements if you can.

How did you do?

Ask another student or your teacher to give you feedback on how well you sequenced your ideas and used paragraphs to guide your reader.

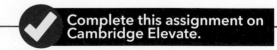 **Complete this assignment on Cambridge Elevate.**

FURTHER PROGRESS

Identify purpose and audience, generate ideas and plan paragraphs for the following task. You can use some of the ideas you generated in Activity 1.

Your local council is running a competition. They are asking for an effective description of the best places to visit in your area. Write your description.

WRITING
Unit 24
Create tone to influence your reader

Make progress (AO5)
- write in Standard English
- understand the differences between formal and informal writing
- create tone through word choice
- use tone to influence your reader.

USE YOUR SKILLS

When you write a letter to email or post, it becomes a permanent record. You need to make sure that what you write and the way you write it is matched to your purpose and audience, so that it helps you get the result you want.

ACTIVITY 1

1 Work in pairs. Jasmine is angry about the way she was treated in a shop. Read the first draft of her letter of complaint to the manager. Use what you know about writing for purpose and audience to help you discuss the appropriateness of the letter.

You might want to think about:

a whether Jasmine clearly explains what has happened
b whether Jasmine makes clear what she wants the manager to do
c whether the way she writes is appropriate for a letter of complaint.

Source A

Dear Mr Smith,

I'm really really angry about the way one of your security guards treated me just coz I'm a teenager. He didn't even ask me about it. He wouldn't of treated an adult so bad. Everyone kept staring at me. I was so embarrassed I could of cried. He was totally out of order.

Me and my friends spend loads of money in your shop and your security guard should of shown me some respect – the same as he would of to anyone else.

I want you to sort it all out so that nobody ever treats me or my friends like that again.

Yours sincerely,

Jasmine

Standard English is the term used to describe grammar, spelling, punctuation and vocabulary that is accepted as being correct by people living throughout the UK. It is the form of English you are taught to write in school. A letter of complaint should be written in Standard English.

ACTIVITY 2

1 Jasmine redrafted her letter to make it suit her audience and purpose. In pairs, read the letter, then answer the questions that follow.

Source B

Dear Mr Wright,

I am very angry about the way one of your security guards treated me in Top Sport yesterday, Saturday 20th June. The security guard, who was called Mike, did not ask me what had happened before he accused me of breaking a mirror in the fitting room. In fact, the mirror was already broken before I went in there. He would not have treated an adult so badly.

While the security guard was shouting at me, other customers were staring, which made me feel extremely **embarrassed**. His behaviour was unacceptable. He treated me like that simply because I am a teenager.

My friends and I spend a lot of money in your shop. Many teenagers do. I think I deserve an apology for what happened and I would like you to train Mike to treat his teenage customers with the same respect that he gives your adult customers.

Yours **sincerely**,

Jasmine Ryan

a List the extra information Jasmine gives to make it clear what happened and what she wants the manager to do.

b Jasmine uses Standard English in her second draft. Copy and complete the following table to show the changes Jasmine makes to her non-standard English.

Non-standard English	Standard English
really really angry	
coz	
he wouldn't of treated an adult so bad	
He was totally out of order	
Me and my friends	
loads of money	

ABC XYZ **S1 embarrassed/ sincerely:** for more information about commonly misspelt words, see Unit 31.

2 When the manager, Mr Smith, replies to Jasmine he will want to show that he has read her letter carefully, that he is sorry for what has happened and that he will take action.

Write the manager's reply. Use some of the phrases in the word bank to help you. Remember to write in Standard English.

> I would like to apologise for …   I would like to offer you …
>
> teenage customers do deserve the same respect …
>
> I have spoken with …   I regret that …
>
> has now been trained …   … will not happen again …

 Watch a video about Standard English on Cambridge Elevate.

UNDERSTAND REGISTER

The term **register** is used to describe how formal or informal writing is.

In the first draft of her letter, Jasmine used words and phrases that she would say to someone she knew well. Her letter sounded informal. When she re-wrote the letter she used Standard English and a more developed vocabulary. Her letter sounded more formal.

ACTIVITY 3

Look at this scale, where 1 is very informal and 5 is very formal.

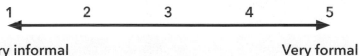

1   2   3   4   5

Very informal   **Very formal**

1 Copy the scale and place the following types of written text on it, matching the letters to the appropriate numbers.

a	a newspaper article	**f**	a letter of application for a job
b	a birthday greeting	**g**	a shopping list
c	a text message	**h**	an essay plan
d	an encyclopedia entry	**i**	a letter to a relative.
e	a school report		

2 Compare your order with that of another student. Discuss the reasons for any differences.

Wanted!

Smart young person needed to help in our café on Saturdays.

You will be 15 or over, reliable, hard-working and polite with customers.

If this sounds like you, please apply by letter or email to:

Sadie Johnson, Café Supreme, 22 Earl Street, London W4; sadiejohnson@total.com

3 Write a letter of application for the job in the coffee shop. Aim to:

a make clear which job you are applying for
b explain why you want the job
c explain why you are suitable for the job
d write in Standard English.

4 Compare your letter with that of another student. Decide which of you would be most likely to get the job, based on the letters you have written.

CREATE TONE

When you speak, you can show your listener how you feel through your tone of voice. When you write, you can also create tone to influence your readers. Here are some of the different tones you can create:

angry   friendly   sad   polite   sympathetic

sarcastic   humorous

Source C

LOS ANGELES

I've always thought that the first few lines of any book would be the hardest to write. Where do I start? How do I begin to tell you, someone I don't **know**, someone I've more than likely never met, about my life? My life? My story. How do I do this? I am only thirty two and, if I'm being completely honest, at least two of those thirty-two years were spent playing Playstation and eating Crunchy Nut cornflakes.

From *May I Have Your Attention, Please?* by James Corden

 S2 know: find out more about the silent 'k' in Unit 31.

162

ACTIVITY 4

1 Match these sentence starters to the correct ending from the box to understand how Corden creates tone.

a He builds a relationship with his reader by …

b He uses questions such as 'How do I do this?' to …

c He refers to Playstation and Crunchy Nut cornflakes to …

d He uses exaggeration when he says 'at least two of those thirty-two years' to …

e He uses an informal register when he writes 'someone I've more than likely never met' to … .

> create a modest, uncertain tone.
>
> create a friendly tone.
>
> addressing the reader directly using 'you'.
>
> create humour.
>
> make him sound ordinary and down-to-earth.

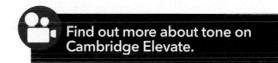
Find out more about tone on Cambridge Elevate.

Now read a later paragraph from the same autobiography. This time, Corden uses tone to persuade his readers and to create more humour.

Source D

I've just realised you may not have actually purchased this book and are doing what I do when buying a book and reading the first page to see if you like it. I'm guessing so far you're not overly impressed. If that is the case, let me start by saying that you look and indeed smell incredible today. Are those new shoes? No? New-ish? Well they're a triumph. They really suit you. I tell you what, don't look now but as you're reading this, everyone around you in the shop is checking you out and saying how hot you are. Seriously. There's something about you holding this book that really brings out the best in you. Now I come to mention it, you look slimmer holding this book.

From May I Have Your Attention, Please? by James Corden

2 Identify where Corden uses each of these techniques to create tone:

a direct address

b flattery

c exaggeration

d an informal register.

3 What does Corden want his reader to do?

PROGRESS PUNCTUATION

In his writing, Corden adopts an informal register. Instead of writing words in full, he uses apostrophes to show omission. The apostrophes are placed in the **exact spot** of the missing letter or letters. For example:

I h̲a̲ve → I've   do n̲o̲t → don̲'t

I a̲m → I'm   you a̲re → you̲'re.

ACTIVITY 5

1 Write the shortened form of each of the following by replacing the underlined letters with an apostrophe.

a we <u>a</u>re
b they <u>ha</u>ve
c can <u>no</u>t
d he <u>i</u>s

e she w<u>i</u>ll
f could n<u>o</u>t
g there <u>i</u>s.

2 Write the shortened form of each of the following. Remember to place your apostrophe in the exact spot of the missing letter or letters:

a we have
b would not
c she is

d they are
e have not
f he will.

3 Learn these two exceptions:

a will not → won't
b shall not → shan't

 Assess your progress

In this unit, you have:

- written in Standard English
- understood the differences between formal and informal writing
- learnt how to create tone through word choice
- examined how tone can be used to influence readers.

James Corden creates a humorous tone, using flattery and exaggeration, in order to persuade his readers to buy his book. He writes in Standard English and uses an informal register.

 Complete this assignment on Cambridge Elevate.

1 Imagine that you have something you want to sell. It could be a bike, an item of clothing or jewellery, a CD collection or something else. Write one or two paragraphs designed to persuade another student to buy it. Aim to:

✔ write in Standard English
✔ create a friendly, informal tone
✔ use flattery, exaggeration and humour to persuade.

How did you do?

Ask another student or your teacher to give you feedback on how successful you have been in using tone and humour to persuade.

FURTHER PROGRESS

Read the following extract, in which the writer creates a friendly, understanding and positive tone.

1 Write a letter to a Year 9 student who is being bullied, advising them on how to cope. Aim to create a friendly, understanding and positive tone.

Being a parent is never easy. Your baby will depend on you for everything. That means constant care and affection twenty-four-seven. Many parents struggle with sleepless nights, unfinished conversations and lack of money. But, when the going gets tough, always remember there is nothing better than the smiles, laughter and love of a happy child.

WRITING
Unit 25
Make choices to organise and write

Make progress AO5
- investigate the structure of some text types
- choose to write in the first or third person
- understand how to write in the present, past and future tense
- structure your writing for order and impact.

USE YOUR SKILLS

Some types of texts almost always follow the same order. There is usually a good reason why they are organised in a particular way.

ACTIVITY 1

1 Read the following jokes. Where does the punch line appear in each one? Why this is the usual position for a punch line?

a I said to the gym instructor, 'Can you teach me to do the splits?' He said, 'How **flexible** are you?' I said, 'I can't make Tuesdays'.

b Police arrested two kids yesterday. One was drinking battery acid and the other was eating fireworks. They charged one – and let the other one off.

ABC XYZ **S1 flexible:** find out more about the suffixes '-ible' and '-able' in Unit 31

2 Answer these questions to identify the usual structure of a recipe.

a What comes first: the list of ingredients or the instructions? Why is this the usual order?

b Why is it important to have recipe instructions in chronological order?

3 Look at these common features of a letter of complaint. Place them in the order they would usually appear:

a the salutation (e.g. 'Yours sincerely')
b details of what you want done
c details about the nature of the complaint
d the greeting (e.g. 'Dear Sir')
e request for a reply within a stated date.

4 Give **two** reasons why a report on a sports match is usually given in chronological order.

 **CHOOSE THE FIRST OR THIRD PERSON**

Most texts are written in either the first person or the third person.

The first person is indicated by the use of 'I' (first person singular) or 'we' (first person plural). For example:

I said to the gym instructor, 'Can you teach me to do the splits?'

The third person is indicated by the use of 'he' or 'she' (third person singular) or 'they' (third person plural). For example:

They charged one – and let the other one off.

ACTIVITY 2

1　Decide which of the following text types:

- is usually written in the first person
- is usually written in the third person
- can be written in the first or third person.

a　a school report
b　a diary or blog
c　an encyclopaedia entry
d　an autobiography (account of the writer's life)
e　a description
f　a biography (account of someone else's life)
g　a letter
h　a story.

2　**a**　Write a short account of where and when you were born using the first person.
　　b　Write the same account using the third person.
　　c　Highlight the differences between the two accounts.

CHOOSE YOUR TENSE

A tense is a verb form that indicates time. English verbs have two basic tenses: past and present. These can be simple or continuous. For example:

present	past
I run (simple)	I ran (simple)
I am running (continuous)	I was running (continuous)
present perfect	**past perfect**
I have run (simple)	I had run (simple)
I have been running (continuous)	I had been running (continuous)

Future time can be expressed in a number of different ways, using 'will' or present tenses:

The new teacher will start on Tuesday.
The new teacher is going to start on Tuesday.
The new teacher will be starting on Tuesday.
The new teacher is starting on Tuesday.
The new teacher starts on Tuesday.

ACTIVITY 3

1 The following sentences are written in the simple present tense. Write them in the continuous present tense.

The boy <u>walks</u> slowly. He <u>wants</u> to sit down. His mother <u>tells</u> him to keep going.

2 The following sentences are written in the present tense, using the simple, perfect and continuous forms. Write them in the past tense.

As I <u>am running</u>, I <u>think</u> about my other sporting ambitions. I <u>have often wondered</u> what it is like to **climb** a mountain. I <u>make</u> this my New Year's resolution.

You can mix tenses in the same sentence as long as it makes sense to do so. For example:

This <u>was</u> once a busy walkway but now it <u>is</u> almost deserted.

3 Read the following sentences. The tenses are incorrectly mixed in them. Rewrite them so that the tenses match.

a When she first visited the school she feels lonely and isolated.

b The day before he had walked into the room and sees the missing painting.

c They sat and wait for the doctor to arrive.

4 The following sentence is written in the future tense. How many other ways can you write it in the future tense?

The parcel will arrive tomorrow morning.

STRUCTURE YOUR WRITING FOR IMPACT

Some texts are structured in certain ways to make sure they achieve their purpose. You give the punch line at the end of a joke – otherwise it would be spoilt. You give recipes or other instructions in chronological order, so that the reader can follow them and complete the task.

However, in many types of writing you can choose how to structure the information for maximum impact on your audience.

 S2 climb: find out more about the silent letter 'b' in Unit 31.

Source A

This trip, I am doing my show at the City Hall, which is by no stretch of the imagination a sweaty room in the back of a pub. However, ten minutes into the show, and I am drenched again. But now it is with a cold, cold sweat. The kind you get when you realize that there are 1,950 people in the room and it just isn't working. 5

Let's see how this happened. I ran out to applause, mentioned a few of the other nights on the tour, hit them with the schtick about how much I was looking forward to chatting to them tonight and then said, 'Right, who's here?' and leaned in towards the front row. And, instinctively, 1,950 people seemed to back away. 10

Have you ever made a room clench? That's what it felt like.

They puckered up. They curled into a ball. They went foetal. It was like doing a show to an alarmed hedgehog.

I managed to frighten a room full of people so badly, their natural defence mechanisms kicked in and they made a smaller target of 15 themselves.

From *Tickling the English* by Dara O Briain

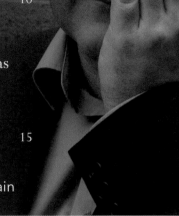

ACTIVITY 4

Read Source A. The writer is a comedian, describing an embarrassing performance on stage in Sheffield.

1 a What does the writer describe in the first paragraph? Which tense does he use?
b What does he describe in the rest of the passage? Which tense does he use most?

2 O Briain uses the present tense to first describe his feelings. Then he uses the past tense to describe what caused them. He does this to make his readers curious and want to read on. Use this structure to write an effective description of an embarrassing occasion. It can be real or imagined.

a In the first paragraph, describe your feelings of embarrassment – write in the present tense.
b In the rest of your writing, describe what led to your embarrassment – write in the past tense.

3 Ask a partner to give you feedback on:

a the effectiveness of your description
b your correct use of the present and past tenses.

STRUCTURE DISCUSSION

When you write to discuss or argue, you can decide how to structure your writing for maximum impact. You could:

- group points and examples together
- cover points in order of importance, ending with the strongest.

ACTIVITY 5

Groups of students were asked to talk about this task:

Family, not friends, have the most influence in our lives. How far do you agree?

Here are the ideas of one group:

a stepdad took me to first match

d learnt about life from my friends

b older sister taught me to swim

c only want what's best for us

f parents got divorced

e brought us up

g go everywhere with friends

Family v. friends influence?

i friends understand better

h know us better than anyone

l Gran taught me to bake

m both help with homework

j paid for everything

k family always there for you

n taught us right from wrong

p my aunt and uncle moved to Australia

q friends can't always be trusted

o tell my best friend everything

r friends got me in trouble

s parents too busy to talk to you

u friends more important in teens

t you have to make new friends if you move

v friends online advise me

To write a good response to this question, you need to consider the influence of both family and friends. Use the letters to group points under the following headings. You can use the same point more than once.

Family more important
Friends more important
Family always there for you
Friends can be unreliable
Family teaches you all you need to know
Friends understand you better
Families split up
Friends change over time

Which five headings would you choose to use in a five-paragraph plan? What order would you place them in?

PROGRESS PUNCTUATION

An apostrophe can be used to show that something belongs to someone or something. Instead of 'the father of the girl' you would write 'the girl's father'. The apostrophe shows that the father belongs to the girl. The 'girl' is the possessor.

When the possessor is singular, as in the case of 'girl', place the apostrophe after the word and add an 's'.

When the possessor is plural and already ends in an 's', add an apostrophe:

the father <u>of the girls</u> → <u>the girls'</u> father

When the possessor is plural but does not end in an 's', add an apostrophe and an 's':

the father of <u>the children</u> → <u>the children's</u> father

The possessive words 'yours', 'his', 'hers', 'its', 'ours', 'whose' and 'theirs' do **not** have an apostrophe.

ACTIVITY 6

1 Reorder the following sentences to make them shorter. Place the apostrophes correctly.

   a the choice of the editor
   b the homework of the student
   c the medicine of the child
   d the weather of Saturday.

FURTHER PROGRESS

1 Plan a response to the following task.

Celebrities are paid too much while other people work hard for too little pay. Discuss.

Talk through your plan with another student. Ask for feedback on how well you have grouped your ideas and ordered your paragraphs.

Assess your progress

In this unit, you have:

- investigated the structure of some text types
- written in the first or third person
- learnt how to write in the present, past or future tense
- structured paragraphs for order and impact.

1 Look again at the paragraph plan you made in Activity 5. Can you improve the content or order of your paragraphs? Use your plan to help you write five paragraphs in answer to the task:

Complete this assignment on Cambridge Elevate.

Family, not friends, have the most influence in our lives. How far do you agree?

Remember to:

- choose to write in the first or third person
- choose and control your use of tenses
- structure your writing for order and impact.

How did you do?

Ask another student or your teacher to give you feedback on how well you have controlled and structured your response.

Unit 26
Test your progress 3

In Units 20–25, you have learnt to:

- write for purpose and audience
- use sentence structures for effect
- choose vocabulary and use imagery for effect
- build and link coherent paragraphs
- structure your writing for effect
- create tone to influence your readers.

Your aim in this test is to show your teacher the best of your writing skills.
You will be assessed on your communication, organisation, vocabulary range,
use of sentence structures and technical accuracy.

Here are a few reminders of what you need to do:

Communication	• write for purpose and audience • choose information and ideas to interest your reader • write in Standard English unless using dialogue • use tone to influence and manipulate your reader
Organisation	• identify purpose, audience and form • generate ideas and plan for paragraphs • develop coherent paragraphs and link them fluently • guide your reader with integrated discourse markers
Vocabulary, sentence structures and accuracy	• choose words to suit purpose and influence readers • show that you have a wide vocabulary range • vary sentence structures to interest readers • use accurate punctuation to guide your reader

Choose one of the following tasks. Plan, write and check your answer.

You have **45 minutes**.

Either

1 Read Source A. Imagine you were walking home when the storm struck. Describe what you saw, heard and felt.

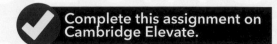

Complete this assignment on Cambridge Elevate.

Or

2 Write a description suggested to you by the picture in Source B.

Source A

VIOLENT STORM STRIKES AT MIDNIGHT

A weather system over the Atlantic crashed onto British shores last night, bringing a month's worth of rain in just eight hours.

Winds reached 100 mph and there were reports of flash lightning and even hailstones. Trees have been uprooted, electric supplies halted and damage is widespread …

Source B

Unit 27
Describe effectively

AO5 AO6

Make progress

- build detail in your descriptions
- vary your sentence length for effect
- create atmosphere though detail and word choice
- use sounds and imagery to create effective descriptions
- experiment with different ways of structuring descriptions.

USE YOUR SKILLS

Writers of both fiction and non-fiction describe a wide variety of things – feelings, places, people, weather and events. They choose their words and details carefully to have an impact on the reader. Complete Activity 1 to discover what you already know about good descriptive writing.

ACTIVITY 1

Read the following descriptions, which describe the same event.

A In September a big storm brought rain onto the fields of Duncton Hill and then into Duncton Wood.

B September. A great grey storm swept pelting rain up the pastures of Duncton Hill and then on into the shadowy oaks and elms of Duncton Wood itself.

1 Description B is clearly better. In pairs, discuss what the writer has done to create an effective description. Think about the use of vocabulary and sentence length.

2 Read the following student's description of a storm. The description is clear but not very exciting. Discuss how you could improve it.

It was a November day and a storm was on its way. It started with rain and then there was some lightning. After that there was some very loud thunder which shook the house and made the windows rattle. All the time it just kept on raining and, when I looked out the window, I could see big puddles on the road and people rushing by with their umbrellas up.

3 Working together, write your improved description.

4 Annotate your description to explain the effects of the changes you have made.

BUILD DETAIL IN DESCRIPTION

To write effective description, you need to think about the effect you want to achieve. Then you must use detail to achieve it.

ACTIVITY 2

Read Source A, in which Charles Dickens describes in detail the face of a character called Quilp.

1 Work in pairs. Investigate Dickens's description of Quilp by answering the following questions:

a Which features of Quilp's face are described in the first sentence?

b Which feature is described in detail in the second sentence?

c Dickens uses a wide range of adjectives to describe Quilp – for example 'his black eyes were restless, sly and cunning'. What adjectives are used to describe Quilp's chin, expression and smile?

d What is Dickens suggesting when he tells us that Quilp's smile seemed to be the 'mere result of habit and to have no connection with any mirthful or complacent feeling'.

e What words does Dickens use to compare Quilp with an animal?

f This is the first time the reader meets Quilp in the story. What overall impression of Quilp do you think Dickens wanted to give his readers?

2 Work on your own. Follow these steps to help you write a detailed description of the face of a real or imagined person.

a Decide first whether you want your reader to find the person unpleasant and fearful or friendly and kind.

b Think about adjectives you could use to make your description effective.

c Aim to write between three and five sentences.

3 Show your writing to another student and ask for feedback on the success of your description.

 Find out about writing techniques on Cambridge Elevate.

Source A

His black eyes were restless, sly, and cunning; his mouth and chin, bristly with the stubble of a coarse hard beard; and his complexion was one of that kind which never looks clean or wholesome. But what added most to the grotesque expression of his face   5 was a ghastly smile, which, appearing to be the mere result of habit and to have no connection with any mirthful or complacent feeling, constantly revealed the few discoloured fangs that were yet scattered in his mouth, and gave him the aspect of a panting dog.   10

From *The Old Curiosity Shop* by Charles Dickens

VARY SENTENCE LENGTH FOR EFFECT

When describing Quilp, Dickens packs a lot of detail into two long sentences. You can also create effective description by using very short sentences.

ACTIVITY 3

Read Source B, in which the writer builds a description of a place. Notice the use of the present tense.

1 The writer of Source B uses two short sentences.

   a What is emphasised in the first short sentence?
   b What 'big point' does the writer emphasise in the final very short sentence?

2 Look at the following short sentences:

   a The sun sets.
   b Snow falls.
   c A switch is clicked.

3 How could they be used to **end** a description of a place? Choose one of them. Write three or four sentences in which you build up descriptive detail about a place before finishing with your selected sentence. Write in the present tense.

Source B

The salt is a dried-up sea from the days when the Sahara was a lush, green, fertile landmass. The weather began changing five thousand years ago and now the dried sea is still mined by slaves, criminals and the men from Arouane. Nothing grows at all in Arouane. Fuel for fires is rabbit-dropping-sized camel dung for which the children search daily, endlessly. There is one well.

From *Geldof in Africa* by Bob Geldof

 S1 well: find out more about homonyms in Unit 31.

CREATE ATMOSPHERE

You can create mood or atmosphere through:

* the details you select
* the words you choose to describe them.

ACTIVITY 4

1 Read the description of a shopping centre. Then answer the questions that follow.

The bustling crowd poured through the main avenue. Excited children pulled parents to the Christmas window displays, shrieking with laughter at the nodding reindeer and grinning puppets. Carols rang through the air and, in the background, coffee machines whirred and tills pinged.

---

a What atmosphere is created in the description?
b What details does the writer focus on to create this atmosphere?
c What words does the writer use to create this atmosphere?

Read the following opening to a mystery thriller. Some of the main descriptive words have been removed.

A **(1)** … mist **(2)** … between the stone statues; **(3)** … figures with **(4)** … , **(5)** … faces and **(6)** … twisted limbs which seemed to move **(7)** … in the **(8)** … yellow **(9)** … of the rising moon. An owl **(10)** … .

---

2 Copy the opening. Create a spooky, chilling atmosphere by choosing words from the word bank to go in the gaps. Use your own words if you prefer.

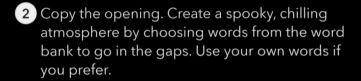

grey	scary	nightmare	grotesquely
pale	shrieked	light	deathly	crept
hideous	menacingly	hooted	dark
threatening	glare	sickly	moved

3 Compare your sentence with a partner. Decide which of you has been most successful in creating a spooky, chilling atmosphere.

4 Think of a real or imagined place that is either:

a calm and peaceful (e.g. the countryside)
b noisy and exciting (e.g. a sports ground just before a match starts).

Write two or three sentences describing the place. Choose details and words to create your chosen atmosphere.

5 Share your story opening with a partner. Ask for feedback on how successful you have been in creating your chosen atmosphere.

Learn about creating atmosphere effectively on Cambridge Elevate.

DEVELOP YOUR DESCRIPTIVE TECHNIQUES

You can improve your descriptive writing by using:

- techniques dealing with the sound of words
- techniques dealing with imagery.

ACTIVITY 5

Read Source C. The underlined parts indicate where the writer has used techniques for effect.

1 Match the underlined sections 1–7 to the following explanations:

a alliteration emphasising the coolness of the potato
b simile comparing the aroma to fire-breathing dragons
c extended metaphor of fire and flame, suggesting the heat and power of the sauce
d **personification** suggesting how his body is brought to life by the flavours
e repetition emphasising how the food made him feel
f onomatopoeia indicating his relish in eating
g metaphor suggesting the amount and thickness of the sauce.

2 Think about your favourite meal. How do you feel when eating it? Use some of the techniques from Question 1 to help you write a description of the experience. Aim to write four or five sentences.

3 Work in small groups. Take it in turn to read your descriptions aloud. Give feedback on the effectiveness of each description.

Source C

I ordered a blue china bowl filled with <u>cubes of cool creamy</u> **(1)** potato <u>swimming in</u> **(2)** a thick, red-flecked yellow sauce. The aroma rose up <u>like dragons breathing on my face</u> **(3)** — chilli, garlic and ginger, sharp and powerful, and the buttery mellowness of turmeric. I <u>slurped</u> **(4)** at the sauce. <u>Savoury fire rushed through my mouth, and my tastebuds sang:</u> 'Alive!' I swallowed and flames coursed down my throat **(5)**. <u>My tummy shouted</u> **(6)**: 'I'm alive, I'm alive!' **(7)**

5

10

From *Fearless Diner* by Richard Sterling

USE CONTRAST IN DESCRIPTION

When you contrast two things, you show the differences between them. You might use opposites such as light and dark or high and low. However, contrasts do not have to be opposites – they just have to be different, such as angry and sad.

ACTIVITY 6

Read Source D, in which the writer contrasts the appearance of two children.

Source D

Sissy and Bitzer both sat in the same ray of sunshine. But, whereas the girl was so dark-eyed and dark-haired, that she seemed to receive a deeper colour from the sun, when it shone upon her, the boy was so light-eyed and light-haired that the same rays 5 appeared to draw out of him what little colour he ever possessed. His short-cropped hair matched the sandy freckles on his forehead and face. His skin was so unwholesomely pale that he looked as though, if he were cut, he would bleed white. 10

From *Hard Times* by Charles Dickens

1 **a** What difference does the writer show in the appearance of the two children?
   b What are the different effects of the ray of sunshine on each child?
   c How does the writer emphasise the paleness of the boy in the final sentence?

2 Write a paragraph contrasting the appearance of two teenagers standing under a streetlamp at night. Before writing, decide:

   a what each teenager looks like
   b how the light affects their appearance
   c how you will show the contrast between them.

3 Share your writing with another student. Ask for feedback on the effectiveness of your contrast.

ZOOM IN FOR EFFECTIVE DESCRIPTION

You can use the technique of 'zooming in' to create an effective description. Begin by describing a 'big picture' and gradually zoom in on a single point of interest. This might be a person or an object.

ACTIVITY 7

1 Read Source E, in which the writer uses the zooming-in technique. Identify and list the different stages of the description.

Source E

The stadium is a vast bow with ten thousand whitewashed seats, every seat occupied, every spectator hushed, eyes fixed on a rectangle of dusty sun-baked grass. The line judges sit silent in their green blazers, leaning forward, eyes 5 trained on the faded lines of the court. The umpire in her chair waits; the pen in her hand hovers above a score-sheet. A weary white-clad figure, her left knee bandaged, her blonde hair dark with sweat, turns to **accept** the offer of 10 the balls and pockets one. She wipes a sleeve across her brow, bounces the ball once, twice, and tosses it high. For a moment it hangs motionless in the air, then with an explosive 'thwack!' the racquet makes contact. Ace! 15

 S2 accept: find out more about commonly confused words in Unit 31.

 Watch a video about descriptive methods in writing on Cambridge Elevate.

2 Copy the following table. Use it to plan a paragraph, in which you 'zoom in' from a silent street to a photograph held in the hand of a tramp huddled in a doorway.

Stage	Image	Descriptive detail
1	**big picture:** silent street	litter blowing along pavement; stray dogs; bus-stop with graffiti
2	row of shops	
3	shop doorway	
4	tramp	
5	**close-up:** photograph	

3 Use your plan to help you write a paragraph about this scene.

4 Share your writing with a partner. Ask for feedback on the effectiveness of your description.

PROGRESS PUNCTUATION

A semicolon can be used instead of a full stop between sentences that are closely linked. In Source E, for example, the writer uses a semicolon to emphasise the close link between the umpire waiting and her hand hovering:

The umpire in her chair waits; the pen in her hand hovers above a score sheet.

A semicolon can also be used to separate items in a list, when the items are too long to be separated by commas. In Source A, for example, the writer uses semicolons to separate the listed features of Quilp:

His black eyes were restless, sly, and cunning; his mouth and chin, bristly with the stubble of a coarse hard beard; and his complexion was one of that kind which never looks clean or wholesome.

ACTIVITY 9

1 Read the following sentence. Rewrite it, adding semicolons as appropriate.

The twins have varied interests: playing games on the internet until the early hours of the morning preparing delicious Mexican dishes using subtle herbs and spices participating in adventure sports such as abseiling and windsurfing.

Assess your progress

In this unit, you have:

- built detail in your description
- varied your sentence length for effect
- created atmosphere through detail and word choice
- used sounds and imagery to create effective descriptions
- experimented with different ways of structuring descriptions.

You are going to write a description **suggested** to you by the photograph in Source F. Notice that you do **not** have to describe the actual photograph.

Look closely at the photograph and read the suggestions for how you could structure your description.

Contrast

Focus on the contrasting scenes in the photograph. Describe the city scene in your first three paragraphs. For example:

- **Paragraph 1:** the buildings
- **Paragraph 2:** the city streets/traffic
- **Paragraph 3:** the people on the streets.

Describe the parkland in your fourth and fifth paragraphs. Make a link between the third and fourth paragraphs with a sentence such as this:

Away from the hustle and bustle of the busy streets, a stream flows quietly through a deserted park.

 Complete this assignment on Cambridge Elevate.

Zoom in

Start by describing the park in the foreground and then gradually zoom in on one thing. For example:

- **Paragraph 1:** the parkland
- **Paragraph 2:** the city streets
- **Paragraph 3:** the tall buildings
- **Paragraph 4:** the view into an office
- **Paragraph 5:** focus on a person working at their desk.

Zoom out

This is the reverse of 'zooming in'. You could be the person working at the office desk – you wander across to the window and look out – you describe the buildings, the streets below and the distant parkland.

1 Choose one of the three methods. Write a detailed five-paragraph plan for a description suggested by the picture in Source F.

2 Use your paragraph plan to help you write an effective description. Remember to:

- build detail
- create atmosphere
- use a range of techniques to make your writing effective.

Spend about 45 minutes on this task, and write about five paragraphs.

How did you do?

Ask another student or your teacher to give you feedback on the effectiveness of your description.

Source F

FURTHER PROGRESS

1 Look at the photographs on page 50 and page 120. Choose one of these and study it closely. Choose one of the methods of structuring a description referred to in Assess your progress.

Write a detailed paragraph plan for a description suggested to you by the photograph you have chosen.

Unit 28
Tell a good story

Make progress (A05) (A06)

- write in the first and third person
- structure stories in different ways to interest your reader
- create believable characters
- use dialogue to develop narrative.

USE YOUR SKILLS

What is your favourite type of story? A ghost story? Science-fiction? Something funny? Something romantic? Whatever you like to read or write, you need to be aware of the **narrative perspective** – the point of view from which the story is told. You can narrate a story in the first person or in the third person. It depends what sort of story you want to tell.

ACTIVITY 1

Read Source A, which is written in the first person.

1 Work in pairs.

a Talk about why the choice of a first person narrative is appropriate for this passage.
b What kind of person do you think the narrator of Source A is?

Now read Source B, which is written in the third person.

Source A

THURSDAY JANUARY 1ST

These are my New Year's resolutions:

I will help the blind across the road.
I will hang my trousers up. [...]
I will not start smoking.
I will stop squeezing my spots.
I will be kind to the dog.
I will help the poor and ignorant.
After hearing the disgusting noises from downstairs last night, I have also vowed never to drink alcohol.

My father got the dog drunk on cherry brandy at the party last night.
If the RSPCA hear about it he could get done. [...]

Just my luck, I've got a spot on my chin for the first day of the New Year!

Adapted from *The Secret Diary of Adrian Mole Aged 13 ¾* by Sue Townsend

Source B

The fair was over.

Nobody had noticed the girl. In her black clothes she stood against the side of the roundabouts, hearing the last feet tread upon the sawdust and the last voices die in the distance. Then, all alone on the deserted ground, surrounded by the shapes of wooden horses and cheap fairy boats, she looked for a place to sleep.

Adapted from 'After the Fair', in *Adventures in the Skin Trade*
by Dylan Thomas

Work in the same pairs.

  a What do you learn about the girl?
  b Talk about how this might be different if it was written in the first person, with the girl as the narrator.
  c Together, write an alternative opening for this story. Write in the first person and from the girl's perspective. Aim to write four or five sentences.

3 Draw up a table with two columns headed 'First person narrative' and 'Third person narrative'.

Decide which of the following statements describes a first person narrative and which describes third person narrative. Copy them into the correct column in your table.

  a The narrator has an overview of everything that happens.
  b The narrator is a character in the story.
  c The narrator is not a character in the story.
  d The narrator can tell you the thoughts and feelings of all the characters.
  e The reader is drawn into the story by their interest in what happens to the narrator.
  f The narrator can only tell you what he or she sees, thinks and feels.

STRUCTURE STORIES

Stories for young children are usually written in chronological order. The narrator keeps the reader interested by saying **what happens next**. For older readers, however, you can start a narrative at different points and use devices such as **flashback** to make your writing interesting.

ACTIVITY 2

The following captions represent episodes of a story in chronological order.

A teenage boy (Phil) receives a postcard from his pen-friend (Yasmina) inviting him to spend Christmas in Australia with her family. →	Phil sits in his seat aboard the aeroplane, with headphones on. →	The view of the wing from his window with an engine on fire.

Phil regains consciousness and finds himself washed up on the beach of a desert island. →	Phil sitting by a camp fire at the top of a beach. →	Phil standing next to the fire looking up to the sky waving his arms as a helicopter hovers. →	Phil and Yasmina embracing at the arrivals lounge of the airport.

1 Work in pairs.

a Copy the captions onto separate cards and arrange them in the order shown.

b Study the sequence and decide a different order for telling the story, using flashback.

c Decide who should tell the story – Phil, Yasmina or a third person narrator.

d Discuss the narrative you might use for each of the episodes.

2 Explain your ideas to another pair. Ask for feedback on:

a the effectiveness of your story sequence

b your choice of narrator.

3 Now work in groups of three. Each choose one of the following as your story starter:

a Have you ever feared for your life? The moment I saw flames blazing at the window of my cabin, I did.

b I was thrilled when Dad said he would pay Phil's airfare. It meant we would be together for Christmas.

c The midday sun blazed down on the lonely figure on the beach. Gradually he stirred and, stumbling to his feet, gazed in confusion at the blue ocean.

Tell your story to the rest of the group.

4 Discuss what difference the change of narrative viewpoint makes.

WRITE STORY OPENINGS

The opening of a story is an important part of its structure. Like a headline in a newspaper, it has to make your reader want to read on.

ACTIVITY 3

Read sources C to F – a selection of story openings.

Source C

'Yes, I know all about that, Tom,' the Captain said through a mouthful of stew. 'But qualifications aren't everything. My personal view is that your friend Dally's an embarrassment to this unit. And I mean to do something about it, do you see?'

Adapted from *My Enemy's Enemy* by Kingsley Amis

Source D

Have you ever wondered how difficult it would be to look after a baby gorilla?

Source E

The interior of the Church was slowly darkening under the close clouds of a winter afternoon. It was Sunday; service had just ended, and the congregation, with a cheerful sigh of release, were rising from their knees to depart. For the moment the stillness was so complete that the surging of the sea could be heard outside. Then it was broken by the sound of footsteps.

Adapted from 'To Please His Wife' by Thomas Hardy

Source F

That evening it was dark early, which was normal for the time of year. It was cold and windy, which was normal.

It started to rain, which was particularly normal.

A spacecraft landed, which was not.

From *So Long, and Thanks for all the Fish* by Douglas Adams

Match each opening to one of the following descriptions.

    a   The writer engages the reader by describing a setting to create atmosphere.
    b   The writer engages the reader by starting with dialogue.
    c   The writer engages the reader by surprising the reader.
    d   The writer engages the reader by addressing the reader directly.

2 Use two of these methods to write **two** different openings for a story with the title 'Kidnapped'.

3 Compare your openings with a partner. Decide:

    a   which opening is most effective
    b   why it makes you want to read on.

 Learn about creating effective story openings and endings on Cambridge Elevate.

BUILD IN CLUES

You can structure a story by building in clues about what is going to happen. This adds impact to the ending, when the reader grasps the significance of the clues.

ACTIVITY 4

Read Source G.

Source G

'Do you sell slippers?' <u>the voice gruff, foreign</u>. Lucy groans inwardly. If only something exciting would happen to relieve the boredom …

Answering the phone in the Shoe Warehouse is not a career choice. Photography, not footware, is her passion. But without 5 her wages, the trip to Canada won't happen.

She remembers the night the trip was suggested. 'Saskwatch! Mysterious giant of the Canadian forest'. She and her fellow 'Monster Hunters', fuelled by beer and pizza discussed the evidence – watched internet footage of a shambling figure 10 amongst the trees. That night she'd dreamed of dawn in the forest, the crackle of soft heavy feet … imagined a glimpse of the shaggy face, a snapshot in her album of <u>a giant</u> pawprint.

Imprisoned now amongst the shelves of boots and trainers, it seems ridiculous – a crazy fantasy. 15

'Slippers? Certainly sir. What size?'

There is an embarrassed pause at the end of the line.

'<u>Twenty-two.</u>'

Twenty two?! She stifles a giggle. 'We'll have to order them, and mail them to your house. Do you live locally?' 20

'Dean Street.'

'That's just around the corner. Who should I address them to?'

'Mr Foot.'

'And your first name?'

'Bernard … Bernard Ignatious George.' Another embarrassed 25 pause, 'My friends just call me BIG.'

185

1 Work in pairs. Answer the following questions:

   a In what way is the ending a surprise?

   b How do the three underlined clues help you understand the ending?

   c At what point in the story does the writer use flashback?

   d What do you think is the purpose of the flashback?

   e The third paragraph contains detailed description. What does this add to the impact of the story?

2 Now work on your own. Plan a story with a surprise ending. You can use one of these 'twists' or come up with your own:

- The bully's victim has a black belt in Karate.
- The detective turns out to be the murderer.
- The new basketball coach is confined to a wheelchair.

   a Think of at least **two** clues that will make sense of the ending you have chosen.

   b Think of where you are going to put them in the story.

   c Decide how you are going to use flashback.

   d Decide how you are going to use description.

3 Write your story. Aim to write no more than 200 words.

4 Read two or three stories written by other students. Comment on:

   a the use of clues to make sense of the ending

   b the use of flashback

   c the use of description.

CREATE BELIEVABLE CHARACTERS

A good story needs believable characters. You can create believable characters by:

- describing appearance
- recording thoughts, speech and actions.

ACTIVITY 5

Read Source H, in which a boy called Huckleberry Finn meets his father for the first time in many years.

Source H

<u>His hair was long and tangled and greasy, and hung down,</u> **(1)** and you could see his eyes shining through <u>like he was behind vines</u> **(2)**. It was all black, no gray; so was his long, mixed-up whiskers. There warn't no **color** in his face, where his face showed; it was white; not like another man's white, <u>but a white to make a body sick, a white to make a body's flesh crawl — a tree-toad white, a fish-belly white</u>. **(3)** As for his clothes — <u>just rags, that was all</u>. **(4)**

From The Adventures of Huckleberry Finn by Mark Twain

 S1 color: find out more about American spellings in Unit 31.

 Learn about creating characters on Cambridge Elevate.

1 Match the following annotations to the numbered parts of the description in Source H (1–4).

   a suggests that he does not care about his appearance

   b suggests that there is something unhealthy and repulsive about him

   c confirms the impression that he doesn't care about himself

   d implies something suspicious about him, as if he spies on others, but does not wish to be seen.

2 Explain how the writer builds detail to describe the father's pale colour.

Now read Source I, in which the writer implies how the characters feel through their actions and words.

Source I

She started crying. She said we should never have left Random Road. We should never have come to this stinking derelict place. She walked back and forward in the kitchen with the baby in her arms. **(1)**

'My little girl,' she murmured. 'My poor little girl.' **(2)**

'The baby has to go back to hospital,' Dad whispered. **(3)** 'Just for a while. So the doctors can keep an eye on her. That's all. She'll be fine.' **(4)**

He stared out of the window into the wilderness. **(5)**

From *Skellig* by David Almond

3 Match the following annotations to the numbered parts of the text (1–5).

  a Her words suggest anger and frustration.
  b His words suggest he is trying to be optimistic and positive.
  c Her actions and words suggest that her anger is due to anxiety.
  d His actions suggests he does not feel as hopeful as he wants to appear.
  e His voice suggests he is gentle with his wife.

4 Did you notice that both writers suggest things about their characters rather than explain them directly? Create a character who could appear in a story about a hospital. Either use physical description or action and speech or combine both approaches.

5 Share your work with another student. Give feedback on:

  a how successfully they have suggested character
  b how believable their character is.

 Watch a video about developing characters on Cambridge Elevate.

USE DIALOGUE TO DEVELOP NARRATIVE

To make dialogue effective in a narrative, you need to:

- make sure it is interesting and moves the story forward
- avoid using too much dialogue, which may bore your reader.

Source J

Remi followed Tom to the gap in the hedge.

'I'm not sure about this', she whispered, 'It's private property. What if someone sees us?'

Tom sneered. He was determined to get his ball back. He'd saved money for weeks to buy a World Cup Special, and was hanged if he'd lose it now because she couldn't control her free kicks.

'Been empty for years,' he growled, hunting in the long grass. 'Anyway, if someone stops us we'll just explain … they won't mind.'

Remi wasn't so confident. She continued to grumble and fret as they searched. Suddenly Tom froze.

'Shhhh!' he hissed. 'I can hear something …'

The writer has found different words for 'said'.

The writer has used narrative rather than dialogue to indicate the character's thoughts.

ACTIVITY 6

Read Source J.

1 Using the annotations to Source I as a guide, continue the passage above by:

   a **writing** one or two sentences of narrative
   b writing two lines of dialogue.

2 Share your work with a partner. Give feedback on how well they have balanced narrative and dialogue.

PROGRESS PUNCTUATION

When three dots are used in a row as punctuation (…) it is called ellipsis. Ellipsis can be used:

- within a sentence to indicate words or thoughts unspoken. For example when Tom says 'Anyway, if someone stops us we'll just explain … they won't mind', the ellipsis suggests that he has some doubts about how to explain or whether the explanation will be convincing.
- at the end of a sentence to create tension or suspense. For example: 'Shhhh!' he hissed. 'I can hear something …' Here the ellipsis leaves it to the reader to imagine what it is Tom can hear.

Ellipsis can be a very effective form of punctuation when used occasionally. Using it too often can spoil its effect.

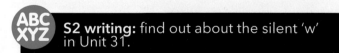

S2 writing: find out about the silent 'w' in Unit 31.

ACTIVITY 7

1 Look back at Source G. Explain the effects of the uses of ellipsis in this text.

2 Look back at the writing you have done in this unit. Identify any point where your writing could have been improved through the use of ellipsis.

WRITE EFFECTIVE ENDINGS

Although it can be difficult to know exactly how your story will end, it is helpful to have some ideas in mind. One technique that often works well is to make a link back to your opening

ACTIVITY 8

1 Copy the following table. Match each of the opening sentences with one of these suggested endings.

   a And, as the red sun set over those distant hills, the children knew their lives would never be the same again.
   b Money? It's not all it's made out to be.
   c The creature disappeared into the darkness. My fears vanished with it.

Opening	Ending
Have you ever wondered what it would be like to win the lottery?	
Fear overtook me. I could not look. I could only wait.	
The mist rose gently over the distant hills as the morning sun gave warmth and light to the earth below.	

2 Look back at the group storytelling exercise in Activity 2. Copy the following table and suggest a possible ending for each opening.

Opening	Ending
Have you ever feared for your life? The moment I saw flames blazing at the window of my cabin, I did.	
I was thrilled when Dad said he would pay Phil's airfare. It meant we would be together for Christmas.	
The midday sun blazed down on the lonely figure on the beach. Gradually he stirred and, stumbling to his feet, gazed in confusion at the blue ocean.	

Assess your progress

In this unit, you have:

- told stories in the first and third person
- structured stories to interest your reader
- created believable characters
- used dialogue to develop narrative
- written effective openings and endings.

You are now going to write a story inspired by this picture.

Follow these steps:

a Before you start, think about how you could:
  - structure your story
  - create believable characters
  - use dialogue to develop the story
  - open and end effectively.

b Plan for five paragraphs.

c Write your story

d Read through your story and improve it if you can.

How did you do?

Ask another student or your teacher to give you feedback on:

✔ the effectiveness of your opening and ending

✔ how well you have structured your story and guided the reader

✔ how well you have created believable characters.

Complete this assignment on Cambridge Elevate.

FURTHER PROGRESS

Look back to Source A. It is from a story about a teenage boy called Adrian Mole, presented in the form of entries in his diary. Write a story based on a week of diary entries. Plan what will happen on each day and how you will develop the story. Remember to write in the first person.

Unit 29
Make your point

Make progress   (AO5) (AO6)

- generate and organise ideas and views
- use discourse markers to link and develop ideas
- make effective links within and between paragraphs
- plan and write a balanced argument.

USE YOUR SKILLS

In your exam, you will be asked to write your viewpoint on a given subject. To do this well, you first need to generate and develop a range of ideas on the subject.

ACTIVITY 1

1 Work in small groups. Discuss the following task. Choose a scribe to record the group's ideas on a big piece of paper. Here are some areas to think about:

1 rules that restrict young people in school

2 rules that restrict young people in public

3 why they seem unfair

> Young people are restricted by **too many rules at school** and in society in general.
>
> **To what extent do you agree with this statement?**

4 rules to do with age e.g. driving, drinking alcohol

5 why rules might be necessary

Examples, facts and anecdotes

<u>School</u>:

mobile phones

uniform

food and drink in class

<u>In public</u>:

2 Think of examples, facts or **anecdotes** to help you develop the different ideas:

Rules ➝ school ➝ mobile phones ➝ examples of personal experience ➝ some opinions on why they should/should not be allowed

3 Share your ideas with another group. Add further useful suggestions.

4 Now work on your own. Choose one point – for example the legal driving age. Write three or four sentences in which you develop ideas on this subject. Use examples, facts or anecdotes.

5 Ask another student to check that your sentences:

a clearly express your ideas
b develop ideas related to your chosen point.

CHOOSE A LOGICAL ORDER

To make sure that your reader can follow your ideas, you need to organise them into coherent paragraphs. This means that the ideas must follow a logical order.

ACTIVITY 2

1 Work in pairs. Look at the following six sentences, written by a student about the rules on using mobile phones in school. Decide a logical order in which to place them.

a The other day I needed to check my homework hand-in reminders on my phone.
b Students may want to use their phones in class to look things up or be reminded about things they need to do in the day.
c We're only allowed to use our phones at dinner time.
d It's against school rules to use your phone in class.
e I don't think it's fair to prevent students from using their phones in class.
f In our school we have to hand our phones in before every exam which does seem reasonable.

Learn more about revising your writing on Cambridge Elevate.

2 Compare your order with that of another pair. Discuss any differences.

3 Work on your own. Write **four to six** sentences on the subject of rules about school uniform. You might want to consider:

a The benefits and disadvantages of uniform
b Other rules on fashion items.

Organise your sentences in a logical order.

USE DISCOURSE MARKERS

Discourse markers are words and phrases that help writers introduce and link ideas fluently (e.g. 'and', 'because'). They work in different ways.

Look at the opening paragraph of one student's response to this task:

Zoos are cruel and unnecessary in the 21st century. To what extent do you agree?

Notice the function of each discourse marker as you read it.

<u>Firstly</u>, zoos do a lot of good work, but this is sometimes invisible to the public. <u>For example</u> many incredible species have been saved from extinction by captive breeding, <u>such as</u> the Giant Panda. Secondly, the idea of animals locked in cages is old-fashioned these days, <u>because</u> most zoos are now like safari parks, with open land for the animals to live on, <u>so</u> people who say that zoos are cruel are focusing on an old-fashioned image of the zoo as a prison. <u>However</u>, it's true that cages and pens are still necessary to keep certain animals separate, so you can understand why some animal liberation protesters get upset, <u>especially</u> as it's now easy to see and learn about animals on the TV and internet.

| introduces idea |
| illustrates idea |
| links idea |
| qualifies idea |
| emphasises idea |

ABC XYZ **S1 invisible:** find out more about the prefixes 'in-', 'il-', 'ir-' and 'im-' in Unit 3

ACTIVITY 3

Look at the following table, which shows a range of discourse markers.

Add to what you've said	Put points into a sequence	Illustrate a point you've made	Show cause and effect
and	first, second, third	for example	so
also	… finally	such as	because

Compare ideas	Qualify something you've written	Contrast different ideas	Emphasise a point
similarly	but	whereas	above all
likewise	however	on the other hand	of course

1 Copy the table. Add two more examples to each category from the word bank.

as well as	meanwhile	for instance	therefore
moreover	then	illustrated by	thus
equally	although	alternatively	especially
in the same way	having said that	unlike	indeed

2 Go back to the sentences you wrote about school uniform in Activity 2. Use your discourse marker table to help you link your sentences into a fluent paragraph.

3 Annotate your work to show:

   a   where you have used discourse markers
   b   the purpose of the discourse markers you have used.

LINK PARAGRAPHS FLUENTLY

Paragraphs are a bit like stepping stones. They guide your reader from one developed point to another. It is important that you link your paragraphs fluently.

Read the beginning of a student's response to the following question:

Not stepping in to stop a bully is just as bad as being one. How far do you agree?

Study the commentary and note how the student uses key words and ideas to link paragraphs.

Do you know how it feels to be picked on because you're different? Would you speak up if you saw this happening to someone else? Of course, everyone feels different, because everyone is frightened of rejection by their classmates and peers. After all, saying someone is 'different' is just another way of saying they're an individual. However, for some young people their difference is so obvious it's an easy target.

> The writer questions the reader about their experience of bullying, and asks whether they would speak up for a victim. He suggests that everyone is 'different' but that some are more liable to be picked on than others.

I'm different. At school my interests seemed crazy to my classmates. They couldn't understand why I was more interested in collecting model cars than playing football or talking about girls. So I was bullied. I wasn't beaten up, but I had to put up with cruel notes left on my desk, and names muttered from the back of the class. The teachers knew.

> The writer links to the previous paragraph with the word 'different'. He develops the idea of being 'picked on' into a description of being 'bullied'.

Why didn't they step in? Because bullying is still thought of as physical violence. If you show no bruises, the bullies get away with it. Even teachers, who are meant to protect you, are frightened to speak up. It makes my blood boil because I know there are thousands like I was, scared of being different.

> The writer links the third paragraph to the second with a question about the teachers. He develops the idea of 'bullying' further and links back to the beginning with ideas of being 'frightened', 'different' and of 'speaking up'.

ACTIVITY 4

1 The student varies his tone to influence his readers. Find examples of the following tones in the essay:

   a sad
   b honest
   c matter-of-fact
   d resentful
   e angry.

2 You are going to write the first two paragraphs of a response to the following task:

Sport is as important as Maths and English in education. To what extent do you agree?

Write an article for your school website explaining your views. Make sure you:

   a generate ideas and plan your paragraphs
   b use discourse markers to link ideas between and within sentences
   c make fluent links between your paragraphs
   d use tone to influence your readers.

 S2 they're: find out more about 'they're', 'their' and 'there' in Unit 31.

3 Annotate your two paragraphs to show:

a your use of discourse markers
b the links you have made between your paragraphs.

ACHIEVE STRUCTURE AND BALANCE

The student writing about bullying presents an effective personal viewpoint. There are times, however, when you need to present a more balanced essay, which considers different points of view.

ACTIVITY 5

Read Source A, the opening paragraphs of an article written about the pros and cons of animal

testing. The annotations show you how the text has been structured.

 a What argument is made in favour of animal testing?
b How is this counter-argued?
c What word is used to introduce this counter-argument?

Now read the writer's concluding paragraph.

While there are numerous pros and cons for animal testing, the simple question of whether it is right or wrong overshadows all of them. In other words, what you, the reader, believe, is what matters. What does your conscience tell you?

Adapted from www.aboutanimaltesting.co.uk

Source A

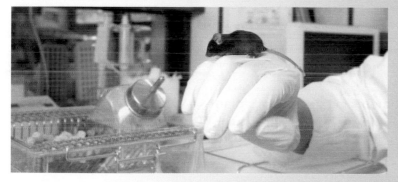

Using Animals for Testing: *Pros Versus Cons*

There are many pros and cons to the practice of animal testing; is it a matter of conscience, or common sense? — introduces topic with single sentence paragraph

The major point in favour of animal testing is that it aids researchers in finding drugs which improve human health. Many treatments have been made possible by animal testing, including cancer and HIV drugs, insulin, antibiotics, and vaccines. However, not all testing is done for this reason; cosmetics are also tested on animals. It might be argued that in order to consider the issue properly, we must first distinguish between the reasons for testing; there are many people who are against animal testing for cosmetics but still support animal testing for medicine.

5

10

makes first point in favour of one side of the argument, adding factual evidence

discourse marker, introducing counter argument

adopts objective tone, does not express personal opinion

counter-argument

Adapted from www.aboutanimaltesting.co.uk

2 Which of the following phrases do you think best describes the writer's conclusion?

    a He expresses his personal opinion.

    b He summarises the points made.

    c He refers to the arguments and asks the reader to decide.

3 Explain why this is an effective way to end a balanced essay.

PLAN A BALANCED ESSAY

To write a balanced essay, you need to consider different viewpoints over a number of paragraphs. Always plan your ideas before writing your response.

ACTIVITY 6

Read the following plan. A student is preparing to answer this question:

Obsession with overnight TV success has made young people forget the value of hard work. To what extent do you agree?

Note how the plan:

- opens with a clear statement
- includes an argument and counter-argument in paragraphs 2 to 4
- ends with a summary and invites the reader to decide.

1 Work with a partner. List any facts, examples or anecdotes that could be used to:

    a support the arguments or counter-arguments in the student's plan

    b support other points that you might make in response to this task.

Para 1 Programmes like X Factor encourage young people to believe in the possibility of overnight success.

Para 2 Argument: young people deluded – believe you only have to want it and you'll achieve your dream. Counter-argument: those who achieve success on these programmes work very hard.

Para 3 Argument: many young people waste time and energy chasing an impossible dream instead of qualifications and employment. Counter argument: dream **not** impossible – some do achieve success.

Para 4: Argument success is short-lived; you need work and security for your whole life. Counter argument if everyone thought this, no one would ever dream of a better life.

Para 5: Conclusion: some say the dream of fame is a delusion which leads to unhappiness, some say it makes life worth living. What do you think?

PROGRESS PUNCTUATION

In Unit 21, you learnt that commas are used to separate parts of a sentence. They:

- separate items in a list – for example: 'Many treatments have been made possible by animal testing including cancer and HIV drugs, insulin, antibiotics, and vaccines.'
- mark off extra information – for example: 'Even teachers, who are meant to protect you, are frightened to speak up.'
- are used after a subordinate clause that begins a sentence – for example: 'If you show no bruises, the bullies get away with it.'

ACTIVITY 7

Read the following paragraph from one student's writing. The commas, full stops and capital letters have been removed.

thousands of young people with or without talent attend auditions for programmes such as the X Factor they all hope to be selected and most of them believe that money fame fast cars are within their grasp only a very few will be selected and they are probably the ones who have worked hardest to get there the truth is you don't get far in anything without effort whether you want to be a rocket scientist or X Factor superstar you still have to give one hundred per cent to achieve your goal

1 Re-write the paragraph, punctuating it correctly.

2 Now read the paragraph aloud. The punctuation you have used should make the meaning clear.

Assess your progress

In this unit, you have:

- generated and organised ideas and views
- used discourse markers to link and develop ideas
- made effective links within and between paragraphs
- considered how to plan a balanced argument.

1 Write a five-paragraph plan for the discursive task below. Your audience is your teacher and other students. Include arguments and counter-arguments. Add examples, facts or anecdotes to support these.

Write a balanced essay in response to the question: Can money really buy happiness?

2 Use your plan to help you write an organised and balanced response. Remember to:

- ✔ use supported argument and counter-argument
- ✔ use discourse markers to link and develop ideas
- ✔ make effective links between paragraphs.

3 Read through your response. Check you have used full stops and commas correctly.

How did you do?

Ask another student or your teacher to give you feedback on how well you organised and balanced your response.

 Complete this assignment on Cambridge Elevate.

FURTHER PROGRESS

The skill of structuring a balanced argument is particularly important in debating.

1 Work in small groups. List a range of points you could make in favour of and against the following proposal:

Young people should spend less time in academic lessons and more time preparing for the world of work.

2 Add examples, facts or anecdotes to support the points in your list.

3 On your own, prepare a speech either in favour of the proposal or against it.

WRITING

Unit 30
Craft your writing

Make progress
- use your skills to assess students' writing
- investigate the qualities of effective writing
- craft your own writing.

USE YOUR SKILLS

In your exam you will be assessed on:

- the way you communicate and organise your ideas
- your technical skills.

You have spent many years developing your skills in writing. Now you need to bring all those skills together to make sure that you show the very best of what you can do. Start by using your skills to assess the writing of other students.

ACTIVITY 1

1 Read the following opening paragraphs from two students' exam writing. They were answering this question:

Too many adults put down the teenagers of today. Discuss.

Decide which student shows the best skills in writing.

> **Student A** I think that adults put down the teenagers of today a lot. There always argueing and telling us what to do. Ive had enough of it cos its not fair. I think adults should treat teenagers with more respect so that they dont argue with us no more and dont tell us what to do all the time. If they stop all the argueing and telling us what to do all the time we would behave better and not get into so much troubble.

Student B When adults and teachers think of teenagers, I know they think of bad things. They think we are difficult, moody, selfish and inconsiderate. Well, although this may be true for a small percentage of teenagers, for most of us it is simply just describing a stereotype. Most teenagers are not like this at all. Being teenagers, we are neither adults nor children. We're stuck in the middle trying to work out who we are and what we want to do. Even so, adults still tend to treat us like children but then they expect us to act like polite adults! It is very confusing.

2 The following comments were used to assess the writing of these students. Which comments do you think match Student A's writing? Which comments match Student B's writing?

a   Uses full stops and capital letters.
b   Punctuation is used accurately throughout.
c   Varied sentences for effect.
d   Opening sentence repeats the question.
e   Communicates ideas clearly.
f   Uses a list for effect.
g   Spells complex words correctly.
h   Some range of vocabulary.
i   Begins to vary sentences.
j   Uses standard English throughout.
k   Communicates clearly and effectively.
l   Uses sophisticated vocabulary.
m   Spelling is usually accurate.
n   Begins to vary sentences.
o   Usually uses standard English.

3 What **three** key pieces of advice would you give Student A to help improve their writing?

COMMUNICATE CLEARLY

When reviewing your own writing skills, the first thing you need to do is make sure you communicate clearly.

Student C was asked to describe a person who was important to them. Look at the first paragraph. It uses some range in vocabulary and the spelling is accurate, but the student fails to show that she can communicate clearly.

Student C The most caring person I have met is my best loving, sweet Mum. Mum is the person where you can be share whatever you want to. Either you private life or others. Mum is the person where whenever you call her and she run toward you. The love and respect you get from your Mum I think you cannot get any other place or from a person. If you wants your best friend under the entire earth then make you mum best friend.

The following student also writes about their mother. They also use some range in vocabulary and spells accurately. In addition to this, they communicate clearly and so get a higher mark.

Student D The most caring person I have ever met in my life is my mother. My mother is the person I love the most in this world. She has looked after me since I was a baby and now she's watching me grow. When I was ill last year, my mother was the only person beside me. She was the one who stayed up all night for me and made sure I was alright. My mother is always the first person who knows when I am in trouble or when I need help.

1 Write an opening paragraph for the task below.

   Describe a person who is important to you.

2 Read through your writing. Make sure you read what you have written and not what you **think** you have written. One good way to do this is to read it aloud. Have you communicated clearly?

3 Ask a partner to check that you have communicated clearly.

COMMUNICATE EFFECTIVELY

Once you are confident you can communicate clearly, the next step is to focus on making your writing effective. Student E is answering the same question as you did. Read his opening paragraph before completing Activity 3.

Student E There are many important people in my life – my parents, my brothers and my friends. But there is one person who holds a special place in my affections. This person has known me all my life, has danced me on his knee when I was little, played football with me when I got older, helped me with my homework; he even gave me advice on what to do when the 'love of my life' dumped me. If I have a problem, I always turn to him first. If something good has happened, he is always the first to know. Who is this person? It is, of course, my Grandad – Peter George Barker.

ACTIVITY 3

1 Work in pairs. Answer the following questions to help you examine Student E's writing and identify what makes it effective.

a Think about how the ideas are organised. How does the student begin? How do they develop the paragraph? What detail is witheld until the end?

b For the second sentence, the student could have written: 'But there is one person who is very important to me.' What phrase does the student actually use to show the person's importance? Notice how this is a more sophisticated way of expressing the idea.

c In the third sentence, the student uses the verb 'danced'. What does this verb make you think of?

d What is the effect of the list used in the third sentence?

e There are two sentences that 'mirror' each other in the way they are structured. Identify these sentences. What is the effect of this mirroring?

f How does the student address the reader directly?

2 Work on your own. Look again at the paragraph you wrote in Activity 2. Rewrite the paragraph. Use Student E's writing as a model by:

a starting with a general statement

b revealing a range of details about the important person

c only revealing who the person is in the last sentence

d using some of the other techniques used by the student.

3 Compare this paragraph with your first one. Is it more effective?

DEVELOP VOCABULARY AND IMAGERY TO INCREASE EFFECT

You can make your writing more effective by using vocabulary and imagery to describe something to your reader and bring it alive in their minds.

ACTIVITY 4

1 Work in pairs. Compare each of the pairs of sentences in Source A and explain why the second sentence is more effective than the first.

2 On your own, use vocabulary and imagery effectively to improve the following sentences:

a When I woke up I could smell burning.

b I managed to crawl out of the car window.

c The car was badly damaged.

Source A

It was winter and it was dark and raining	It was winter and, despite it being just six-thirty, the sky was as black as coal and thick globules of rain were falling like bullets.
Cars kept going past with their bright headlights.	At regular intervals, fierce yellow eyes would appear out of the gloom, race past and then disappear from view.
The car was out of control and crashed into a wall.	There was a squeal of tyres, a titanic crashing sound, screams, and then only the silence of the grave.

3 Compare your sentences with your partner's. Decide whose are the most effective.

ORGANISE EFFECTIVELY

Student E organised and linked their ideas to write a coherent, effective paragraph. In an exam, you need to organise and link a series of paragraphs effectively. Spending a few minutes on planning will help you do this. You need to:

1: Identify your form, purpose and audience:
Form: A story? A description? A letter? An article?
Purpose: To narrate? To describe? To argue? To discuss? To explain?
Audience: Judges of a creative writing competition? Readers of a national newspaper? A Member of Parliament? And always your examiner!

2: Generate ideas: What are you going to write about? Gather a wide range of ideas to choose from.

3: Plan for paragraphs: Sort your ideas into a coherent order. Discard or add ideas as you sort. Plan five coherent paragraphs (even though you may end up writing more than five).

1 You have five minutes to plan for the task below. Use the three stages of planning to help you.

> You are going to enter a creative writing competition.
>
> Your entry will be judged by a panel of professional writers.
>
> Write a story that starts or ends with 'He walked away and never looked back'.

Think again about your plan. Could you use one of the following ideas to give your story a stronger structure?

- Make a link between your opening and ending.
- Tell your story in a different, more interesting order.
- Introduce a contrast.
- Include a flashback to reveal something that had happened in the past.

2 Now work in groups of three or four. Talk through your plans. Be prepared to ask questions and make suggestions to help other students develop their plans.

3 How well did you plan? Make a note of ways you could plan more efficiently.

LINK PARAGRAPHS FLUENTLY

Your paragraphs should guide your reader through your story. Each paragraph will introduce a new focus but should link back to what has gone before and on to what follows. Read the opening of Student F's story and think about how the paragraphs are linked. Then complete Activity 6.

Student F *They had done their best to make him feel that he would be missed. They had even made a cake for him and given him a present but he knew that really they were glad to see the back of him. He had worked at Graingers for ten years and now he hated every minute of it. Every day was the same – the same people, the same dull routine, the same clocking in and clocking off. He had not always felt this way. There had been a time when he even enjoyed his work.*

He thought back to the first day he had walked through the doors of Graingers. He was only eighteen. His Mum had made sure he woke up early and had breakfast before his first day at work. It was his first job after leaving Cloiston Secondary and he was pleased to have got it. There had been over one hundred applicants for three vacancies and he had been one of the lucky ones. At least that's what he thought then. And things had gone well for the first five years.

Now, however, he did not feel lucky …

ACTIVITY 6

1 Explain how:

   a paragraph 2 is fluently linked with paragraph 1
   b paragraph 3 is fluently linked with paragraph 2.

2 Now write the first three paragraphs of your story. Make sure you link your paragraphs fluently and move your story forward.

3 Ask another student to comment on how well you have linked your paragraphs.

PRESENT YOUR VIEWPOINT

So far in this unit, you have investigated descriptive and narrative writing. When you write to present your viewpoint you also need to:

- plan efficiently
- communicate clearly and effectively
- link your paragraphs fluently.

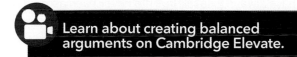

Learn about creating balanced arguments on Cambridge Elevate.

Read Student G's response to the following task, including their plan:

'**Teenagers today have a better life and a better future than any previous generation.**' **Write an article for a magazine for parents of teenagers in which you explain your point of view on this statement.**

Student G

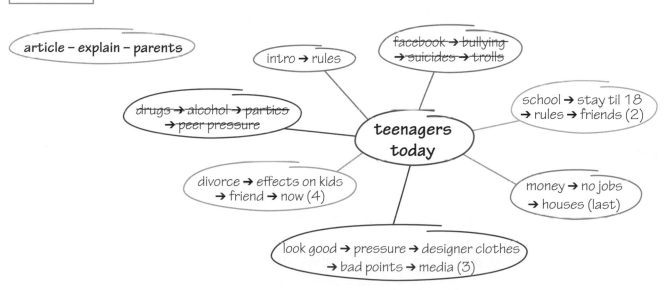

Student G

The life of teenagers these days is much as it has always been – full of endless rules, which are supposed to be there to 'protect' you. All they really *do* is stop you from becoming the adult you want to be and doing the things you want to do. Sometimes they even stop you from thinking what you want to think.

Let's start with school. We still have to go every day. We still get homework and have to sit exams, just like every other generation. The only difference is that we have to spend more years there than they did. When my Mum was at school she could leave when she was sixteen but I have to stay until I'm eighteen. Of course, personally, I think school's a great idea. How else would I spend my days except for sleeping, gaming, reading, socialising, exercising and generally learning more useful things about the world around me?

But it's not just school that makes life challenging for teenagers today. Appearance is also a subject for concern. People look at each other and judge them by their appearance. You're either too fat, too skinny, too tall, too short, have too big a nose, too small a nose; but nobody ever comments on your good points. Too many teenagers have issues about their appearance and the media doesn't help. All you ever see on TV are perfect people – even their teeth are perfectly straight and perfectly white. This pressure to look good may have always existed but it's never been as destructive as it is today.

On top of that, this generation of teenagers has to deal with more dysfunctional family breakdowns than ever before. More and more parents are getting divorced and it's us who suffer because of it. A friend of mine found out that his parents were divorcing on Christmas Day and that his father was going to work in Germany. He had to decide whether to go with him or stay with his Mum. He couldn't make up his mind what to do but then his Mum asked him not to leave her and so he decided to stay. Since that day, he hasn't seen his Dad. That's not really a 'better life' is it – not to see your Dad any more?

The last thing I want to write about is money. People are always saying that teenagers have more money than ever before but that's only true if you have wealthy parents. Most of us do jobs around the house or babysit to get extra pocket money and when we leave school it's very difficult to find a job these days. On top of that, we will never be able to buy a house of our own because they are too expensive – I mean, how will I ever save £200,000? That means that I'll probably have to stay at home until I'm 102 and if that's a 'better future' then you've got to be joking!

Student G plans efficiently and links paragraphs fluently. They also communicate effectively. Work in pairs or small groups on Activity 7.

ACTIVITY 7

Investigate tone

1 What are the implications of the underlined words in the following extract?

full of <u>endless</u> rules, which are <u>supposed</u> to be there to '<u>protect</u>' you.

2 The student writes: 'Of course, personally, I think school's a great idea', when she clearly does not. Why do you think she does this?

3 'How else would I spend my days except for sleeping, gaming, reading, socialising, exercising and generally learning more useful things about the world around me?' What does this long list suggest to the reader?

4 What words would you use to describe Student G's tone? Find other examples to support your choices.

Investigate technique

5 Look again at the two paragraphs that end with questions. How is each one used to influence the reader?

6 The student uses an anecdote in the fourth paragraph. What is the effect of this?

7 The student ends with exaggeration. What does he exaggerate? What is its effect?

Investigate vocabulary

8 Student G uses a range of vocabulary for clarity and effect. Examine the range of words used and find examples of what you consider to be 'sophisticated' uses of words.

Investigate sentence structures

9 Examine how the student varies sentence structures for effect in the second paragraph.

TECHNICAL SKILLS

Student G demonstrates good control of technical skills, using:

- a range of **vocabulary** for clarity, purpose and effect
- a range of **sentence structures** for clarity, purpose and effect.

Student G also:

- spells accurately
- punctuates effectively.

It is important that you spell and punctuate your writing as accurately as you can. Spelling and punctuation are part of good communication and errors can lose you marks. The best way to do well in spelling and punctuation in your exam is to:

- know the kind of errors you frequently make and how to correct them
- allow time to read through, check and correct your writing.

207

ACTIVITY 8

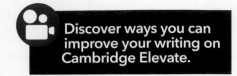
Discover ways you can improve your writing on Cambridge Elevate.

1 Look back through the writing you have done over the past three months:

   a   Make a note of any errors you have made in spelling and punctuation.

   b   Highlight the errors that you make frequently.

   c   If you do not understand the errors, ask your teacher to explain them to you.

2 Look again at the paragraphs you have written in this unit. Check them for accuracy in spelling and punctuation. Make corrections where needed.

 Assess your progress

In this unit you have:

- investigated the qualities of effective writing
- practised writing paragraphs for effect
- developed your skills in efficient planning.

1 Use what you have learnt to show the very best of your writing skills.
You have 45 minutes to carry out the following task:

'Young people are too often, and too easily, blamed for everything that is wrong with society today.' Write an article for a newspaper in which you explain your point of view on this statement.

Before you write:

- Spend four or five minutes planning your writing. Think about content and organisation.

When you write:

- Link your ideas fluently within and between paragraphs.
- Choose your words and sentence structures for maximum effect.

After you write:

- Read through what you have actually written – not what you think you have written. It helps to say each word aloud or in your head.

Check that you have:

✔ communicated clearly and effectively
✔ linked your paragraphs fluently
✔ been accurate in your spelling and punctuation.

2 Ask another student or your teacher for feedback on your writing.

Complete this assignment on Cambridge Elevate.

FURTHER PROGRESS

A good way of developing and extending your ideas on a range of topics is to listen to broadcasted arguments. Listen to *A Point of View*, a Radio 4 podcast, in which a range of contributors reflect on topical issues.

WRITING

Unit 31
Spell accurately

Make progress   AO1
* focus on specific areas of spelling
* develop your accuracy in spelling.

The activities in this unit refer to spellings that you can find throughout the Writing section of this book. You can work through the activities all at once in the order they appear here, or do them as you come across them throughout the units.

USE YOUR SKILLS

Did you know that some students:

* often cross out correct spellings and replace them with incorrect spellings, simply because they lack confidence in their spelling?
* believe themselves to be bad spellers even though they spell over 95% of words correctly?
* can spot mistakes in other students' writing which they cannot see in their own?
* will only use words they are certain they know how to spell?

ACTIVITY 1

1 Work in pairs. Look back over some pieces of your partner's writing. Make a note of any spelling errors your teacher has highlighted. Teachers rarely correct all spelling errors; can you spot any other mistakes? Make a note of these. Share your findings.

2 Now that you know something about each other's spelling skills, read the following statements and talk about which ones apply to you:

a I spell more words correctly than incorrectly.
b I frequently make the same spelling mistake.
c I've always been a good speller.
d I know how to use a dictionary quickly to check spellings.
e I can read words even if I don't know how to spell them.
f I can spot my own spelling mistakes.
g I make careless mistakes – I do know how to spell the words.
h I only use words I know how to spell correctly.

3 Based on your selections, set each other targets to improve spelling.

UNIT 20

S1: Plurals

To form most plurals, you simply add 's' to the singular form. For example:

tadpole → tadpoles   finger → fingers
sock → socks   noise → noises

There are some exceptions you need to know:

- When the singular form ends in '-s', '-x', '-ch' or '-sh', add '-es' to make it plural. For example:

  dress → dresses   tax → taxes
  church → churches   flash → flashes

- If a word ends in '-y' and has a consonant before the last letter, change the 'y' to an 'i' and add 'es'. For example:

  baby → babies   city → cities
  sentry → sentries

- If a word ends in '-o' you usually just add '-s'. However, there are a few commonly used words that need '-es' to make them plural:

  hero → heroes   tomato → tomatoes
  potato → potatoes

- If a word ends in '-f' or '-fe' you usually change the '-f' or '-fe' to '-ves'. For example:

  wolf → wolves   knife → knives

But there are a few exceptions, where the plural for just takes an 's':

roof → roofs   chief → chiefs   reef → reefs

There are also a few irregular plurals. For example:

child → children   man → men
formula → formulae   sheep → sheep
mouse → mice   crisis → crises
tooth → teeth   person → people
stimulus → stimuli

1 Using the rules outlined in this section, write the plurals of the following words. There are a few exceptions included in the list.

branch	blush	gas
holiday	comedy	lie
beach	cactus	coach
lady	hoax	key
atlas	witch	dish
inch	berry	doorman
woman	essay	

2 Check your spellings with another student. If you have different answers, use a dictionary to see who is correct.

S2: Simple past tense

The writer of Source B has written in the past tense. To form the simple past tense you have to change the base form of the verbs you use. The base form is often called the **infinitive**. For example:

to walk   walk_ed_
the infinitive   the simple past tense

Make sure you know these rules for forming the simple past tense:

- The past tense for many verbs is formed by adding 'ed' to the infinitive. For example: _to_ want → want_ed_.
- Where the present tense of the verb ends in an 'e', it is normal to simply add 'd'. For example: _to_ decide → decid_ed_; _to_ settle → settl_ed_
- Where the present tense of the verb ends in a consonant and is preceded by a short vowel sound, it is normal to double the consonant and add 'ed'. For example: _to_ stun → stun_ned_; _to_ rot → rot_ted_.

1 Use these rules to help you correctly form the simple past tense of these verbs:

ask	remind	pick	drag
shun	grasp	fade	
spot	squeeze	shuffle	

UNIT 21

S1: Irregular past tense

There are quite a lot of irregular verbs in the English language. With these, the usual rules for forming the past tense do not apply. For example:

to fly → flew   *to* see → saw

You will already know many of these.

1 Write the simple past tense for each of the following verbs. Try putting 'he' in front of each word first to make sure you get it right. For example: begin → he began.

bite	do	get	pay
become	drive	give	ring
bring	eat	hang	rise
build	fall	have	shake
catch	feel	keep	swear
choose	fight	know	teach
cling	find	leave	tell
dig	freeze	make	write

2 Check your spellings with another student. If you have different answers, use a dictionary to see who is correct.

S2: Syllables

A syllable is a unit of sound. A word might contain:

- one syllable: 'they', 'dog'
- two syllables: thun/der, a/way
- three syllables: ex/pec/ted, se/ve/ral
- or more: de/va/sta/ting.

Breaking a word into syllables and sounding each syllable aloud, or in your head, can help you spell it correctly. For example saying the word 'diff/i/cult' aloud will remind you of the letter i in the middle.

1 Copy the following words. Break them into syllables using a forward slash (/). Say them aloud to make sure you have identified the syllables correctly.

surprise	environment
character	parliament
disappointed	

UNIT 22

S1: Change adjectives to adverbs

Adverbs can be used to give extra meaning to a verb:

The girl <u>quietly</u> watched the rising sun.

Many adverbs are formed by adding 'ly' to an adjective. For example:

quiet → quiet*ly*   fearful → fearful*ly*

When adding 'ly' to adjectives that end in a consonant followed by 'y', change the 'y' to 'i'. For example:

steady → stead*ily*   happy → happ*ily*

Some adjectives end in 'ic'. To form the adverb, you need to add 'ally'. For example:

frantic → frantic*ally*   basic → basic*ally*

1 Change the following adjectives into adverbs:

quick	reluctant	nasty
angry	temporary	rapid
accidental	gloomy	emotional
slow	historic	willing
dreamy	worthy	
romantic	quiet	

2 Check your spellings with another student. If you have different answers, use a dictionary to check who is correct.

S2: 'sc'

Many words contain the sequence of letters 'sc'. Where the 'c' has a hard sound, the spelling is relatively straightforward (e.g. 'scaling', 'describe'). However, where the 'c' has a soft sound, the spelling may not be obvious (e.g. 'muscles').

1 Copy the following words. Highlight the 'sc' sequence in each one. Learn the correct spelling.

fascinate	luscious
conscience	miscellaneous
descendant	obscene
discipline	muscle
fluorescent	resuscitate

2 Work with another student. Test each other on these 10 spellings.

UNIT 23

S1: the 'f' sound

The 'f' sound in a word is usually spelt with 'f' or 'ff':

frost   family   effectively

However, it is sometimes spelt with 'ph':

paragraph   photograph

Many words using the 'ph' pattern come from the ancient Greek language.

1 Complete the following words by using 'f', 'ff' or 'ph'.

a	hy_en	**i**	con_lict
b	gra_ iti	**j**	al_abet
c	_oreign	**k**	baili_
d	_uneral	**l**	para_in
e	claustro_obic	**m**	brie_ly
f	_antom	**n**	_iloso_y
g	em_asise	**o**	_rase
h	tra_ic		

2 Check your spellings with another student. If you have different answers, use a dictionary to check who is correct.

S2: Prefixes: 'dis-' and 'un-'

You can add the prefix 'dis-' to a base word to indicate:

- reversal (e.g. appear/disappear)
- negation or lack of (e.g. trust/distrust).

When added to a base word, the prefix 'un-' can indicate:

- reversal (e.g. cover/uncover)
- not or opposite to (e.g. certain/uncertain)
- removal from or release (e.g. chained/unchained).

The correct spelling is formed by simply adding the prefix to the base word. There is no need to do anything else.

1 Attach the correct prefix, 'un-' or dis-', to the following words. Make sure you spell them correctly:

similar	natural	service
necessary	credit	scratched
official	grace	

UNIT 24

S1: Commonly misspelt words

Jasmine correctly spells two words that are often misspelt by students in exams: 'sincerely' and 'embarrassed'. Here are some more commonly misspelt words:

address	experience	interest
altogether	favourite	marriage
business	government	necessary
definite	guarantee	patience
different	holiday	separate
exaggerate	immediately	soldier

1 How many of these words do you know how to spell? There are 20 words altogether, including those that Jasmine spells correctly. Work with a partner and test each other on them.

2 Write down any words you spell incorrectly. Use this well-known sequence to help you learn the correct spelling:

Look at the word first for a few seconds.
Cover the word and try to 'see' it in your mind.
Say the word by breaking it up into syllables. and pronouncing each bit.
Write the word from memory.
Check the spelling of the word.

S2: Silent 'k'

While you can hear the 'k' at the start of words such as 'kettle' and 'keep', it is silent when followed by an 'n'. This means it cannot be heard when the word is pronounced.

1 Learn how to spell these commonly used words with a silent 'k':

know	knit	knee
knew	knot	knife
known	knock	knight
knowledge	knuckle	

UNIT 25

S1: Suffixes: '-able' and '-ible'

Many adjectives end in '-able' (e.g. 'likeable', 'adaptable', 'capable', 'fashionable'). However, some adjectives end in '-ible' (e.g. 'flexible').

There is no clear rule to help you know which ending is correct. The best thing to do is to make sure you know the most commonly used '-ible' endings.

2 Look at this list of '-ible' words that students often spell incorrectly. Make sure you know their meanings, as well as how to spell them:

sensible	edible	compatible
horrible	gullible	plausible
possible	visible	reversible
responsible	incredible	accessible
terrible	feasible	

S2: Silent 'b'

You can hear the 'b' sound in words such as 'but' and 'between'. However, 'b' can also be a silent letter. This means that it cannot be heard when the word is pronounced, as in the word 'climb'.

1 Say the following words aloud:

thumb	comb	limb
doubt	bomb	crumb
plumber	subtle	debt
succumb	lamb	tomb

2 Spend two minutes memorising the words. Then close your book and ask another student to test your spelling of them.

UNIT 27

S1: Homonyms

A **homonym** is one of a group of words that share the same spelling and the same pronunciation but have different meanings. For example:

well (a hole drilled in the ground for water, oil, and so on)
well (in good health)

A **homograph** is one of a group of words that share the same spelling, but not the same pronunciation, and which have different meanings. For example:

minute (a measure of time)
minute (very small)

A **homophone** is one of a group of words that share the same pronunciation but which have different meanings and spellings. For example:

sea (an area of water)
see (to perceive through the eyes)

These three types of words are often grouped together under the general heading of 'homonyms'. There are many homonyms in the English language.

1   For each of the following, write a word that has the same pronunciation but is spelt differently and has a different meaning:

a	weather	**e**	which
b	sun	**f**	where
c	mined	**g**	one.
d	hear		

S2: Commonly confused words

It is easy to confuse words that sound similar, even though they have different spellings. In Source E, the writer correctly uses the word 'accept', which means 'receive'. Many students confuse this word with 'except', which means 'not including'.

1   Work with another student. Look at the following pairs of words that students often confuse. Discuss the different meanings of the words in each pair. Use a dictionary if you are not sure. Make a note of any that you often confuse.

a	advice / advise	**g**	draw / drawer
b	aloud / allowed	**h**	practice / practise
c	altar / alter	**i**	dual / duel
d	ensure / insure	**j**	cue / queue
e	envelop / envelope	**k**	desert / dessert
f	coarse / course	**l**	storey / story

UNIT 28

S1: American spellings

Huckleberry Finn was written by an American author. The word 'colour' is spelt as 'color'. If you use the internet a lot, you will know that the spelling of words in American Standard English can be different from the spelling in British Standard English.

The most common differences in spelling are shown in this table.

British	American English	Examples
words ending in 're'	often end in 'er'	centre → center metre → meter
words ending in 'our'	usually end in 'or'	neighbour → neighbor colour → color
words ending in 'ogue'	sometimes end in 'og'	catalogue → catalog analogue → analog

You need to make sure that you:

- know what the differences are
- always use British Standard spelling in examinations.

1 Choose the British Standard spelling of the following words. Then copy out each one.

    a   litre / liter   **e**   fiber / fibre
    b   humour / humor   **f**   labour / labor
    c   theatre / theater   **g**   savior / saviour
    d   flavor / flavour   **h**   dialogue / dialog.

S2: Silent 'w'

You can hear the 'w' sound in words such as 'we', 'walked', 'whispered', 'window', 'wilderness'. However, when the letter 'w' is followed by an 'r', the 'w' becomes silent, as in the word 'wrap'.

1 Check this rule against the following commonly used words:

wrath	wreckage	wretch	wring	wrist
wreck	wren	wriggle	wrinkle	wrong

2 Aim never to make a mistake with the words in the box or with the following four words that students often spell incorrectly:

write	wrote	written	writing

UNIT 29

S1: Prefixes: 'in-', 'il-', 'ir-', 'im-'

One meaning of the prefix 'in-', when added to a base word, is 'not' or 'the opposite of'. For example:

- 'visible' means that something can be seen; '*in*visible' means it cannot be seen
- 'credible' means that something is believable; '*in*credible' means that something is not believable.

'In-' is the most common form of this prefix, but there are exceptions:

- If the base word starts with 'r' the prefix is spelt 'ir-'. So if something is not regular, you say it is '*ir*regular'.
- If the base word starts with an 'm' or a 'p', the prefix is spelt 'im-'. So if someone is not mature, they are '*im*mature'; if something is not perfect, you say it is '*im*perfect'.
- If the base word starts with 'l', the prefix is spelt 'il-'. So if something is not legal, it is '*il*legal'.

1 Attach the prefix 'in-', 'il-', 'ir-' or 'im-' to the following base words to suggest their opposite:

capable	offensive	efficient	rational
mortal	moral	finite	consistent
possible	direct	separable	legible
responsible	logical	personal	
literate	reversible	legal	

S2: their, there and they're

Many students confuse the use of these three words and then end up spelling them incorrectly.

Look at the correct use of these words in Source B.

… everyone is frightened of rejection by <u>their</u> classmates and peers.

… is just another way of saying <u>they're</u> an individual.

… because I know <u>there</u> are thousands like I was …

---

1 Copy the following passage. It shows the thoughts of a teacher about a class she teaches. Fill in the blanks with the correct use of 'their', 'there' or 'they're'.

… are twenty-five students in this class. They generally work well but … are times when … simply not in the mood. They can be distracted by … classmates or … phones or a wasp or even by the weather outside. When that happens, … work suffers and … is little I can do to settle them. Nevertheless, I think … a great group of students. … lively and interesting and … are some real characters amongst them.

2 Check your answers with those of another student. Discuss any differences and decide who is correct.

Assess your progress

Read the following extract from one student's exam writing, in which they are discussing the pressures facing young people today.

It's not just school life that is suffocating us; it's also the pressure to 'fit in', 'be cool', and simply just be excepted by people our age. When I first moved to this area I wasent at all confident and if it hadent been for my mother going out of her way to ensure I met girls my age and invited them for tea and sleepovers, I'm not sure how I would have survived. Now, even though I feel secure in myself and my friends, I'm still aware of the weight of pier pressure – a weight that sits heavily on most young people's shoulders. It's pier pressure that often takes us to places we dont really want to go to and that makes us do things we dont really want to do.

The student communicates clearly and quite effectively using a range of vocabulary and punctuation for effect. However, there are two areas in which this student could improve their accuracy:

- The student knows how to use apostrophes for omission to spell the words 'I'm' and 'It's' correctly. However, they need to strengthen their understanding of this and apply it more generally:

  was not → wasn't   had not → hadn't
  do not → don't

- The student needs to be extra careful with homonyms and ensure they know the meanings of words that sound similar but are spelt differently:

  excepted **or** accepted?   pier **or** peer?

1 Look closely at samples of your own writing. Identify the main areas of spelling that you need to work on in order to improve your spelling accuracy. Make a note of these and ensure you take extra care in these areas in the future.

FURTHER PROGRESS

1 Always correct spelling errors highlighted by your teacher or another student. Use a dictionary to make sure that your correction is right.

2 When you come across words you do not know:

a look in a dictionary to find out their meaning
b write them three times to help you remember how to spell them.

Unit 32
Test your progress 4

In Units 27–31 you have learnt to:

- communicate effectively
- structure descriptions and narratives
- present a point of view
- write a balanced argument
- craft your writing
- check and correct your work.

This unit contains two tests. In Test A you need to present your point of view. In Test B you need to write a story. Your aim in each test is to show your teacher the best of your writing skills. Here are a few reminders of what you need to do:

Communication	• write effectively for purpose and audience • engage your reader with interesting ideas • write in fluent Standard English • influence and manipulate your reader
Organisation	• identify purpose, audience and form • generate ideas and plan for paragraphs • sustain coherence though fluently linked paragraphs • seamlessly integrate discourse markers
Vocabulary, sentence structures and accuracy	• demonstrate a wide vocabulary range • use language creatively and imaginatively • vary sentence structures to influence readers • achieve high level accuracy in punctuation and spelling

TEST A

Plan, write and check your answer to **one** of the questions below.

You have 45 minutes.

At the start: Allow three to five minutes for planning.
While writing: Read through after each paragraph to make sure you are producing a coherent and effective piece of writing.
At the end: Allow three minutes to check your punctuation and spelling.

Either

'It's all too clear that the place in which you grow up has a major impact on the person you become.'

Write an article for a newspaper in which you explain your point of view on this statement.

Or

'Too many young people are wasting their lives on Facebook, Twitter and the like; there must be better things for them to do!'

Write an article for a newspaper in which you explain your point of view on this statement.

TEST B

Plan, write and check your answer to one of the questions below.

You have 45 minutes.

At the start: Allow three to five minutes for planning.
While writing: Read through after each paragraph to make sure you are producing a coherent and effective piece of writing.
At the end: Allow three minutes to check your punctuation and spelling.

You are going to enter a creative writing competition.

Your entry will be judged by a panel of published writers.

Either

Write a story that begins or ends with this sentence:

'As the long day drew to an end, the noises in the corridor faded and the cell doors were locked on the outside.'

Or

Write the opening part of a story suggested to you by this picture.

✓ Complete this assignment on Cambridge Elevate.

Preparing for your exam

At the end of your GCSE course in English Language you will sit an exam. This exam consists of two papers, which are designed to test your skills in reading and writing.

PAPER 1: EXPLORATIONS IN CREATIVE READING AND WRITING

Section A: Reading

You will be asked to read and answer four questions on one fiction text.

Section B: Writing

You will be asked to write to describe or to narrate.

PAPER 2: WRITERS' VIEWPOINTS AND PERSPECTIVES

Section A: Reading

You will be asked to read and answer four questions on two texts. One of these will be non-fiction and one will be literary non-fiction.

Section B: Writing

You will be asked to write to present a viewpoint.

The time allowed in both papers is 1 hour 45 minutes. Each paper counts for 50% of your final GCSE mark.

PREPARING FOR THE EXAM

Sit Practice Paper 1, taking note of the teacher's advice. Then read and assess other students' answers alongside your own, and make improvements to your responses.

Once you have done Practice Paper 1, sit Practice Paper 2 and repeat the process.

At the end of this unit there are two further practice papers for you to sit. These papers test your skills in the following six assessment objectives:

AO1:
- Identify and interpret explicit and implicit information and ideas.
- Select and synthesise evidence from different texts.

AO2: Explain, comment on and analyse how writers use language and structure to achieve effects and influence readers, using relevant subject terminology to support their views.

AO3: Compare writers' ideas and perspectives, as well as how these are conveyed, across two or more texts.

AO4: Evaluate texts critically and support this with appropriate textual references.

AO5: Communicate clearly, effectively and imaginatively, selecting and adapting tone, style and register for different forms, purposes and audiences. Organise information and ideas, using structural and grammatical features to support coherence and cohesion of texts.

AO6: Use a range of vocabulary and sentence structures for clarity, purpose and effect, with accurate spelling and punctuation.

Set 1 Practice Paper 1

Explorations in creative reading and writing

Section A: Reading

In your exam, you will be given an exam paper with an insert. The insert will contain Source A, which will be an extract written in the 20th or the 21st century. You are advised to spend some time reading through the source and thinking about all five of the questions before writing your answers. Use the time to read the source closely and to make notes on the answers you could give to the questions in Section A.

Source A

This extract is from a novel by Margaret Atwood, first published at the beginning of the 21st century. In this section, a character closely examines a photograph that was taken many years before.

The Blind Assassin

She has a single photograph of him. She tucked it into a brown envelope on which she'd written *clippings*, and hid the envelope between the pages of *Perennials for the Rock Garden*, where no one else would ever look.

5　She's preserved this photo carefully, because it's almost all she has left of him. It's black and white, taken by one of those boxy, cumbersome flash cameras from before the war, with their accordion-pleat nozzles and their well-made leather cases that looked like muzzles, with straps and intricate buckles. The photo is of the two of them together, her and this man, on a picnic. *Picnic* is written on the back, in pencil – not his name or hers, just *picnic*. She knows the names, she doesn't need to write them down.

10　They're sitting under a tree; it might have been an apple tree; she didn't notice the tree much at the time. She's wearing a white blouse with the sleeves rolled to the elbow and a wide skirt tucked around her knees. There must have been a breeze, because of the way the shirt is blowing up against her; or perhaps it wasn't blowing, perhaps it was clinging; perhaps it was hot. It was hot. Holding her hand over the picture, she can still feel the heat coming up from it, like the heat from
15　a sun-warmed stone at midnight.

The man is wearing a light-coloured hat, angled down on his head and partially shading his face. His face appears to be more darkly tanned than hers. She's turned half towards him, and smiling, in a way she can't remember smiling at anyone since. She seems very young in the picture, too young, though she hadn't considered herself too young at the time. He's smiling too – the whiteness
20　of his teeth shows up like a scratched match flaring – but he's holding up his hand, as if to fend her off in play, or else to protect himself from the camera, from the person who must be there, taking the picture; or else to protect himself from those in the future who might be looking at him, who might be looking in at him through this square, lighted window of glazed paper. As if to protect himself from her. As if to protect her. In his outstretched, protecting hand there's the stub end of a cigarette.

25　She retrieves the brown envelope when she's alone, and slides the photo out from among the newspaper clippings. She lies it flat on the table and stares down into it, as if she's peering into a well or pool – searching beyond her own reflection for something else, something she must have dropped or lost, out of reach but still visible, shimmering like a jewel on sand. She examines every detail. His fingers bleached by the flash or the sun's glare; the folds of their clothing; the leaves of
30　the tree, and the small round shapes hanging there – were they apples, after all? The coarse grass in the foreground. The grass was yellow then because the weather had been dry.

Over to one side – you wouldn't see it at first – there's a hand, cut by the margin, scissored off at the wrist, resting on the grass as if discarded. Left to its own devices.

The trace of blown cloud in the brilliant sky, like ice cream smudged on chrome.
35　His smoke-stained fingers. The distant glint of water. All drowned now.

Drowned, but shining.

From *The Blind Assassin* by Margaret Atwood

Have you fully understood the passage? If not, read the questions and then read the passage again.

Section A: Reading

Practice questions

Answer **all** questions in this section.
You are advised to spend about 45 minutes on this section.

0 1 Read again the first part of the source, lines 1 to 9.

List **four** things from this part of the text about the photograph.

[4 marks]

0 2 Look in detail at this extract from lines 16 to 24 of the source:

> The man is wearing a light-coloured hat, angled down on his head and partially shading his face. His face appears to be more darkly tanned than hers. She's turned half towards him, and smiling, in a way she can't remember smiling at anyone since. She seems very young in the picture, too young, though she hadn't considered herself too young at the time. He's smiling too – the whiteness of his teeth shows up like a scratched match flaring – but he's holding up his hand, as if to fend her off in play, or else to protect himself from the camera, from the person who must be there, taking the picture; or else to protect himself from those in the future who might be looking at him, who might be looking in at him through this square, lighted window of glazed paper. As if to protect himself from her. As if to protect her. In his outstretched, protecting hand there's the stub end of a cigarette.

How does the writer use language here to describe the photograph?

You could include the writer's choice of:

- words and phrases
- language features and techniques
- sentence forms.

[8 marks]

Prompts (margin notes):

Read all the questions before you start to answer Question 1. Use the marks indicated by each question to help you decide how much time to spend on it.

Take note of these – you will not get marks for material taken from outside the stated lines.

This question is worth 4 marks.

Take note of these – you will not get marks for material taken from outside the stated lines.

These are prompts to help you.

Think about how the writer uses words for effect.

This might include features such as repetition, **figurative language** and punctuation used for effect.

Focus on variations in sentence lengths and structures for effect.

This question is worth 8 marks.

You need to consider the complete passage.

0 3   You now need to think about the **whole** of the source.

This text is from the early part of a novel.

How has the writer <u>structured</u> the text to interest you as a reader?

You <u>could</u> write about:

- what the writer focuses your attention on at the beginning and end
- how the writer develops her ideas
- any other structural features that interest you.

[8 marks]

Structure can be at a whole text level (for example beginnings, endings, shifts in perspective); at a paragraph level (for example topic changes, paragraph cohesion, single sentence paragraphs) or at a sentence level (for example sentence length, sentence variation).

These are prompts to help you.

This question is worth 8 marks.

0 4   Focus on **lines 25 to the end**.

'The writer successfully creates an air of mystery around the photograph.'

To what extent do you agree with this statement?

In your response, you <u>could</u>:

- examine how the writer creates an air of mystery around the photograph
- evaluate the extent to which the writer is successful in doing this
- support your opinions and judgements with quotations from the text.

[20 marks]

Take note of these – you will not get marks for material taken from outside the stated lines.

These are prompts to help you.

This question is worth 20 marks.

Section B: Writing

Practice questions

You are advised to spend about 45 minutes on this section.
<u>Write in full sentences.</u>
<u>You are reminded of the need to plan your answer.</u>
<u>You should leave enough time to check your work at the end.</u>

0 5   You are going to enter a creative writing competition.

Your entry will be judged by a <u>panel of professional writers</u>.

Either:

Write a story in which a photograph plays a significant part.

Or:

Write a description suggested by this photograph:

(24 marks for content and organisation
16 marks for technical accuracy)
[40 marks]

You must also write in Standard English unless you are writing dialogue.

Planning helps you structure your writing.

Check your answer for technical accuracy. You can also make other improvements at this stage.

Your audience is professional writers; your audience is also your examiner; you will be assessed on how well you craft your creative writing.

In this practice paper you have a choice of a narrative or descriptive task. In your exam, you may have this choice or you may have two narrative tasks or two descriptive tasks.

Notice how the marks are awarded for your different writing skills.

Section A: Reading

Question 1

0 1	Read again the first part of the source, lines 1 to 9.

List **four** things from this part of the text about the photograph.

[4 marks]

This question tests you on your skill in identifying and interpreting explicit and implicit information and ideas (AO1).

It is a relatively straightforward question. It is asking you to identify four distinct things about the photograph.

1 Check your answers against the following list and decide how many you identified correctly:

- It is the only one she has of him.
- It was hidden in an envelope between the pages of *Perennials for the Rock Garden*, where no one else would ever look.
- It had been carefully preserved.
- It was almost all she had left of him.
- It was black and white.
- It was taken by one of those boxy, cumbersome flash cameras.
- It was taken from before the war.
- It was of the two of them together on a picnic.
- *Picnic* is written on the back, in pencil.

You may have written something else, such as 'the photograph was very important to the woman'. This is correct, but you will only be awarded the points if you have given evidence from the text to support it – i.e. 'because it was hidden where no one else would ever look' or 'because it was all she had left of him'.

Question 2

0 2   Look in detail at this extract from lines 16 to 24 of the source:

> The man is wearing a light-coloured hat, angled down on his head and partially shading his face. His face appears to be more darkly tanned than hers. She's turned half towards him, and smiling, in a way she can't remember smiling at anyone since. She seems very young in the picture, too young, though she hadn't considered herself too young at the time. He's smiling too – the whiteness of his teeth shows up like a scratched match flaring – but he's holding up his hand, as if to fend her off in play, or else to protect himself from the camera, from the person who must be there, taking the picture; or else to protect himself from those in the future who might be looking at him, who might be looking in at him through this square, lighted window of glazed paper. As if to protect himself from her. As if to protect her. In his outstretched, protecting hand there's the stub end of a cigarette.

How does the writer use language here to describe the photograph?

You could include the writer's choice of:

- words and phrases
- language features and techniques
- sentence forms.

[8 marks]

This question tests your skill in examining and commenting on the writer's use of language – her phrases, language features, language techniques and sentence forms (AO2).

You should:

- show that you understand the writer's use of language
- examine and analyse the effects of the writer's language choices
- select and use relevant quotations
- use appropriate subject terminology to discuss language use. You might, for example, comment on the writer's use of adjectives or similes. 'Adjectives' and 'similes' are both appropriate subject terminology.

Look at the following responses of four students to this question. They are placed in order of merit. The comments show you what each student achieves.

Student A

The writer says that the man is wearing a light-coloured hat and that his hat is at an angle. She is very young and he's smiling. He's holding up his hand as if to protect himself but she's not sure if he's trying to protect her.

Identifies some details about the photograph – no comment on writer's use of language.

Student B

The writer describes what's in the photograph and she tells us every little detail about the man and herself. She says that his face is more darkly tanned than hers, which makes me think he's been on holiday. She uses a simile to describe his teeth 'like a scratched match flaring'. This helps me to picture his teeth. She says that the photograph is a 'square, lighted window of glazed paper' which makes me think that you can see through it.

identifies technique

simple comment

identifies technique

uses quotation

simple comment

uses quotation

simple comment

Student C

The writer uses adjectives to describe the man. He is wearing a 'light-coloured' hat and his face is 'darkly tanned'. These help the reader imagine what he looks like. A simile is used to describe his teeth. They are compared with 'a scratched match flaring'. This makes them sound very white and bright and maybe a bit dangerous. The writer includes lots of detail about the photograph to describe it. She tells us that the woman is turned towards the man and that he's holding up his hand. She also uses repetition of the word 'protect' to make the reader think that the man is trying to protect the woman to show that he cares about her. There's a range of sentence forms. The writer uses sentences of different lengths to have an effect on the reader and to make it more interesting to read.

identifies technique

uses quotation

identifies technique

uses quotation

explains effect

identifies technique

identifies technique

uses quotation

not quite right

identifies technique

not supported with examples

Student D

The writer uses a range of techniques to describe the photograph. She uses the [identifies technique]

simile 'like a scratched match flaring' to describe the man's smile. The word 'flaring' [uses quotation]

makes it seem sudden and has connotations of danger. She repeats the word [starts to examine]

'young' three times in one sentence to describe the woman and emphasises this [explains effect]

even more by saying twice that she is 'too' young. This makes it seem as though [uses quotation]

she shouldn't have been there with this man because she wasn't old enough. She [explains effect]

also uses repetition later in the paragraph when she repeats the word 'protect' in [identifies technique]

the sentences: 'As if to protect himself from her. As if to protect her.' These two [identifies technique]

sentences are structured in very similar ways but they have a different meaning and [uses quotation]

the short words 'as if' at the start of each sentence make the reader realise that [identifies technique]

she doesn't know why the man was holding up his hand and it maybe shows that she [starts to examine]

wasn't very sure about him. [developed comment on effect]

The writer also uses an effective metaphor near the end. She calls the photograph [identifies technique]

a 'square lighted window'. A window is something that you look through to see [uses quotation]

something and it is often square. It makes me feel as though I am looking through a [developed comment on effect]

window into the world of this man and woman.

Notice how the best response:

- identifies and examines a range of techniques
- uses quotations to support the points made
- explains and develops comments on effect
- uses appropriate subject terminology.

2 Annotate your answer to show what you have achieved. Then make notes on how you could improve your answer.

Question 3

---

03   You now need to think about the **whole** of the source.

This text is from the early part of a novel.

How has the writer structured the text to interest you as a reader?

You could write about:

- what the writer focuses your attention on at the beginning and end
- how the writer develops her ideas
- any other structural features that interest you.

[8 marks]

This question tests your skill in examining and commenting on the writer's use of structure (AO2).

You should:

- show that you understand features of structure
- examine and analyse the effects of the writer's choice of structural features
- select and use relevant examples
- use appropriate subject terminology to discuss structure.

Structural features can be:

- at a whole text level – for example beginnings, endings and shifts in focus
- at a paragraph level – for example topic changes, single-sentence paragraphs
- at a sentence level – for example sentence lengths.

3 Look at these two examples of student responses to this question and the two comments. Match the comment to the correct response.

a   Which student has written the best answer?
b   Which student response most closely matches your own?

Student E

The writer starts by telling the reader about the woman and the photograph that she keeps hidden. Then she describes the photograph in a lot of detail so that the reader can imagine what it looks like. At the end she says that there's a hand cut off on the photograph and we don't know whose hand it is. The first two paragraphs start with 'She' and the next one starts with 'They're' so now she's writing about both the man and the woman. In the fourth paragraph she starts with 'The man' and then in the next one she goes back to 'She'. The last paragraph is very short to emphasise what she is saying and it says that they're 'drowned, but shining' which makes you wonder what has happened to them.

Student F

The text is all about a photograph and we find out more about it as we read on. The writer starts with the simple sentence 'She has a single photograph of him'. The second sentence is longer and shows the reader that the photograph is a secret and that the woman keeps it hidden. The second paragraph also links the woman and the photograph at the beginning: 'She's preserved this photo carefully'. In it we find out more about the photograph and how it was taken. The man and the woman are linked together by the use of the pronoun 'they're' at the start of the third paragraph although it is mainly about the woman. However, at the start of the fourth paragraph the focus shifts onto 'The man' and it's mainly about him. The next paragraph picks up on the idea that the photograph is a secret because the woman only looks at it when she's alone. It also emphasises the fact that it was hot when it was taken because it says that the grass was yellow.

After the five main paragraphs, there are three very short ones. The writer introduces something new – a hand 'cut by the margin' – so there must have been someone else with them but we don't know who and the paragraph isn't very long so maybe it wasn't that important. The last paragraph is the shortest of them all: 'Drowned, but shining'. It emphasises the idea of someone being dead but still important and it's like it sums up the importance of the man in the photograph to the woman.

---

1 The student identifies the beginning and the end and has some awareness of shifts in focus. He makes links between the openings of paragraphs and begins to explain effects. He has some awareness of variation in paragraph length for effect and selects a few relevant examples.

2 The student understands how paragraphs are linked and used to shift focus. She also has some awareness of variation in sentence length. She uses relevant examples to support points. She links content with paragraph length and clearly explains the effect of the final short paragraph.

Did you work out that student F had written the best answer? Even though it is good, the student could have said more about the structure of the passage.

4 Work in pairs. The following questions will help you think more deeply about structure. Make notes on your answers.

a   In what ways is the passage structured like an investigation?

b   Look at the use of pronouns at the start of sentences. How many times is 'she' used? How many times is 'he' or 'his' used? What does this tell you about the main focus of the passage?

c   Look at the opening sentences of the first and second paragraphs:

'She has a single photograph of him.'
'She's preserved this photo carefully, because it's almost all she has left of him.'

What **three** points of connection are there between these sentences?

d Look again at the final three short paragraphs:

Over to one side — you wouldn't see it at first — there's a hand, cut by the margin, scissored off at the wrist, resting on the grass as if discarded. Left to its own devices.

The trace of blown cloud in the brilliant sky, like ice cream smudged on chrome. His smoke-stained fingers. The distant glint of water. All drowned now.

Drowned, but shining.

What does the writer do to create a sense of the woman's thought processes?

e The references to the man's smoking habit are a structural feature of the passage. Identify where these appear in the passage.

---

0 4 Focus on **lines 25 to the end**.

'The writer successfully creates an air of mystery around the photograph.'

To what extent do you agree with this statement?

In your response, you could:

- examine how the writer creates an air of mystery around the photograph
- evaluate the extent to which the writer is successful in doing this
- support your opinions and judgements with quotations from the text.

[20 marks]

This question tests your skill in evaluating texts critically and supporting this with appropriate textual references (AO4).

You should:

- clearly evaluate the text
- offer examples from the text to explain your views
- explain the effect of writer's choices
- select relevant quotations to support your views.

5 This is a good response to the question. Identify where the student:

a evaluates clearly

b uses examples from the text to explain views

c explains effects

d uses quotations to support judgements.

Student G

The writer creates an air of mystery around the photograph right from the start when she 'slides the photograph out from among the newspaper clippings'. This shows how it's hidden away and she has to look at it secretly. She stares at it as if 'searching for something else' which makes it sound mysterious. She then says it's like looking into a 'well or pool'. When you do this you see your own reflection at first and you have to look hard to see what is really under the water. This makes it sound as though the photograph, as well as being a secret, holds secrets that can't be seen on the first look. The woman then examines the photograph in 'every detail' and notices things that haven't been mentioned before like the 'folds of their clothing'. Because she's looking so closely, the reader expects her to find something and solve the mystery of the photograph but she never does.

There's also a mysterious hand in the photograph and we don't know if the photograph's been cut or if the person was never in it and we never find out who the person is so that's another mystery. We also learn that there is 'the distant glint of water' in the photograph and this comes just before she says 'All drowned now'. It's not clear who they all are and whether they really drowned. There's something sad and happy in the last sentence 'Drowned, but shining' as though the memories that the photograph bring back are precious to her.

I think the writer does successfully create an air of mystery around the photograph. She tells us lots of things about it but she never really answers all the questions we have about it.

6 Compare your answer with the example answer. Make notes on things you could have said to improve your response.

Annotate this response on Cambridge Elevate.

Section B: Writing

Question 5

> **0 5** You were asked to write an entry for a creative writing competition, which would be judged by a panel of professional writers. You could:
>
> **Either**:
>
> Write a story in which a photograph plays a significant part.
>
> **Or**:
>
> Write a description suggested by the photograph on the practice paper.
>
> (24 marks for content and organisation
> 16 marks for technical accuracy)
>
> **[40 marks]**

You should:

- communicate clearly and effectively
- match tone, style and register to your purpose and audience
- develop, organise and structure your information and ideas
- make clear links within and between paragraphs
- make effective use of structural features
- choose vocabulary for effect
- use a range of sentence structures for effect
- spell and punctuate accurately.

7 Student H chose to 'Write a story in which a photograph plays a significant part'. Read Student H's answer, then use the bullet points to help you assess their work.

When you have done this, write a comment for the student. Identify:

a **three** things that they do well

b **two** things you think they should work on to improve their writing.

Student H

Write a story in which a photograph plays a significant part

Mary a mother of two children Sam and Tom lived with her husband in a small house

in the countryside. Marys husband had lost his job and started to drink and when

he got drunk he would beat Mary and sometimes the two children. Mary was very

unhappy and one day she was looking in a drawer and she saw a photograph of her

mum and dad and her when she was a kid.

Mary remembered how happy she was and she decided that she would take Sam

and Tom to stay with her mum and dad and she would leave her husband and not

tell him. Mary took what money she could find and got on a bus with Sam and Tom

hoping that the bus would take her all the way to her parents house but it would

not. They all stayed on the bus for as long as possible but the bus only went half way

to her parents house so they would have to walk the rest of the way. Mary new that

it was going to be a very big challenge to walk the rest of the way but she had no

money left so she had no choice.

The three of them set off and after one hour of walking they were tired so they

sat on the side of the road for a bit hoping that someone would give them a lift and

they got lucky because a lorry stopped and took them to her parents house. They

got there very late at night and her parents were in bed but they woke up and they

were very surprised to see them. When Mary told them what had happened they

said that Mary and Sam and Tom could stay with them. Mary was very happy and

she still keeps the photograph on the side of her bed.

8 Student I also chose to write a story. Read it carefully. Student I wrote a better response than Student H. Can you work out why? List the reasons.

Student I

Write a story in which a photograph plays a significant part.

The photograph took pride of place on the mantelpiece. I had often dusted it and sometimes, when I was really annoyed, stuck it in a drawer just to annoy him.

But now I picked it up and looked at it. It bought back so many memories.

I remembered how it had been a cold, wet night and was getting dark. I was part of a group. I had knew these people for two years now and I knew I was safe. Twenty miles we had to walk to get our adventure medals. We had only compleated ten. By this time things were looking a bit unpredictable. The rain was stoping and starting, the wind would suddenly pick up and then gradualy slow down. Time was not on our side. We had to be back for 11.00 pm and it was now already 6.00 pm. We carried on climbing up the hills and rocks till all of a sudden one of our members out of the group fell.

He fell a few feet and gave out a yell, this was just the beginning of a nightmare. We all rushed down to see how bad he was hurt. He was in pain and it looked as though his ankle was broken.

We all realised at this point that he could not go on. He was dissappointed and so were we. We were all told that if someone was injured that one or two people should stay with that person. I agreed to stay with him while the rest of the group carried on. As soon as the rest of the group reached the next checkpoint they would get someone to find and help us get back to the camp.

I helped him to a suitable position nearby, so he would be comfortable. We expected to see someone about 9.00, only two hours from when the rest of the group carried on. It was now 8.30. Only 30 minutes to go we both thought.

We were both getting really tiered at this point. The darkness was setting in and fog was beginning to settle. We were up high on a huge mountain. It was dangerous and one false move and we could of been off the side.

When it got to 11.30 I decided at this point that we should get prepared to spend the night here as it did not seem like we would be going anywhere. I thought maybe I should go and try and get help but Mark asked me to stay. I didn't really know him all that well but we started to talk properly to each other to pass the time. He told me all about his family and how he was really interested in sport and wanted to be a trainer when he was older. I told him about my Mum and how she had brought us up after Dad died. I also told him that I wanted to go to Uni once I'd finished all my exams. We were almost falling asleep when we heard a sound and suddenly a bright light appeared from nowhere. It was waving around near by and I heard my name being called out from a distance. I felt so relieved. They had finally found us through all the mist and darkness.

I felt really glad and proud that I had stayed with Mark but that wasn't the best bit. After that night we started going out together. The photo that I'm looking at is of him and me on our wedding day over twenty years ago now.

9 Student J chose to 'Write a description suggested by the photograph'.
Student J wrote a better response than both Student H and Student I.
Can you work out why? List the reasons.

Student J

Write a description suggested by the photograph

They can't see me but I watch them nearly every day. There are usually hordes of them, but today there's only four. There they are now in their ragged clothes and with their bright, innocent smiles looking as though they haven't a care in the world. I can hear their laughter and sometimes their cries when one of them falls over and hurts his knee or rips his jumper. The cries don't usually last for long. Sometimes one of their mothers comes out to see what the problem is but most of the time they just get back to the game.

They don't seem to notice the chaos all around them. There's just a few of the houses still standing on our street now and most of them have broken windows and gates swinging creakily on their hinges. This used to be a busy, bustling street. There was a baker's shop on the corner and a Post Office facing it, and a little further down the street there was a café where I used to go for a cup of tea after I'd finished all my housework. The tables there were all neatly laid with pink and white tablecloths and delicate china cups and saucers.

Now all there is is piles of rubble where the bombs have made direct hits on the houses and shops. The baker's shop was destroyed on the very first night of the bombings; there was a loud explosion and then the piercing sound of the air-raid sirens. When I got back from my shelter the sun was shining brightly in a clear blue sky. All I could see of the baker's shop was an empty frame of bricks like a skeleton with no clothes or flesh. The roof was gone and so was the house front but I could still see the empty bed on the first floor. That was just the start of it.

After that I used to hurry to my shelter as soon as those sirens sounded. Every time I returned home there was more damage, more destruction and more houses like skeletons.

As I watch the children playing, I notice another child standing shyly on the corner. He's all by himself and looks as though he'd like to join in the game. I recognise him as the boy who used to live in number 12. I heard he had lost his mum the night his house was destroyed and was now living in Baker Street. Slowly he is walking towards the boys who are playing. I watch as they turn and recognise him. With big smiles they invite him to join in. They play a game of soldiers fighting a battle with pretend guns. And then the sirens sound.

10 Use what you have learned from assessing the responses of Students H, I and J to help you identify:

a what you did well in your writing
b how you could improve your writing.

Writers' viewpoints and perspectives

Section A: Reading

You are advised to spend up some time reading through the source and all five questions you have to answer.

You should make sure you leave sufficient time to check your answers.

- **Source A:** A magazine article called *Social notebook*.

- **Source B:** 'The Sunday Morning Markets': an extract from a book called *London Labour and the London Poor*.

> In your exam you will be given an exam paper with an insert. The insert will contain two sources – A and B. One of these will have been written in the 19th century. You are advised to spend some time reading through the sources and thinking about all five of the questions before writing your answers.

Source A:

Social notebook

by Paul Barker, 20 February 1996

The bridge carrying the M25 southwards into Kent juts up, like an awkward insect, beyond the dumpy dome and ready-made cornices of the Thurrock Lakeside shopping centre. The centre and the retail park next to it occupy about two million square feet. Three-and-a-half million people live within 30 minutes' drive, and on a Saturday most of them seem to be trying to get into its car park.   5

Lakeside is a strange mixture of flashiness and plain grot. A 'vertical feature' tells you the time and temperature as you drive along the M25. Then you turn off past the Essex Arena (for car racing) and the War Zone (for paintball games). A 20 acre lake offers windsurfing and an imitation Mississippi riverboat.   10

Opened only six years ago, by Princess Alexandra, its magnetism already terrifies Oxford Street, where traders muse about the attraction of roofing their street over, and perhaps having their own security guards. Malls are mocked as a parody of a traditional city. But Jane Jacobs, heroine of the urban conservation movement, wrote that 'the bedrock attribute of a successful city district is that a person must feel personally secure among all these strangers.' Enclosed and video-scrutinised, they make people, especially women, feel safe. No panhandlers here.   15
No need to carry bags slung across your chest.

The new centres are different from the basic air-conditioned shopping mall. The first in Britain opened at Brent Cross, North London, 20 years ago. But today's luxuriant, baroque centres are like mini-cities. Drive past the Meadowhall Centre outside Sheffield, and look down on its green dome in the old wasteland of the lower Don Valley. Apart from the shops, there are two office parks. Warner has opened an 11-screen multiplex cinema.   20
Sheffield's first supertram line runs from the old city centre to Meadowhall. Locally, high hopes for regeneration are placed on the 'rippling-out' effect of Meadowhall.

Nobody planned that this should happen. When T Dan Smith, regional planning's flawed hero, started to weave motorways around and through Newcastle, the Gateshead MetroCentre was no part of his vision. Britain's first out-of-town shopping centre exploited a tax break intended to woo industry, not a retail heaven. It sometimes   25
seems that the only people who like the centres are the millions of people who use them. Many of the complaints have the giveaway taint of snobbery – in direct line of descent from 1930s moans about vulgar supercinemas or 1950s moans about unsightly television aerials.

I love these centres. The first time I went into the MetroCentre, I had been travelling the grey streets of the north-east. If the alternative was Sunderland High Street or Peterlee, then the MetroCentre is where I would shop. In design the centres have as much in common with theme parks as with department stores: perhaps more. At the Metro you can leave your children while you shop, in a pick 'n' mix amusement zone like the late-lamented Fun House at Blackpool Pleasure Beach. Shoppers go about with cheerful, sprightly step. They have dressed up to come here.   30

On the upper floor there is a classical corner with Corinthian columns and statues in creamy fibreglass, and box trees made of plastic. A sign welcomes you to 'Roman Shopping.' In architects' drawings of their city schemes, you find little groups of tables with happy urbanites chatting under the sunshades. A bit like a tourist brochure. You seldom see this in Britain in real life. But you see it in the Roman Forum at the MetroCentre, where the electricity always shines.   35

Adapted from an article in *Prospect Magazine* by Paul Barker

Source B:

by Henry Mayhew, first published in 1851

Henry Mayhew was a social researcher in favour of social reform. In this extract, he describes a Sunday morning market in London in the mid-19th century.

The Sunday Morning Markets

Nearly every poor man's market does its Sunday trade. For a few hours on the Sabbath morning, the noise, bustle, and scramble of the Saturday night are repeated, and but for this opportunity many a poor family would pass a dinnerless Sunday. The system of paying the mechanic late on the Saturday night – and more particularly of paying a man his wages in a public-house – when he is tired with his day's work lures him to the tavern, and there the hours fly quickly enough beside the warm tap-room fire, so that by the time the wife comes for her husband's wages, she finds a large portion of them gone in drink, and the streets half cleared, so that the Sunday market is the only chance of getting the Sunday's dinner.   5

Of all these Sunday-morning markets, the Brill, perhaps, furnishes the busiest scene; so that it may be taken as a type of the whole.   10

The streets in the neighbourhood are quiet and empty. The shops are closed with their different-coloured shutters, and the people round about are dressed in the shiney cloth of the holiday suit. There are no 'cabs,' and but few omnibuses to disturb the rest, and men walk in the road as safely as on the footpath.

As you enter the Brill the market sounds are scarcely heard. But at each step the low hum grows gradually into the noisy shouting, until at last the different cries become distinct, and the hubbub, din, and confusion of a thousand voices bellowing at once again fill the air. The road and footpath are crowded, as on the over-night; the men are standing in groups, smoking and talking; whilst the women run to and fro, some with the white round turnips showing out of their filled aprons, others with cabbages under their arms, and a piece of red meat dangling from their hands. Only a few of the shops are closed, but the butcher's and the coal-shed are filled with customers, and from the door of the shut-up baker's, the women come streaming forth with bags of flour in their hands, while men sally from the halfpenny barber's smoothing their clean-shaved chins. Walnuts, blacking, apples, onions, braces, combs, turnips, herrings, pens, and corn-plaster, are all bellowed out at the same time. Labourers and mechanics, still unshorn and undressed, hang about with their hands in their pockets, some with their pet terriers under their arms. The pavement is green with the refuse leaves of vegetables, and round a cabbage-barrow the women stand turning over the bunches, as the man shouts, 'Where you like, only a penny.' Boys are running home with the breakfast herring held in a piece of paper, and the side-pocket of the apple-man's stuff coat hangs down with the weight of the halfpence stored within it.   15   20   25

Presently the tolling of the neighbouring church bells breaks forth. Then the bustle doubles itself, the cries grow louder, the confusion greater. Women run about and push their way through the throng, scolding the saunterers, for in half an hour the market will close. In a little time the butcher puts up his shutters, and leaves the door still open; the policemen in their clean gloves come round and drive the street-sellers before them, and as the clock strikes eleven the market finishes, and the Sunday's rest begins.   30

Have you fully understood the passages? If not, read the questions and then read the passages again.

Section A: Reading

Practice questions

Answer **all** questions in this section
You are advised to spend about 45 minutes on this section.

> Use the marks indicated by each question to decide how much time to spend on it.

0 1   Read **Source A** again, from lines 1 to 15.

> Re-read these lines only.

Choose **four** statements below which are TRUE according to the passage.

- Write the letters of the four true statements
- Choose a maximum of four statements.

> You need to read the statements and check whether they are true. Be careful – some of them are partly but not wholly true.

A   The M25 runs close by the Thurrock Lakeside shopping centre.

B   The Lakeside shopping centre alone occupies about two million square feet.

C   You can go windsurfing on a nearby lake.

D   Princess Alexandra opened Lakeside in 1990.

E   The time and temperature are displayed on the dome of Lakeside.

F   Shopping malls are like a traditional city.

G   The Lakeside shopping mall is like a war zone.

H   Women in particular like the security offered by shopping malls.

[4 marks]

> This question is worth 4 marks.

0 2   You need to refer to **Source A** and **Source B** for this question:

> You need to refer to both sources.

Use details from **both** sources. Summarise the different reasons why people went to shopping malls in the 20th century and why they went to the Sunday morning markets in the 19th century.

[8 marks]

> This question is worth 8 marks.

0 3 Read again lines 13 to 31 in **Source B**.

How does Henry Mayhew use language to show the reader what the Brill market is like?

You could include the writer's choice of:

- words and phrases
- language features and techniques
- sentence forms.

[12 marks]

0 4 For this question, you need to refer to **Source A** and **Source B**.

Compare how the two writers convey their attitudes to the places they describe.

In your answer, you could:

- compare their attitudes
- compare the methods they use to convey their attitudes
- support your ideas with quotations from **both** sources.

[16 marks]

Take note of these – you will not get marks for material taken from outside the stated lines.

These are prompts to help you.

Think about how the writer uses words for effect.

This might include features such as repetition, figurative language and punctuation used for effect.

This question is worth 12 marks.

Focus on variations in sentence lengths and structures for effect.

You need to refer to both sources.

These are prompts to help you.

This question is worth 16 marks.

Section B: Writing

Practice questions

Answer **all** questions in this section.
You are advised to spend about 45 minutes on this section.
You are reminded of the need to plan your answer.
You should write in full sentences.
You should leave enough time to check your work at the end.

0 5 'People waste away their weekends mindlessly in shopping malls when they could be doing so much more with their free time.'

Write an article for a national newspaper in which you explain your point of view on this statement.

(24 marks for content and organisation
16 marks for technical accuracy)

[40 marks]

Take note of these instructions. They are given to help you.

Your audience is newspaper readers; your audience is also your examiner; you will be assessed on how well you craft your writing.

In Practice Paper 1, you focused on what makes a good answer. The emphasis here is also on how to produce a good answer. You are advised to make focused notes. This needs practice and the advice here will help you get started. The more exam practice you do, the more efficient you will become in making focused notes. These skills are transferrable to Paper 2. You can start to make your notes in your reading time.

Section A: Reading

Question 1

> | 0 | 1 | Read **Source A** again, from lines 1 to 15.
>
> Choose **four** statements below which are TRUE according to the passage.
>
> - Write the letters of the four true statements
> - Choose a maximum of four statements.
>
> **[4 marks]**

This question tests you on your skill in identifying and interpreting explicit and implicit information and ideas (AO1).

It is a relatively straightforward question. It is asking you to identify four true statements.

1 Check your answers against the following four correct choices and decide how many you identified correctly.

A The M25 runs close by the Thurrock Lakeside shopping centre.
C You can go windsurfing on a nearby lake.
D Princess Alexandra opened Lakeside in 1990.
H Women in particular like the security offered by shopping malls.

Question 2

> **02**   You need to refer to **Source A** and **Source B** for this question:
>
> Use details from **both** sources. Summarise the different reasons why people went to shopping malls in the 20th century and why they went to the Sunday morning markets in the 19th century.
>
> **[8 marks]**

This question assesses both bullet points of AO1:

- Identify and interpret explicit and implicit information and ideas.
- Select and synthesise evidence from different texts.

To do well in this answer you need to:

- show that you understand the reasons and the differences between them
- show that you can interpret the detail given in each source
- make clear connections between the texts
- refer to detail and use quotations to support the points you make.

It is important to focus closely on the question. You are not being asked to compare the reasons why people went to these places. You are being asked to summarise them. It is a good idea to quickly list the reasons before writing your answer. For example:

20th century

Convenient transport – M25/supertram

Like a day out for family – cinema/

wind surfing/MetroCentre amusement zone

People feel safe – video-scrutinised

You can see things you can't see in real life, e.g.

Roman Forum

19th century

Transport not an issue – on foot

Men went to smoke and talk – social reasons –

barber's

Women went to buy food for Sunday dinner –

all other shops closed - necessity

Mainly food market – lots of different things:

walnuts, apples – boys went to buy herrings

You can then use your lists to help you write your answer. For example:

There are lots of reasons why people go to shopping malls in the 20th century. The writer tells us that there is good transport, like the M25 for Lakeside or the supertram to Meadowhall. In the 19th century most people would have walked to the markets. It's like a day out for people in the 20th century. There's lots of things to do, such as go to the cinema at Meadowhall or go windsurfing at a lake near Lakeside. At the Sunday markets there was mainly just food to buy. Most of the women went there because they had to buy the food for the Sunday dinner but some men went to smoke and chat and the labourers and mechanics just 'hang about'. There wasn't a lot else to do but the men sometimes went to go to the barber's.

Children go to the shopping malls and their parents can put them in the amusement zone at the MetroCentre but in the 19th century the boys went to buy herrings for breakfast. In the 20th century women like to go to malls because they feel safe there as they are video-scrutinised but in the 19th century, women had to go to buy food though it sounds as though it was fairly safe. All the other shops were closed so this was the only place they could go to.

2 Compare your answer with the sample given. Did you miss some points you could have included? Make a note of them. Did you include some other points? Check that all the points you made are relevant to the question.

Question 3

| 0 3 | Read again lines 13 to 31 in **Source B**. |

How does Henry Mayhew use language to show the reader what the Brill market is like?

You could include the writer's choice of:

- words and phrases
- language features and techniques
- sentence forms.

[12 marks]

This question tests your skill in examining and commenting on the writer's use of language – words, phrases, language features, language techniques and sentence forms (AO2). You should:

- show that you understand the writer's use of language
- explain the effects of the writer's language choices
- select and use relevant quotations
- use appropriate subject terminology to discuss language use. You might, for example, comment on the writer's use of adjectives or groups of three. 'Adjectives' and 'groups of three' are both appropriate subject terminology.

3 Develop your skills in making useful notes by:

- identifying things to write about
- selecting examples
- reminding yourself to write about effects.

For this question, start by identifying three features in lines 13 to 31 that seem important. For example:

Sounds: simple sentence – 'sounds are scarcely heard'; long sentence – 'low hum' to 'noisy shouting' to 'the different cries become distinct' to 'the hubbub, din, and confusion of a thousand voices bellowing at once'. These sounds 'fill the air'. Discuss effects – verbs, nouns and adjectives.

Movement: starts 'as you walk through the market'; then 'at each step' – like walking with him; changes to 3rd person – 'road and footpath are crowded'; men are 'standing'; women 'run to and fro' – contrast – men 'sally' or 'hang about' while women 'streaming forth' and boys 'running'. Discuss effects – 'you' + contrast.

Use of lists: captures detail: the hubbub, din and confusion (nouns); the men are standing in groups, smoking and talking (verbs); Walnuts … corn-plaster (nouns)'. Discuss effects – build up.

Notes like these will help you write three good paragraphs. A paragraph based on the notes for 'Sounds' is shown below.

Henry Mayhew uses language to show the reader what the market is like. He shows us the sounds of the market. He starts with a short simple sentence, which says that at the entrance to the market sounds are 'scarcely heard'. He then follows this ← *Sentence structure understood.*

with a contrasting long, complex sentence which he uses to show the gradual build-up of sounds. At the start there is a 'low hum' and this grows to noises that 'fill the air'. He uses a wide range of nouns to describe the sounds and show how they grow from ← *Uses correct terminology.*

'hum' to 'shouting', 'cries', 'hubbub' and 'din'. The noun phrase 'confusion of a thousand ← *Quotes are relevant.* voices bellowing at once' is effective because it gives a number and the verb 'bellowing' makes the reader think of a very loud sound like a herd of cattle would make. ← *Effects are closely examined.*

4 Use the notes for 'Movement' and 'Use of lists' to help you add to your answer to this question. Remember to show that you can examine and analyse the effects of the writer's language choices.

Question 4

> **0 4**   For this question, you need to refer to **Source A** and **Source B**.
>
> Compare how the two writers convey their attitudes to the places they describe.
>
> In your answer, you could:
>
> - compare their attitudes
> - compare the methods they use to convey their attitudes
> - support your ideas with quotations from **both** sources.
>
> **[16 marks]**

This question tests your skill in comparing writers' ideas and perspectives, as well as how these are conveyed (AO3). You should:

- show that you understand the ideas and perspectives
- make clear comparisons between the ideas and perspectives
- explain and compare the methods used to convey the ideas and perspectives
- use relevant quotations from both texts to support your comparison.

| Point out similarities and differences | | Viewpoint and perspective – what does tone show? |

Compare how the two writers convey their attitudes to the places they describe.

| Methods: language? structure? use of evidence? tone? |

You cannot point out the similarities and differences until you have worked out the perspectives, viewpoints and methods.

The chart can help you to:

- identify similarities and differences
- write an organised answer.

	Source A	Source B
Perspective / purpose / audience	20th-century journalist – Barker – mag. Article – adults Describes and argues and gives personal opinion – tries to persuade – has visited malls	19th-century social reformer – Mayhew Social record? Educated readers – future? Describes – has visited – doesn't persuade – shows positives
Viewpoint	In favour: 'I love these centres.' Biased? – sees them as 'fantasy' places – not real life	Distant observer – doesn't interact with place or people – seems to like it - real place – shopping for Sunday dinner
Tone	Sometimes sarcastic, mocking, humorous	Impartial – informing – educating – addresses reader directly once
Language	Conveys tone: 'dumpy dome'; 'a strange mixture of flashiness and plain grot'; adjectives/verbs persuade: 'Shoppers go about with cheerful, sprightly step'; 'the electricity always shines'	Sounds/movements/lists (see Q3)
Structure	Third person at first – moves from one mall to another – explains attractions – personal viewpoint at end	Third person throughout – explains and then describes – ends with close of market
Use of evidence	Only positive details given – avoids negative – quotes expert to support argument	Details about place, e.g. sounds, movements – own experience only

5 Look again at your answer to this question. How many of the things in the chart did you mention in your answer?

Read the first paragraph of a good response based on the first two rows of the chart.

> The writers of the sources have different purposes and audiences. Barker is a journalist writing for a magazine and a 20th-century audience that will probably already know about shopping malls. Mayhew is a social reformer. He is probably writing for educated people who would not have visited the Sunday market. Barker clearly has a strong personal opinion in favour of shopping malls. He says: 'I love these centres.' Mayhew seems to quite like the Sunday market but he doesn't 'love' it and doesn't seem to be trying to persuade his readers to love it either. His purpose seems to be to inform and describe and maybe to record for the future. There are other differences in their attitudes. Barker seems to see shopping malls as 'fantasy' places that are not like real life, whereas Mayhew presents the Sunday market as a place where ordinary people go to buy food.

6 Use the detail in the third and fourth rows of the chart to help you write a detailed paragraph in which you compare:

    a   the tone of the writers

    b   the ways the writers describe the places.

Section B: Writing

Question 5

> **0 5**   'People waste away their weekends mindlessly in shopping malls when they could be doing so much more with their free time.'
>
>   Write an article for a broadsheet newspaper in which you explain your point of view on this statement.
>
>   (24 marks for content and organisation
>   16 marks for technical accuracy)
>   **[40 marks]**

In order to do well in your writing, you need to:

* communicate clearly and effectively
* match tone, style and register to your purpose and audience
* develop, organise and structure your information and ideas
* make clear links within and between paragraphs
* make effective use of structural features
* choose vocabulary for effect
* use a range of sentence structures for effect
* spell and punctuate accurately.

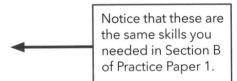

Notice that these are the same skills you needed in Section B of Practice Paper 1.

7 Work with a partner. Use the bullet points to help you assess the work of Students A and B.

8 Student A does some things well, but Student B's article is better. Can you work out why?

9 List three pieces of advice you would give Student A to help improve their writing.

10 Use what you have learned from assessing the responses of Students A and B to help you identify:

    a   what you did well in your writing

    b   how you could improve your writing.

Student A

My name is Helen Smith and I'm going to explain why I think shopping malls are good places to go to at the weekend. I live in Sheffield and I go to Meadowhall with my friends on almost every Saturday.

I don't think it's fair to say that it's a waste of time as we always have a really good time there. There are lots of things to do at Meadowhall, for example you can watch films at VUE or do lots of shopping and you can also find lots of different places to eat. We usually spend most of our pocket money there on a Saturday and we think it's money well spent!

We usually start the day by catching a tram from Middlewood which is where I live to Meadowhall. It doesn't take very long and if you miss one another one soon comes along. When we get there we start by looking around the shops and we try lots of things on but we usually wait until later to decide what to buy. Early on there's not too many people there so we often go for a drink before the cues start to get really long. If we go to Pizza Express I always have an Appletiser but if we go to Macdonalds I have a delicus milk shake.

Sometimes in the afternoon we go to see a film. The last film I saw there was Annabelle and that was really scary. We all sat in the back row I had to sit with my hands over my eyes when the really bad bits came on. Luckily my friend wasn't scared at all so she could tell me what was going on. If we don't go to see a film we'll just walk around and chat and maybe go back and buy some clothes that we tried on in the morning.

Then when we've had enough of walking we go to have a burger and chips and even though there not good for you they do taste delicus. After that we usually catch the tram home. When I get home my Dad always says did you have a good day and I always say yes the best. And that's why I think it's not a waste of time. It's the best day of the week for me and my friends cos we get to do everything we want to and we have lots of fun.

Student B

Did you know that there has been a 60% increase in the number of people visiting shopping malls in the last ten years? Maybe it's time that we stopped and thought about why this is happening.

I was at school yesterday and everyone was talking about what they were going to do at the weekend. At least half of my friends said that they were going to our local shopping mall, which is called the Bullring.

I was simply shocked by this. It was a Saturday and they had nothing better to do than go and walk around a place like that. Let me tell you, it is not a very nice place to be. There are usually loads of people there and all they do is walk around all the time. There are a few nice shops there and some good places to eat but there's nothing much else to do. Would you like to spend a whole day there? I know I wouldn't and yet lots of people do.

And it doesn't stop there! Some people go there more than once a week and some of my friends were planning to go on Saturday and Sunday! I mean to say! One day is surely enough! Why don't they find better things to do with their time?

There are lots of things that people can do at the weekend depending on where they live and what they like. If they live in Birmingham they could go paintballing at Deltaforce or they could spend the day in a park. Birmingham has more parks than any other city in Europe – and that includes London! The best park is Cannon Hill Park and you can do all different things there like boating and tennis and you can go and have a picnic there. Birmingham also has lots of canals which you can walk along. There's so many things you can do why would you want to spend all day in the Bullring?

If you go to the Bullring you will find lots of families there. The kids are often whingeing and not happy because they don't want to be there. You can see them crying and pulling at their Mum and Dad's hands because they want to go home. It's not good enough! They should be outside running about and enjoying the fresh air and getting fit and healthy. It's no wonder that so many children don't run any more when they spend all their weekends stuck inside a shopping mall.

Their parents should find better things for them to do. When I was little my Dad took me to watch the football every weekend. He would never have taken me to a shopping mall. We spent some really good times together and it was really good fun. He still asks me if I want to go with him and sometimes I do. That's the kind of thing parents should be doing with their children. They should be having fun with them at weekends and not dragging them round somewhere they don't want to be.

Quite frankly, I think it has to stop. So many people going there week after week is just appalling. We should make sure that there are better things for everyone to do with their time at weekends. I don't know about you but I always find that if people know there are better things to do, they will do them. So let's work together and make sure that everyone does something different at a weekend.

Explorations in creative reading and writing

Section A: Reading

- You are advised to spend some time reading Source A and thinking about the questions you have to answer.
- You should make sure you leave sufficient time to check your answers.

Source A

This is the opening of a short story, in which a boy ventures out into the early morning with only his dogs and his gun.

A Sunrise on the Veldt

Every night that winter he said aloud into the dark of the pillow: Half-past four! Half-past four! till he felt his brain had gripped the words and held them fast. Then he fell asleep at once, as if a shutter had fallen; and lay with his face turned to the clock so that he could see it first thing when he woke.

5   It was half-past four to the minute, every morning. Triumphantly pressing down the alarm-knob of the clock, which the dark half of his mind had outwitted, remaining vigilant all night and counting the hours as he lay relaxed in sleep, he huddled down for a last warm moment under the clothes, playing with the idea of lying abed for this once only. But he played with it for the fun of knowing that it was a weakness that he
10   could defeat without effort; just as he set the alarm each night for the delight of the moment when he awoke and stretched his limbs, feeling the muscles tighten, and thought: Even my brain – even that! I can control every part of myself.

Luxury of warm rested body, with the arms and legs and fingers waiting like soldiers for a word of command! Joy of knowing that the precious hours were given to sleep
15   voluntarily! – for he had once stayed awake three nights running, to prove that he could, and then worked all day, refusing even to admit that he was tired; and now sleep seemed to him a servant to be commanded and refused.

The boy stretched his frame full-length, touching the wall at his head with his hands, and the bedfoot with his toes; then he sprung out, like a fish leaping from water. And
20   it was cold, cold.

He always dressed rapidly, so as to try and conserve his night-warmth till the sun rose two hours later; but by the time he had on his clothes his hands were numbed and he could scarcely hold his shoes. These he could not put on for fear of waking his parents, who never came to know how early he rose.

25   As soon as he stepped over the lintel, the flesh of his soles contracted on the chill earth, and his legs began to ache with cold. It was night: the stars were glistering, the trees standing black and still. He looked for signs of day, for the greying of the edge of a stone, or a lightening in the sky where the sun would rise, but there was nothing yet. Alert as an animal he crept past the dangerous window, standing poised with his
30   hand on the sill for one proudly fastidious moment, looking in at the stuffy blackness of the room where his parents lay.

---

35 Feeling for the grass edge of the path with his toes, he reached inside another window further along the wall, where his gun had been set in readiness the night before. The steel was icy, and numbed fingers slipped along it, so that he had to hold it in the crook of his arm for safety.

40 Then he tiptoed to the room where the dogs slept, and was fearful that they might have been tempted to go before him; but they were waiting, their haunches crouched in reluctance at the cold, but ears and swinging tails greeting the gun ecstatically. His warning undertone kept them secret and silent till the house was a hundred yards back: then they bolted off into the bush, yelping excitedly. The boy imagined his parents turning in their beds and muttering: Those dogs again! before they were dragged back in sleep; and he smiled scornfully. He always looked back over his shoulder at the house before he passed a wall of trees that shut it from sight. It looked so low and small, crouching there under a tall and brilliant sky. Then he turned
45 his back on it, and on the frowsting sleepers, and forgot them.

He would have to hurry. Before the light grew strong he must be four miles away; and already a tint of green stood in the hollow of a leaf, and the air smelled of morning and the stars were dimming.

From 'A Sunrise on the Veldt' by Doris Lessing, in *This Was the Old Chief's Country*

Section A: Reading

Practice questions

Answer **all** questions in this section.
You are advised to spend about 45 minutes on this section.

0 1 Read again the first part of the source, lines 1 to 16.

List **four** things that the boy does between going to bed at night and getting out of bed in the morning.

[4 marks]

0 2 Look in detail at this extract from the source:

> As soon as he stepped over the lintel, the flesh of his soles contracted on the chill earth, and his legs began to ache with cold. It was night: the stars were glistering, the trees standing black and still. He looked for signs of day, for the greying of the edge of a stone, or a lightening in the sky where the sun would rise, but there was nothing yet. Alert as an animal he crept past the dangerous window, standing poised with his hand on the sill for one proudly fastidious moment, looking in at the stuffy blackness of the room where his parents lay.

How does the writer use language here to describe the scene?

You could include the writer's choice of:

- words and phrases
- language features and techniques
- sentence forms.

[8 marks]

0 3 You now need to think about the **whole** of the source.

How has the writer structured the text to interest you as a reader?

You could write about:

- how the writer shifts the focus
- how the writer develops her ideas
- any other structural features that interest you.

[8 marks]

0 4 Focus this part of your answer on **lines 29 to the end**.

'In these lines, the writer successfully captures the secrecy of the boy's actions and makes me worried about what might happen to him.' To what extent do you agree with this statement?

In your response, you could:

- explain what you learn from the boy's actions
- evaluate the extent to which the writer captures the secrecy of the boy's actions and makes the reader worried about what might happen to the boy
- support your opinions with quotations from the text.

[20 marks]

Complete this assignment on Cambridge Elevate.

Section B: Writing

Practice questions

You are advised to spend about 45 minutes on this section.
Write in full sentences.
You are reminded of the need to plan your answer.
You should leave enough time to check your work at the end.

0 5   You are going to enter a creative writing competition.

Your entry will be judged by a panel of published writers.

Either:

Write a story suggested to you by this photograph.

Or:

Write a story in which a secret plays an important part.

(24 marks for content and organisation
16 marks for technical accuracy)
[40 marks]

Complete this assignment on
Cambridge Elevate.

Writers' viewpoints and perspectives

Section A: Reading

Insert

You are advised to spend up to 15 minutes reading through the source and all five questions you have to answer.

You should make sure you leave sufficient time to check your answers.

- **Source A:** An account about the hardships of factory life in the 19th century from *A Narrative of the Experience and Suffering of William Dodd*

- **Source B:** A newspaper article from *The Guardian,* 2013

Source A:

Dear Reader, – I wish it to be distinctly and clearly understood that I am not actuated by any motive of ill-feeling to any party with whom I have formerly been connected; on the contrary, I have a personal respect for some of my former masters; but having witnessed the efforts of some writers (who can know nothing of the factories by experience) to mislead the minds of the public upon a subject of so much importance, I feel it to be my duty to give the world a fair and impartial account of the working of the factory system, as I have found it in twenty-five 5
years' experience.

Of four children in our family, I was the only boy; and we were all at different periods, as we could meet with employers, sent to work in the factories. My eldest sister was ten years of age before she went; consequently, she was, in a manner, out of harm's way, her bones having become firmer and stronger than ours, and capable of withstanding the hardships to which she was exposed much better than we could. My second sister went at 10
the age of seven years, and, like myself, has been made a cripple for life, and doomed to end her days in the factories or workhouse. My youngest sister also went early, but was obliged to be taken away, like many more, the work being too hard for her.

I was born on the 18th of June, 1804; and in the latter part of 1809, being then turned of five years of age, I was put to work at card-making, and about a year after I was sent, with my sisters, to the factories. I was then a fine, 15
strong, healthy, hardy boy, straight in every limb, and remarkably stout and active. It was predicted by many of our acquaintance, that I should be the very model of my father, who was the picture of robust health and strength.

From six to fourteen years of age, I went through a series of uninterrupted, unmitigated suffering, such as very rarely falls to the lot of mortals so early in life, and such as I could not have withstood, had I not been strong and of a good constitution. 20

My first place in the factories was that of piecer, or the lowest situation. The piecers are the servants of the spinners, and both are under an overlooker; and liable to be dismissed at a week's notice. In order to induce the piecer to do his work quick and well, the spinner has recourse to many expedients, such as offering rewards of a penny for a good week's work; as a last resource, when nothing else will do, he takes the strap, or the billy-roller, which are laid on most unmercifully, accompanied by a round volley of oaths. 25

On one occasion, I remember being thrashed with the billy-roller till my back, arms and legs were covered with ridges as thick as my finger. This was more than I could bear and I stole off home, along some by-ways, so as not to be seen. Mother stripped me, and was shocked at my appearance. The spinner had to beg that mother would let me go again, and promised not to strike me with the billy-roller any more. He kept his promise, but instead of using the roller, he used his fist. 30

A Narrative of the Experience and Suffering of William Dodd

Source B:

Admit it. You love cheap clothes. And you don't care about child slave labour

Until three years ago I did not believe in magic. But that was before I began investigating how western brands perform a conjuring routine that has cast a spell over the world's consumers.

This is how it works. Well Known Company (WKC) makes shiny, pretty things in India or China. *The Observer* reports that the people making the shiny, pretty things are being paid buttons and, what's more, have been using 5 children's nimble little fingers to put them together. There is much outrage, WKC professes its horror that it has been let down by its supply chain and promises to make everything better. And then nothing happens. WKC keeps making shiny, pretty things and people keep buying them. Because they love them. Because they are cheap. And because they have let themselves be bewitched.

In the last few years, companies have got smarter. It is rare now to find children in the top level of the supply 10 chain, because the brands know this is PR suicide. But the wages still stink, the hours are still brutal, and the children are still there, stitching away in the backstreets of the slums.

Drive east out of Delhi for an hour or so and take a stroll down some of the back lanes. Take a look through some of the doorways. See the children stitching the fine embroidery and beading? Now take a stroll through your favourite mall and have a look at the shelves. Recognise some of that handiwork? You should. 15

Suppliers now subcontract work out from the main factory. The work is done out of sight, the pieces sent back to the main factory to be finished and labelled. And when the auditors come round the factory, they can say that there were no children and all was well.

Need fire extinguishers to tick the safety box? Hire them in for the day. The lift is a deathtrap? Stick a sign on it to say it is out of use and the inspector will pass it by. We, the consumers, let them do this because we want the 20 shiny, pretty thing.

But times are tough, consumers say. Here's some maths from an *Observer* investigation last year in Bangalore. We can calculate that women on the absolute legal minimum wage, making jeans for a WKC, get 11p per item. Now wave your own wand and grant them the living monthly wage – the £136 needed to support a family in India today. It is going to cost a fortune, right? No. It will cost 15p more on the labour cost of each pair of jeans. 25

A young boy working in a textile factory in Delhi, India

The very fact that wages are so low makes the cost of fixing the problem low, too. Someone has to absorb the hit, be it the brand, supplier, middleman, retailer or consumer. But why make this a bad thing? Why be scared of it?

Here is the shopper, agonising over ethical or cheap. What if they can do both? What if they can pluck two pairs of jeans off the rail and hold them up. One costs £20. One costs £20.15. It has a big label on it, which says 'I'm proud to pay 15p more for these jeans. My jeans were made by a happy worker who was paid the fair rate   30
for the job.'

Go further. Stitch it on to the jeans themselves. I want those jeans. I want to know I'm not wearing something stitched by kids kept locked in backstreet godowns, never seeing the light of day, never getting a penny. I want to feel clean. And I want the big brands and the supermarkets to help me feel clean.

I want people to say to them: 'You deceived us. You told us you were ethical. We want you to change. We want   35
you to police your supply chain as if you care. We want to trust you again, we really do, because we love your products. Know what? We don't mind paying a few pennies more if you promise to chip in too.'

And here's the best part: I think they would sell more. I think consumers would be happier and workers would be happier. And if I can spend less time trawling through fetid backstreets looking for the truth, I'll be happier.

Adapted from an article in *The Guardian* by Gethin Chamberlain

Section A: Reading

Practice questions

Complete this assignment on Cambridge Elevate.

Answer **all** questions in this section.
You are advised to spend about 45 minutes on this section.

01 Read **Source A** again, from lines 1 to 13.

Choose **four** statements below which are TRUE according to the passage.

- Write the letters of the four true statements
- Choose a maximum of four statements.

A   The writer has no ill feeling towards his former masters.   ⬭

B   Some writers have tried to mislead the public about factory life.   ⬭

C   There are many other reliable accounts of children's lives in the factory system.   ⬭

D   The writer had four sisters.   ⬭

E   The four children all started factory work at the same age.   ⬭

F   One of his sisters was strong enough to withstand the hardships of factory work.   ⬭

G   His second sister ended up in a workhouse.   ⬭

H   Factory work was too hard for the writer's youngest sister.   ⬭

[4 marks]

0 2 You need to refer to **Source A** and **Source B** for this question:

Use details from **both** sources. Write a summary of the different hardships faced by children in the 19th and 21st centuries.

[8 marks]

0 3 Read again **lines 1 to 14** in **Source B**.

How does the writer use language to influence the reader's opinion?

You could include the writer's choice of:

- words and phrases
- language features and techniques
- sentence forms.

[12 marks]

0 4 For this question, you need to refer to **Source A** and **Source B**.

Compare how the two writers convey their attitudes to child labour.

In your answer, you could:

- compare their attitudes
- compare the methods they use to convey their attitudes
- support your ideas with quotations from **both** sources.

[16 marks]

Section B: Writing

Practice questions

Complete this assignment on Cambridge Elevate.

You are advised to spend about 45 minutes on this section.
You are reminded of the need to plan your answer.
You should write in full sentences.
You should leave enough time to check your work at the end.

0 5 'Unless ordinary people speak out about things they believe to be wrong, nothing will ever change.'

Write a letter to your local Member of Parliament about something that you believe to be wrong. Explain your views and persuade him or her to take action.

(24 marks for content and organisation, 16 marks for technical accuracy)
[40 marks]

Glossary

adjective a word used to enhance the meaning of a noun

adverb a word that adds to the meaning of a verb, adjective or another adverb (e.g. 'very', 'easily')

alliteration repetition of the initial letter in adjacent words (e.g. 'dark, dank dungeon')

anecdote a personal story

audience the intended readers of a piece of writing

closed question a question that typically only requires a 'yes' or 'no' response

complex sentence a sentence consisting of a main clause and at least one subordinate clause

compound sentence a sentence formed from two simple sentences using 'and', 'but', 'so' or 'or' (e.g. 'he ate supper and went to bed')

connotation an additional associated meaning of a word

coordinating conjunction a conjunction such as 'and', 'but' or 'or'

dialogue a conversation, or part of a conversation, in a piece of writing

direct speech a way of reporting speech by repeating the exact words that someone said

discourse marker words or phrases that are used to organise and link what you write or to express an attitude (e.g. 'anyway', 'okay', 'well', 'so', 'right')

emotive language using words to influence how a person feels

figurative language non-literal use of language

first person the form of a verb or pronoun used when you are speaking or writing about yourself

flashback a scene or description that is set at an earlier time than the main story

homograph a word that shares the same spelling as another word, but is pronounced differently and has a different meaning

homonym a word that shares the same spelling and punctuation with another word, but has a different meaning

homophone a word that shares the same pronunciation as another word, but has different meanings and spellings

imagery the use of words to create a picture or scene

imperative a verb form used to issue a command, often with an exclamation mark (e.g. 'Listen!', 'Stop!')

inference something that is suggested or implied rather than stated openly

infinitive the base form of a verb

intonation the rise and fall of the pitch of the voice when speaking

main clause a clause that makes sense as a sentence, having a subject and a verb

metaphor a word or phrase that describes one thing as something else

narrative perspective the point of view from which something is written (e.g. first person, third person)

noun a word that refers to a person, place or thing

noun phrase a group or words that act like a noun

objective a piece of writing presented without emotion or bias

open question a question that requires a full, descriptive response

pace the perceived speed of a piece of writing or speech

personification giving human attributes to non-human things

pronoun a word that replaces, or is used in place of a noun phrase

pun a joke based on two different meanings of a word

purpose the reason something has been written

register the level of formality in a piece of writing

rhetorical question a question that is asked for effect rather than to obtain information

simile a comparison using 'as' or 'like' (e.g. she was like a fish out of water)

simple sentence a sentence consisting of a single main clause

Standard English the form of English most commonly used in formal situations

subjective a piece of writing based on personal opinion, thoughts and feelings

subordinate clause a clause that functions in the same way as a noun, adjective or adverb, but cannot stand as a sentence on its own

subordinating conjunction a conjunction that precedes a subordinate clause, such as 'although', 'if', 'because'

suffix a common group of letters at the end of a word that change the form of the word

synonym a word or a phrase with a similar meaning to another word

third person the form of the verb or pronoun used when you are speaking or writing about another person

tone the mood or attitude the writer conveys in a piece of writing

verb a word that conveys an action in a sentence

Acknowledgements

The authors and publishers acknowledge the following sources of copyright material and are grateful for the permissions granted. While every effort has been made, it has not always been possible to identify the sources of all the material used, or to trace all copyright holders. If any omissions are brought to our notice, we will be happy to include the appropriate acknowledgements on reprinting.

p. 10, 11 and 12 *Old Mali and the Boy* by D R Sherman (Copyright © D R Sherman, 1964) Reproduced by permission of A.M. Heath & Co Ltd.; p. 13 © 2015 FirstGroup plc. All Rights Reserved; p. 15 Copyright © 2012 PublishYourArticles.net, All rights reserved; pp. 23 and 25 From *Behind the Beautiful Forevers: Life, Death and Hope in a Mumbai Slum* by Katherine Boo, published by Portobello Books Ltd . Reproduced by permission of The Random House Group Ltd.; p. 28 © Copyright D.C.Thomson & Co. Ltd., 2015; p. 32 David Attenborough Productions Ltd; p. 33 Kevin Gardam; p. 34 © Shelter 2015; p. 37 From *Pies and Prejudice* by Stuart Maconie, published by Ebury Press. Reproduced by permission of The Random House Group Ltd.; p. 38 From *No Man's Land* by Eula Biss. Copyright © 2009 by Graywolf Press. Reprinted by permission of Graywolf Press; p. 39 Adapted from www.aviewoncities.com/london/londoneye.htm; p. 41 'The Rain Horse' by Ted Hughes in *The Penguin Book of Modern British Short Stories*, Faber and Faber Ltd; p. 44 Extract from *Mr Proudham and Mr Sleight in A Bit of Singing and Dancing.* © Copyright Susan Hill. Reproduced by permission of Sheil Land Associates Ltd.; pp. 46 and 47 Contains public sector information licensed under the Open Government Licence v3.0; pp. 48 and 50 *How to Speak Brochurese* by Keith Waterhouse (1993) from *Travel Writing* (Oxford Literature Resources). By permission of Oxford University Press; p. 53 *Raymond's Run* (1993) by Toni Cade Bambara (Oxford Literature Resources) By permission of Oxford University Press; p. 56 141 words (p19) from *Of Mice and Men* by John Steinbeck (Penguin Classics 2006) Copyright © John Steinbeck; p. 58 179 words (p38) from *Of Mice and Men* by John Steinbeck (Penguin Classics 2006) Copyright ©

John Steinbeck; p. 60 313 words (p140-141) from *Of Mice and Men* by John Steinbeck (Penguin Classics 2006) Copyright © John Steinbeck; p. 64 (t) From *How To Be a Woman* by Caitlin Moran, published by Ebury Press. Reproduced by permission of The Random House Group Ltd.; p. 64 (b) 70 words (p1) from *All Points North* by Simon Armitage (Penguin 2009) Copyright © Simon Armitage; p. 65 34 words (p13) from *Is That It?* by Bob Geldof (Penguin 2006) Copyright © Bob Geldof; p. 66 *The Times* 2014; p. 68 Mandy Southgate/ www.addictedtomedia.net with permission; p. 71 451 words From *I Used to Live Here Once* by Jean Rhys in *Sleep It Off Lady* (Penguin 1979) Copyright © Jean Rhys; p. 75 *Metro* 2014; p. 77 (t) *Fun Run and other oxymorons* by Joe Bennett, Simon & Schuster UK; p. 77 (b) copyright © Telegraph Media Group Limited; p. 86 Mail online; p. 87 *Mirror*; p. 88 *The Independent*; p. 89 *The Lion Children* by Angus, Maisie and Travers McNeice, Orion Children's Books, an imprint of the Hachette Children's Group, London; p. 90 *Two Dianas in Somaliland* by Agnes Herbert (1993) from *Unsuitable for Ladies - Anthology of Women Travellers* by Jane Robinson (Oxford Paperbacks). By permission of Oxford University Press; p. 94 *Daily Mail* 2013; pp. 100 and 102 Reproduced with permission of Ian Fleming Publications Ltd., London, *Silver Fin* by Charlie Higson Copyright © Ian Fleming Publications Ltd. 2007 www.ianfleming.com; p. 103 *I know why the caged bird sings* by Maya Angelou, published by Constable, an imprint of Little, Brown Book Group/Excerpt from *I know why the caged bird sings* by Maya Angelou, copyright © 1984 by Maya Angelou. Used by permission of Random House Inc; p. 105 *Roots* by Alex Haley, published by Hutchinson. Reproduced by permission of The Random House Group Ltd/adapted from *Roots*, published by Vintage (Alex Haley, © 1994); p. 107 David Attenborough Productions Ltd; p. 109 David Brainard, 1940, Pan Macmillan; p. 111 Reprinted by permission of HarperCollins Publishers Ltd © 1974 Louise Francke; p. 113 © William Boyd, 2009, *Ordinary Thunderstorms*, Bloomsbury Publishing Plc.; p. 114 Naseem Rakha, 2010, Pan Macmillan; p. 115 (t) From THE LOLLIPOP SHOES by Joanne Harris Published by Doubleday Reprinted by permission of The Random House Group Limited;

p. 115 (b) Reprinted by permission of HarperCollins Publishers Ltd © 2005 Susan Fletcher; p. 116 *The Tooth Fairy* by Graham Joyce, The Orion Publishing Group, London; p. 119 *A High Wind in Jamaica* by Richard Hughes, Vintage Digital, 2011; p. 120 225 words (p223) from *White Teeth* by Zadie Smith (Penguin 2001) Copyright © Zadie Smith; p. 122 *The Sunday Times*; p. 125 (t) *The Independent*; p. 125 (m) *The Independent*; p. 125 (b) *Ugly Love* by Colleen Hoover, Simon & Schuster UK; p. 135 406 words (p75) from *A Kestrel for a Knave* by Barry Hines (Penguin Classics 2000) Copyright © Barry Hines; p. 138 From THE ACCIDENTAL NATURALIST by Ben Fogle. Published by Bantam Press. Reprinted by permission of The Random House Group Limited; p. 141 *Oxford Reading Tree Read With Biff, Chip, and Kipper: First Stories: Level 4: Dragon Danger* by Cynthia Rider. By permission of Oxford University Press; p. 151 From CATCHING FIRE by Suzanne Collins. Copyright © 2009 by Suzanne Collins. Reprinted by permission of Scholastic Inc; p. 152 Simon Winchester; pp. 162 and 163 From MAY I HAVE YOUR ATTENTION PLEASE by James Corden Published by Century. Reprinted by permission of The Random House Group Limited; p. 168 406 words (p75) from *Tickling the English* by Dara O Briain (Penguin) Copyright © Dara O Briain; p. 175 From *Geldof in Africa* by Bob Geldof, published by Century. Reproduced by permission of The Random House Group Ltd; p. 177 *How to Eat Around the World: Tips & Wisdom (2nd edition)* by Richard Sterling Travelers' Tales, 2005 Copyright © Richard Sterling 2005; p. 181 *The Secret Diary of Adrian Mole Aged 13 ¾* by Sue Townsend published by Puffin. Reproduced with permission of Curtis Brown Ltd; p. 182 Dylan Thomas, *After the Fair*, Orion 1933; p. 184 (tl) From *My Enemy's Enemy* by Kingsley Amis with permisison fo the Wylie Agency; p. 184 (br) Douglas Adams, 2009, Pan Macmillan; p. 187 (t) *Skellig* by David Almond published by Hodder; p. 195 AboutAnimalTesting; p. 221 Reproduced with permission of Curtis Brown. *The Blind Assassin* by Margaret Atwood Copyright © Margaret Atwood; pp. 240–241 Copyright Paul Barker, *Prospect* magazine, London, February 1996. Paul Barker is a senior research fellow, Young Foundation, London. His books include *The Freedoms of Suburbia*; pp. 254–255 Reprinted by permission of HarperCollins Publishers Ltd © 2003 Doris Lessing; pp. 259–260 Copyright Guardian News & Media Ltd 2013.

Picture credits

Cover (c) 2013 Fabian Oefner www.fabianoefner.com; p. 6 (t) klenova/Thinkstock; p. 6 (b) IR Stone/Shutterstock; p. 7 Helen Hotson/Shutterstock; p. 8 Alexander Zhegalov/Shutterstock; p. 10 Steve Davey Photography/Alamy; p. 11 Laurin Rinder/Shutterstock; p. 12 Labrador Photo Video/Shutterstock; p. 13 Radiokafka/Shutterstock; p. 14 Panmaule/Thinkstock; p. 15 Goran/Thinkstock; p. 16 Dmitry Rukhlenko/Thinkstock; p. 18 Andrew Barker/Alamy; p. 20 (t) italianestro/Thinkstock; p. 20 (1) Steve Hix/Fuse/Thinkstock; p. 20 (2) PathDoc/Shutterstock; p. 20 (3) Riccardo Piccinini/Shutterstock; p. 20 (4) Stokkete/Shutterstock; p. 21 AF Archive/Alamy; p. 23 Nick Cunard/Alamy; p. 25 Matyas Rehak/Shutterstock; p. 27 Rawpixel/Shutterstock; p. 28 (l) egal/Thinkstock; p. 28 (r) Zurijeta/Thinkstock; pp. 30–31 Jacob Ammentorp Lund/Thinkstock; p. 32 efired/Thinkstock; p. 33 (t) DaveBolton/Thinkstock; p. 33 (b) John Gomez/Thinkstock; p. 34 koya79/Thinkstock; p. 35 Heritage Image Partnership Ltd/Alamy; p. 36 Lebrecht Music and Arts Photo Library/Alamy; p. 37 SAKhanPhotography/Thinkstock; p. 39 (t) venemama/Thinkstock; p. 39 (b) Bruce Bennett/Thinkstock; p. 40 Valentina Gabusi/Thinkstock; p. 41 Lars Lentz/Thinkstock; p. 42 The Granger Collection/Topfoto; p. 44 ThaiMyNguyen/Thinkstock; p. 45 Ingram Publishing/Thinkstock; p. 46 Eyematrix/Thinkstock; p. 47 Pavel L Photo and Video/Shutterstock; p. 48 mtr/Shutterstock; p. 50 a-image/Shutterstock; p. 51 AntonioGuillem/Thinkstock; p. 53 igor vorobyov/Thinkstock; p. 54 Semmick Photo/Shutterstock; p. 55 Atthapol Saita/Thinkstock; p. 56 Moviestore Collection Ltd/Alamy; p. 57 YAY Media AS/Alamy; p. 58 Pictureguy/Shutterstock; p. 60 Photos 12/Alamy; p. 62 icsnaps/Shutterstock; p. 63 hxdbzxy/Thinkstock; p. 64 (t) monkeybusinessimages/Thinkstock; p. 64 (b) Stocktrek Images/Thinkstock; p. 66 Galyna Andrushko/Shutterstock; p. 67 TobiasBischof/Thinkstock; p. 68 v.s.anandhakrishna/Shutterstock; p. 70 VladimirFLoyd/Thinkstock; p. 71 David Hughes/Shutterstock; p. 73 (t) donvictorio/Shutterstock; p. 73 (b) Greg Balfour Evans/Alamy; p. 75 WENN UK/Alamy; p. 77 (t) Serg Shalimoff/Thinkstock; p. 77 (b) Bubbles Photolibrary/Alamy; p. 79 The Print Collector/Alamy; p. 80 (t) sam74100/Thinkstock; p. 18 (bl) luckyraccoon/Thinkstock; p. 80 (br) naumoid/Thinkstock; p. 82 (l) Lecic/Thinkstock; p. 82 (r) Africa Studio/Shutterstock; p. 85 (t) Pictorial Press Ltd/Alamy; p. 85 (b) chuyu/Thinkstock; p. 87 (t) RobThomson/Thinkstock; p. 87 (b) Peter Phillips/Alamy; p. 89 MaggyMeyer/Thinkstock; p. 90 FishTales/Thinkstock; p. 92 GlobalP/Thinkstock; p. 94 (T) Noel Hendrickson/Thinkstock; p. 94 (b) David J. Green/Alamy; p. 96 vanillasky/Alamy; p. 97 Ociacia/Thinkstock; p. 98 Pictorial Press Ltd/Alamy; p. 99 makeitdouble/Thinkstock; p. 100 photography-wildlife-de/Thinkstock; p. 101 GlobalP/Thinkstock; p. 102 Jupiterimages/Thinkstock; p. 103 thislife pictures/Alamy; p. 105 The Art Archive/Alamy; p. 106 deamles for sale/Shutterstock; p. 107 StrahilDimitrov/Thinkstock; p. 108 Interfoto/Alamy; p. 109 Toni Scott/Thinkstock; p. 110 sborisov/Thinkstock; p. 111 extremechan/Shutterstock; p. 113 volodymyr yanchuk/Thinkstock; p. 115 IPGGutenbergUKLtd/Thinkstock; p. 116 Vladimír Vítek/Thinkstock; p. 118 Craig McCausland/Thinkstock; p. 119 Ig0rZh/Thinkstock; p. 120 welcomia/Thinkstock; p. 122 Severe/Shutterstock; p. 124 AZ68/Thinkstock; p. 125 Taylor Hinton/Thinkstock; p. 126 Stocktrek Images/Getty Images; p. 128 HowardPerry/Thinkstock; p. 130 Stockbyte/Thinkstock; p. 131 monkeybusinessimages/Thinkstock; p. 134 uharosio/Thinkstock; p. 135 Havana1234/Thinkstock; p. 136 Leszek Kobusinski/Thinkstock; p. 138 Vonschonertagen/Thinkstock; p. 141 (t) LindaMarieB/Thinkstock; p. 141 (b) Elenarts/Thinkstock; p. 144 edstrom/Thinkstock; p. 146 Nerthuz/Thinkstock; p. 147 Gabriele Maltinti/Thinkstock; p. 148 Artush/Thinkstock; p. 150 Wavebreakmedia Ltd/Thinkstock; p. 151 AF Archive/Alamy; p. 152 pkphotoscom/Thinkstock; p. 153 alexaldo/Thinkstock; p. 154 (tl) kadmy/Thinkstock; p. 154 (tr) Horsche/Thinkstock; p. 154 (bl) Mike Watson Images/Thinkstock; p. 154 (br) Ammit/Thinkstock; p. 156 wavipicture/Thinkstock; p. 158 Lynne Nicholson/Shutterstock; p. 159 (t) Alexlukin/Thinkstock; p. 159 (b) Evgeny Karandaev/Thinkstock; p. 162 (t) Andreka/Thinkstock; p. 162 (b) Lester Cohen/Getty Images; p. 164 Dmitrii Kotin/Thinkstock; p. 165 david franklin/Thinkstock; p. 168 Edd Westmacott/Alamy; p. 169 Brand X Pictures/Thinkstock; p. 171 sezer66/Thinkstock; p. 172 Daniel Fung/Shutterstock; p. 173 (t) La_Corivo/Thinkstock; p. 173 (b) matsilvan/Thinkstock; p. 174 Mary Evans Picture Library/Alamy; p. 175 adisa/Thinkstock; p. 176 ricardoreitmeyer/Thinkstock; p. 177 AlexPro9500/Thinkstock; p. 180 redswept/Shutterstock; p. 181 (t) Svetl. Tebenkova/Thinkstock; p. 181 (b) daboost/Thinkstock; p. 182 dutourdumonde/Thinkstock; p. 183 silvae /Shutterstock; p. 185 Chris Rogers/Thinkstock; p. 187 KrivosheevV/Thinkstock; p. 189 Jessica Nelson/Thinkstock; p. 190 Johan Swanepoel/Shutterstock; p. 192 Fuse/Thinkstock; p. 193 Galushko Sergey/Shutterstock; p. 195 anyaivanova/Thinkstock; p. 197 Dundee Photographics/Alamy; p. 198 IPGGutenbergUKLtd/Thinkstock; p. 199 IakovKalinin/Thinkstock; p. 200 amanalang/Thinkstock; p. 201 (t) Creatista/Thinkstock; p. 201 (b) Tsokur/Thinkstock; p. 203 Elenathewise/Thinkstock; p. 207 Aaron Amat/Shutterstock; p. 209 Sergey Nivens/Thinkstock; p. 218 Biletskiy_Evgeniy/Thinkstock; p. 219 Matthew Mawson/Alamy; p. 220 msgrafixxy/Shutterstock; p. 224 Keystone/Getty Images; p. 240 Robert Estall photo agency/Alamy; p. 257 pgaborphotos/Thinkstock; p. 259 Paul Prescott/Alamy.

Produced for Cambridge University Press by

White-Thomson Publishing
www.wtpub.co.uk

Managing editor: Sonya Newland
Designer: Kim Williams